SECOND EDITION

TEACHER'S SURVIVAL GUIDE

GIFTED EDUCATION

SECOND EDITION

TEACHER'S SURVIVAL GUIDE

GIFTED EDUCATION

A First-Year Teacher's Introduction to Gifted Learners

Julia Link Roberts, Ed.D., and Julia Roberts Boggess, M.A.

Routledge
Taylor & Francis Group
NEW YORK AND LONDON

Library of Congress Cataloging-in-Publication Data

Names: Roberts, Julia L. (Julia Link), author. | Boggess, Julia Roberts, 1972- author.
Title: Teacher's survival guide : gifted education : a first-year teacher's introduction to gifted learners / Julia L. Roberts, Julia Roberts Boggess.
Description: 2nd ed. | Waco, TX : Prufrock Press Inc., 2020. | Includes bibliographical references. | Summary: ""Teacher's Survival Guide: Gifted Education" is packed with practical information, up-to-date resources, tips for success, and advice from experts in the field"-- Provided by publisher.
Identifiers: LCCN 2020025891 (print) | LCCN 2020025892 (ebook) | ISBN 9781646320714 (paperback) | ISBN 9781646320721 (ebook) | ISBN 9781646320738 (epub)
Subjects: LCSH: Gifted children--Education. | Teachers of gifted children. | First year teachers.
Classification: LCC LC3993 .R6125 2020 (print) | LCC LC3993 (ebook) | DDC 371.95--dc23
LC record available at https://lccn.loc.gov/2020025891
LC ebook record available at https://lccn.loc.gov/2020025892

First published in 2020 by Prufrock Press Inc.

Published in 2021 by Routledge
605 Third Avenue, New York, NY 10017
2 Park Square, Milton Park, Abingdon, Oxon OX14 4RN

Routledge is an imprint of the Taylor & Francis Group, an informa business

Copyright © 2020 Taylor & Francis Group

Cover and layout design by Shelby Charette

ISBN: 9781032144337 (hbk)
ISBN: 9781646320714 (pbk)

DOI: 10.4324/9781003238553

Dedication

This book is the third one that we have written as a mother-daughter team, and we would like to dedicate it to Elizabeth, Caroline, Jane Ann, and Claire—Julia's four grand-girls—and Julie's daughter, Claire, and nieces.

In addition, we would like to dedicate this book to all of the children and young people with whom we have worked over the years in schools as well as in summer and Saturday programs. They enhance our understanding of their needs that are so often overlooked as their strengths disguise needs.

Table of Contents

ACKNOWLEDGMENTS

So many people have offered ideas included in this book. We are especially appreciative of our colleagues across the country who have written pieces that highlight their areas of expertise and interests. These pieces written by experts add so much to the learning for our readers.

We are also grateful to Gail Hiles for the careful, professional work on the tables and figures included in this book.

INTRODUCTION

Teacher's Survival Guide: Gifted Education is a starting point for educators and others who are new to gifted education or who need an update on what is current in gifted education. This book is a collection of information, advice, resources, and suggestions that we hope readers will turn to again and again. Leonardo da Vinci once said, "He who loves practice without theory is like the sailor who boards a ship without a rudder and compass, and never knows where he may land." This book provides the rudder as you navigate your entry or reentry into the field of gifted education.

This survival kit is filled with basic information on gifted education and strategies for helping gifted kids soar. The goal is to help readers recognize and address the needs of gifted children that are often created by their strengths, encourage their creativity, and implement strategies to remove the learning ceiling. Although written for educators, the information can be shared with parents and decision makers, as the book is an easy-to-read resource for introducing gifted education. After all, it was written as a "survival guide."

The chapters in this book are short and to the point, even though each could be the topic for a longer work, even a book. They are written this way to bring you key information and resources on the many topics pertinent to understanding and supporting gifted and advanced learners. The resources in each chapter's Survival Toolkit will guide readers as they learn about gifted education, with the goal that resources will help readers thrive, not just survive. Several chapters have short pieces called Survival Secrets, written by experts in the field of gifted educa-

DOI: 10.4324/9781003238553-1

tion who share their experiences and provide advice that will help you understand specific topics in gifted education. Chapters also include leading questions to guide your thinking, tips to highlight important points, and quotations that you may want to remember.

As a mother-daughter team, we truly have enjoyed writing this book. Julie is a librarian at Pearre Creek Elementary School in Williamson County, TN. She has had experience as a gifted resource teacher and as a kindergarten and first-grade teacher as well as serving as an elementary librarian. She has taught many sessions of summer and Saturday programs for young people in grades 1–8 who are gifted and talented. Julia is a teacher educator who has prepared hundreds of gifted resource teachers and other educators in gifted education in the course of their graduate study. As the founding and current Executive Director of The Center for Gifted Studies at Western Kentucky University, she has directed more than 3 decades of summer programming for hundreds of gifted children. She has shared ideas and strategies with many parents and provided professional learning opportunities for numerous parent and teacher groups. She has held leadership positions in gifted organizations, including serving as president of the World Council for Gifted and Talented Children.

We hope that you will learn much from *Teacher's Survival Guide: Gifted Education* and share the important information with your colleagues and friends.

Happy reading. Welcome to the world of gifted education!

—Julia Link Roberts and Julia Roberts Boggess

Chapter 1

Let's Start at the Very Beginning

Who Are Gifted Children?

"Gifted children are perishable."—Troy Coleman, parent

Key Question

- What definition for gifted children is current and used in your school, school district, and state?

What Does "Gifted and Talented" Mean?

Let's start the conversation by looking at children who are gifted and talented. Who are they? What terminology is used in the United States in reference to these young people? What are gifted children called in your school, district, and state? What categories of giftedness are recognized where you teach or where your child or children are in school?

Children and young people who are gifted and talented constitute a group that is quite diverse. They come from all ethnic and racial backgrounds, all socioeco-

DOI: 10.4324/9781003238553-2

nomic backgrounds, and all geographic locations. They may speak any language, and they may have both disabilities and advanced abilities. Gifted children represent a variety of interests and talent areas. Even within any category of giftedness, there is a wide range of ability and talent, and the level of achievement and talent development often depends upon available opportunities or opportunities taken. Many gifted individuals learn to underachieve early in their educational experience, but that is not always the case. Others have numerous and ongoing opportunities that allow them to thrive in school. Indeed, "diverse" is the descriptor that best characterizes children and young people who are gifted and talented as well as the experiences and interests they bring to classrooms and other learning communities.

Perhaps the type of giftedness that most people understand most readily is athletic giftedness. Recently, headlines in a local paper used the term *gifted* to describe both an outstanding quarterback and a highly sought-after basketball recruit. The public admires those who are gifted in these athletic abilities, whether the talent is demonstrated in basketball, football, tennis, baseball, or golf. Some young people have natural athletic abilities, and consequently, they get coaching to develop their abilities, and they are even sought after by coaches who recognize obvious athletic potential. If every young person receives the same intensity of coaching, would they all qualify for the varsity team? Of course not. They would not all develop into outstanding athletes, yet all children deserve the opportunity to try—to see if they will develop their skills and abilities to a high level. Those who demonstrate exceptional athletic abilities should not be held back because the other children around them do not perform at the same high level, just as those who are academically gifted should not be held back or made to do the work their age-mates are doing when they are ready for more advanced learning.

Several states include children who are gifted and talented as one category of exceptional or special education. The main difference between gifted children and other exceptional children is that a gifted child is identified by their strength or strengths rather than by a deficiency or an area that requires support in order to achieve. Strengths do not make children look needy (they don't create sympathy for children who are gifted and talented), yet strengths create needs just as deficiencies do. Gifted children are just as different from average learners as are children who are exceptional due to a disability. For example, a gifted child may be able to learn information quickly and at complex levels, while a child with a learning disability may need more time to learn and a basic presentation of the materials to make adequate progress. Or a gifted child may be advanced in one or more content areas, while another child of the same age may need to begin at a different level. All exceptional children, including gifted children, require special accommodations in order for each one to make continuous progress. Of course, ongoing learning is the purpose of going to school.

Definitions of Giftedness

The specific word used to refer to gifted children differs by state and organization. The National Science Board (2010) "alternately refers to the children and young people who have the most potential to become STEM innovators as 'talented and motivated' or 'high-ability' or 'gifted'" (p. 6). Some states choose to call these children *advanced learners* or *gifted and talented*. Still other terms used to refer to gifted children are *highly able*, *highly capable*, or *high potential*. Some people think it is important to put the word *children* first, as in *children who are gifted and talented* and *children with gifts and talents*. No matter the terminology used, the designation is for children who are demonstrating the ability or potential for learning at advanced levels or beyond where age-mates are learning. The most important point to remember is to know the terminology used to refer to children who are gifted and talented in your district and state and then to use that terminology. The goal of all terminology is to designate the need for learning at advanced levels, as indeed, gifted children are capable of learning beyond grade level.

States also differ in the categories of giftedness that they recognize. Some states focus specifically on intellectual giftedness, while other states name several categories of giftedness. Six categories were included in the Marland Report (1972): general intellectual ability, a specific academic area, creative or productive thinking, leadership, the visual and performing arts, and psychomotor abilities. Soon after the Marland Report was issued, psychomotor ability was eliminated as one of those categories. Of course, psychomotor giftedness continues to be important, but, as mentioned earlier, schools and the public readily support athletic talent development, so gifted education funding could not also be used to support sports programs (psychomotor ability). A child can be identified as gifted in one or more of the five remaining categories.

The Jacob K. Javits Gifted and Talented Students Education Act of 1988, now the Jacob K. Javits Gifted and Talented Students Education Program (2015), defined gifted children as:

> Children and youth with outstanding talent perform or show the potential for performing at remarkably high levels of accomplishment when compared with others of their age, experience, or environment.
>
> These children and youth exhibit high performance capability in intellectual, creative, and/or artistic areas, possess an unusual leadership capacity, or excel in specific academic fields. They require services or activities not ordinarily provided by the schools.
>
> Outstanding talents are present in children and youth from all cultural groups, across all economic strata, and in all areas of human endeavor. (as cited in U.S. Department of Education, 1993, p. 3)

5

The federal definition of giftedness is as follows:

> (22) GIFTED AND TALENTED.—The term "gifted and talented", when used with respect to students, children, or youth, means students, children, or youth who give evidence of high achievement capability in areas such as intellectual, creative, artistic, or leadership capacity, or in specific academic fields, and who need services or activities not ordinarily provided by the school in order to fully develop those capabilities. (No Child Left Behind Act, P.L. 107-110 [Title IX, Part A, Definition 22]; 2002)

The National Association for Gifted Children (NAGC, 2019a) defined giftedness as follows:

> Students with gifts and talents perform—or have the capability to perform—at higher levels compared to others of the same age, experience, and environment in one or more domains. They require modification(s) to their educational experience(s) to learn and realize their potential. Students with gifts and talents:
> - Come from all racial, ethnic, and cultural populations, as well as all economic strata.
> - Require sufficient access to appropriate learning opportunities to realize their potential.
> - Can have learning and processing disorders that require specialized intervention and accommodation.
> - Need support and guidance to develop socially and emotionally as well as in their areas of talent.
> - Require varied services based on their changing needs.

In states in which gifted children are included within the category of exceptional children, the terminology from special education may be that used for gifted children. The definition may include a statement that the educational performance of the young person is adversely affected, indicating the general curriculum alone is inadequate to appropriately meet the student's educational needs.

Conclusion

Find the definition of gifted children used by your school, school district, and state, and then clarify its meaning. Make it your responsibility to discover and understand the definition that will guide the identification of gifted children where you live and teach. Are they called "advanced learners" or "children with gifts and talents"? The name is only the starting point, but what you do to recognize their needs and develop their potentials makes lifelong differences for these children and young people.

Various labels for gifted children will be used in this book. The next chapter discusses the responsibilities of teachers of gifted students. School and district leaders need to know about responsibilities set by law, policy, and regulations at district and state levels. Parents, too, need to be aware of what is in place in order for their child to make continuous progress, even when that is going beyond grade-level learning.

Questions to Get Started

- Does your state have a definition of gifted children? Perhaps that seems like an unusual question, but please note that all states do not have a definition.
- Is the definition of gifted in your district or state included as a category of exceptional children? This information will be important to know from the beginning.
- Do teachers in your school seem to know the definition of gifted children? If not, this information is a clue that professional learning is needed.

Survival Tips

A gifted child's area of greatest strength is also their area of greatest need, as that is what distinguishes them from age-mates. Remember that a gifted child's needs are just as intense and different from the average child's as are the needs of any other exceptional or special learner. Teachers need to share this information with colleagues and parents, as gifted children and young people do not look needy, yet their strengths create their needs.

Parents, educators, and policymakers need to know the definition of giftedness used in their state as well as the working definition in the school and school district.

Survival Toolkit

- NAGC (https://www.nagc.org) offers numerous resources to educate on gifted children. It is a great place to explore for topics related to gifted children.
- Your state may have two websites with information on the definition of giftedness in your state—that of the organization of gifted education and your state department of education. These should be rich resources for information about gifted education in your state, and the definition of giftedness should be readily available.
- Joseph Renzulli discusses his conception of giftedness in this video: https://www.youtube.com/watch?v=L8OlKSNQAIU.

Chapter 2

Find Out What You Do First

"A good program for the gifted increases their involvement and interest in learning through the reduction of the irrelevant and the redundant."—Sidney P. Marland, Jr.

Key Question

- What are the laws, policies, and regulations for gifted education in your school, district, and state?

Asking Questions: The Best Way to Get a Good Start

Getting a job offer or a new teaching assignment is both exciting and daunting. You may be starting as a gifted resource teacher. You may be assigned to a single classroom, multiple classrooms, an entire school, or pull-out services. It is also possible that you are a classroom teacher with a new interest in addressing the needs of gifted students in your classroom, or you have a new interest as your

DOI: 10.4324/9781003238553-3

school has a new focus on ensuring that all children, including those who are gifted and talented, make continuous progress. Whether you are a veteran teacher or new to teaching, you are about to embark on an exciting new role—one that involves teaching with a high interest in ensuring that advanced young learners are learning. This survival guide is written with the goal of helping you launch yourself into this new role in a highly successful style.

Perhaps you are starting your graduate classes or have completed a graduate program in gifted education and are beginning a new position. It is even possible that your state does not require teachers to take gifted classes before teaching in a gifted program or providing services for advanced learners, so your education will come via workshops or classes you take because you want to learn more about teaching children who are gifted and talented. No matter your preparation, your most pressing questions are likely "Where do I start?" and "What should I do first?"

Your starting place may be to do some homework on what is mandated or expected for gifted education in your school, district, and state. The website of your state department of education will be a profitable place to explore to know what is required in the way of services for children who are gifted and talented. NAGC also has links to all of the state associations for gifted children to assist you in finding information about the state organization with a focus on gifted children (see https://www.nagc.org/information-publications/gifted-state). Does your state have laws that include children who are gifted and talented and list requirements for their education? Does your state have a regulation for gifted education? Does your school board have a policy on gifted education? Does your school district have a handbook of policies and procedures for gifted education? Are there state or district policies in place about acceleration (more than 20 types of acceleration)? If the answer to any of these questions is yes, then you need to locate and save copies of the laws, policies, and regulations to guide you as you prepare for your new responsibilities.

Roles and Responsibilities

Another early question to ask is: "What are my responsibilities in my new position or within the new emphasis in my school?" There are many variations in programming and services for children and young people who are gifted and talented. Which ones characterize your new teaching responsibilities? Does your state refer to services offered to gifted children or to programs for them? It is important to define your role, as you can't be everything to everyone! That is why it is so important to ask about your responsibilities so you can focus on them.

The role of a gifted resource teacher has many variations. You may have an entire class of students who are gifted and talented. You may be the resource teacher who is responsible for delivering services within a school. More challenging, you may be the educator responsible for delivering services for gifted children in more than one school within the district or across an entire school district. Yet another possibility is that you will be a teacher in a magnet program for gifted children, which could incorporate a one-day-a-week service model, allowing you only one day each week to teach your students. Another possibility is that you have a classroom of gifted students in a magnet school.

Asking questions will be your way to begin defining your responsibilities. For example, you will need to ask who your supervisor is because you will need to pose questions to that individual. What expectations does your supervisor have for you in your new position? Who is responsible for establishing your schedule, and who can suggest input about that schedule? Talk with the person who had your position previously in order to see the "lay of the land." Also talk with your supervisor (who may be a district gifted coordinator or a building principal) to make sure that you fully understand all of their expectations for you in your position.

Perhaps you do not have a new position, but rather a new emphasis in your school or in your professional learning community (PLC) on being certain that gifted kids are stretched in terms of what they are capable of learning. What is your plan for ensuring that you know how to challenge all children in the classroom? What strategies will allow you to differentiate instruction in order to address the wide range of learning needs? Even if you have an entire class of young people who are all gifted and talented, remember that gifted children represent diverse needs and have a range of abilities and interests. The one-size-fits-all approach, even with an above-grade-level approach, will not remove the learning ceiling for all students.

Most of all, you need to know the basics about gifted education in your situation prior to starting your new position. You must be clear on which categories of giftedness are recognized in your school, district, and state. In some states, the category of gifted is limited to intellectually gifted children. In a few states, there are five categories of giftedness—intellectual giftedness as well as giftedness in a specific academic area, creativity, leadership, and the visual and performing arts. In each case, the programming or services must match the category of giftedness. Remember, gifted children don't appear on the surface to have learning needs, as their areas of strength create their needs. The gifted teacher's role is to support the whole gifted child, which includes providing social-emotional support as well as academically challenging them. That support certainly includes providing opportunities for each student to make continuous progress in their areas of strength or giftedness.

Understanding Terminology: Programs and/or Services?

You must understand and use appropriate terminology when communicating with gifted children, their educators, and parents. Do you talk about a gifted program or gifted services for children in your school? The terms *gifted program* and *gifted services* are not synonymous, although you may find they are used interchangeably.

Gifted program tends to communicate that there is one service for gifted children. The downside of calling your service "the gifted program" is that it implies that children are either gifted or not. The other possibility is to give the program a specific name, such as Project Challenge or SOAR (just examples), so it is one of several services, including such options as acceleration in math or reading and differentiation in the classroom.

Speaking about services rather than the gifted program allows you to share the responsibility for addressing the needs (remember—needs stem from students' strengths) of gifted children. You need all staff members to feel responsible for ensuring that all children, including those who are gifted and talented, make continuous progress. Services are offered by various educators and not just by the gifted resource teacher or teachers.

Terminology makes a difference in your message, so check out what terms describe gifted education practices in your school, district, and state. You also should know the key resources for basic information about gifted education, including:

- your state's gifted regulations,
- state laws that impact the education of gifted young people,
- your school district's school board policy on gifted education, and
- your school district's handbook for gifted education.

Knowing the Standards

NAGC's 2019 Pre-K–Grade 12 Gifted Programming Standards are a useful reference that will guide you, as well as educators in your school and district, as you develop services for children who are gifted and talented. Being familiar with the standards will provide confidence in your practices and will assist you as you assess progress in reaching those standards. The standards provide the background for understanding and implementing all aspects of programing for students with gifts and talents.

Note that parents and guardians of children need to know where to locate laws, policies, and regulations related to gifted education in the state and school district. Such information informs them as to what to expect in terms of services at various levels—elementary, middle, and high school. If parents see gaps in services at the next level, it is good to ask questions and perhaps address the need to advocate for additional services at the next level.

Conclusion

Getting started in your new position or with a new or renewed interest in gifted education is admirable. Locate important information from your school, district, and state to ensure that you make a positive start. Find the people who can help you know the laws, policies, and regulations, as well as the terminology, for you to incorporate in ways that will be beneficial for the children and young people you are teaching. It always pays off to educate yourself before you launch into a new area of education. Then, you will be ready to work with others who also want to learn about gifted education opportunities in your school and district.

Survival Tips

Launch yourself into gifted education by first finding out the "lay of the land" in your school, district, and state. Make sure you know what your school, district, and state have as laws, policies, and regulations that establish what services will be offered or could be available for young people who are gifted and talented. Then, be sure to post this information on the school district and school websites so educators and parents can readily access this information.

Survival Toolkit

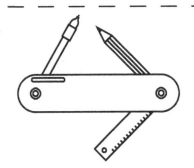

- NACG's 2019 Pre-K–Grade 12 Gifted Programming Standards (https://www.nagc.org/resources-publications/resources/national-standards-gifted-and-talented-education/pre-k-grade-12) focus on Learning and Development, Assessment, Curriculum Planning and Instruction, Learning Environments, Programming, and Professional Learning.
- The Davidson Institute for Talent Development (https://www.davidsongifted.org) has a ready source of current information on gifted education in all states.

- The State of the States in Gifted Education report (https://www.nagc.org/resources-publications/gifted-state/2014-2015-state-states-gifted-education) by the Council of State Directors of Programs for the Gifted and NAGC provides information about what your state does or does not do for children who are gifted and talented. The State of the States provides an overview of definition, policy, and funding for gifted education in your state.
- A compilation of state policies is also accessible in *A Guide to State Policies in Gifted Education* (2nd ed.), by E. W. Lord and J. D. Swanson, 2016, National Association for Gifted Children.

Survival Toolkit, continued

Chapter 3

Building Broad-Based Support for Gifted Education

"The education needs of top students are all but invisible in federal and state law and practice." (Smarick, 2013, p. 13)

Key Questions

- With whom should you be prepared to advocate for gifted education?

- What is your elevator speech as you speak out on behalf of children who are gifted and talented?

Why Advocate for Gifted Children?

To advocate means to speak out on behalf of someone or something. Speaking out in support of gifted education is incredibly important. Here are a few rea-

DOI: 10.4324/9781003238553-4

sons why gifted children need advocates and support for appropriate educational opportunities:

- The purpose of school is for children to learn on an ongoing basis. It is the school's responsibility to ensure that all children make continuous progress, including those who are gifted and talented.
- Gifted children will provide a disproportionate number of leaders for our future. Those are leaders that your community, state, and country need.
- Myths about gifted children are so widely believed that advocates need to be prepared to dispel them and provide accurate information. Debunking myths about gifted children is important in order for educators and parents to understand the needs of gifted young people—a prerequisite for challenging them at appropriate levels. Unless educators believe it is important, they are unlikely to make accommodations.
- Children who are not challenged actually may lose ground in school, both in terms of brain development (more dendrites result from novelty) and achievement (every child should make at least a year's achievement gain for each year spent in school). Much to the surprise of many people, advanced students often do not make a year's achievement gain in a year, as they frequently are not challenged in school.
- Quality educational opportunities for all children (all children includes advanced learners) constitute an economic development strategy. Businesses and industries that value and depend upon innovation will want to locate in places where quality educational opportunities are readily available. The advantage is both for the children and their future employers.
- Your future and the future of our country depend upon the children who are currently in school. What an important reason that is to support gifted education!

Expert Lynette Baldwin highlights the responsibility of and opportunities for educators, parents, and citizens to become advocates. She encourages all interested parties to advocate for children with special needs, including those who are gifted and talented.

Survival Secrets for Gifted Teachers

Lynette Baldwin

The job description for a teacher of gifted and talented children is expected to include identifying gifted students, providing a variety of differentiated services to meet the students' needs, and doing the myriad volumes of paperwork that gather in piles on the desk. The missing piece of the job description, and the piece that may cause great surprise to the many new teachers of gifted and talented children assume that colleagues and parents are as eager as they are to see that gifted children are challenged. It's wonderful when the support is there. It can be disheartening when it's missing. That's when the role of the advocate must kick in.

What does one do to become an advocate?

- First of all, believe in the importance of meeting the needs of gifted children. Develop the passion.
- You are the resident expert. Know your stuff. Know the laws and regulations. Know the research on gifted and talented children—their nature and needs as well as appropriate educational opportunities. Know the myths and the truths about gifted students. Know the individual students.
- From the information and knowledge of your audience(s), craft a clear message and state it often.
- Find supporters of gifted education and nurture them. Educate those who are not supporters in a positive way. There are many ways to do this—some overt, some . . . maybe not! At the same time, you are developing positive relationships among colleagues, parents, and members of the community, and those relationships go far toward strengthening acceptance of giftedness and the need for GT services.
- Be persistent. Rome wasn't built in a day, and neither will be support for gifted and talented services. However, over time, the number of supporters will increase, and changes for the better will be made.

Being a teacher advocate for gifted students is just as important as the other aspects of the job description for educators of gifted children. You believe in what you're doing and want others to believe in appropriate opportunities for gifted and talented children as well. This passion will give you courage. Go forth, teacher-advocator! Make a difference!

—Lynette Baldwin
Executive Director, Kentucky Association for Gifted Education Paducah, KY

Who Should Advocate for Gifted Children, and How Do They Do So?

Parents, educators, and citizens need to advocate for appropriate educational opportunities for gifted young people, and they need to have strong, accurate voices. As an advocate for gifted children, you have many ways to be an advocate. One of those ways is to be a member of decision-making groups like school councils so that you can be a voice representing young people who are gifted and talented.

You also can advocate in organizations in which you are active. Joining your state's gifted organization is a great way to learn about opportunities and new developments, so that you are current about best practices in gifted education. You can also be an important influence with parents, informing them of their child's rights and learning needs. Overall, the best way to advocate is to look for ways that you can help fellow educators and parents better understand the unique and diverse needs of children who are gifted and talented.

Advocacy involves speaking out on an issue as well as educating others on that issue or cause. All must be educated so that they can support addressing the needs of gifted children in order for them to learn on an ongoing basis. Sometimes that may mean correcting the myths about gifted children that are spoken so freely because they are believed so readily. Sometimes that may mean going to a seminar on the social-emotional needs of gifted children. Sometimes it is speaking up at a meeting to ask the questions highlighted in *Mind the (Other) Gap!* (Plucker et al., 2010). The report noted two questions that should be posed whenever educational decisions are made (by legislators, educators in the central office or at the school level, and parents).

1. How will this [decision] affect our brightest students?
2. How will this [decision] help other students begin to achieve at high levels? (p. 30)

Asking these two questions increases the awareness of the needs of children who are ready to learn at advanced levels and who will have progress impeded if ongoing challenge is not offered and continuous progress is not made possible.

What Parents Must Know

Parents must know the regulations and policies for the education of gifted children in the school district and state. Essential questions to ask are: "Are children making continuous progress?" and "Is your child working hard to achieve at high levels?" If the answers are no, then policies and practices to ensure continuous progress should become the focus of advocacy efforts.

Policies put best practices in place without the need to fight the battle for each child who needs accommodations. Policies need to facilitate learning rather than putting up barriers to slow down young people who are ready to proceed in their learning at matching and advanced levels. The following are examples of useful policies for keeping children learning on an ongoing basis (see other examples in Chapter 18, which include the Gold Standard School checklist):

- cut-off dates for starting school (a few children are ready sooner than others);

- requirements for graduation from high school—for example, the requirement to have a math class each year in high school differs from requiring four math credits (one requirement hampers early graduation, while the other doesn't);
- performance-based credit—such a policy makes it possible to demonstrate what one knows and is able to do to meet established standards for a course and opt out of that particular class or requirement; and
- universal screening—a policy to require universal screening is a first step in eliminating bias in recommending students to be assessed for their potential to be identified as gifted and talented.

Support Gifted Education at All Levels by Joining Advocacy Groups

Most states have a state organization with a focus on advocating for gifted education. You should become a member of your state advocacy group for several reasons. You will stay up to date with information, as the group will have newsletters and other ways of communicating with members. The state organization will hold an annual conference as well as other annual workshops—another way to stay current and to enhance your professional learning. And remember that numbers count when the organization is advocating at the state level with the state board of education, members of the state legislature, or other state-level organizations (superintendents, principals, boards of education, Chamber of Commerce, etc.).

Perhaps you will assist parents and educators in setting up a local advocacy organization if one is not already established. Your state gifted education organization will have guidelines for you in terms of setting up a local affiliate group. Groups can be specifically for parents or for educators, but they seem to be more effective when parents and educators work together to understand and advocate for children who are gifted and talented. NAGC (2011) published *Starting and Sustaining a Parent Group to Support Gifted Children* as a valuable resource. Remember that it is good practice to look around for materials that have already been developed, as these ready-made materials will save time and allow you to take advantage of available expertise. Of course, you must give appropriate credit to those who have developed any materials you choose to use.

There are also national and international organizations that focus on advocacy for children who are gifted and talented. They offer resources as well as professional development opportunities to learn more about strategies for addressing the needs of gifted children. Here are the websites for some of the most active organizations that teachers can join:

- The Association for the Gifted, the Council for Exceptional Children (CEC-TAG): https://www.cectag.com
- National Association for Gifted Children: https://www.nagc.org
- Supporting Emotional Needs of the Gifted (SENG): https://www.sengifted.org
- The World Council for Gifted and Talented Children (WCGTC): https://www.world-gifted.org

Numbers count in advocacy. The Prichard Committee of Academic Excellence in Kentucky created the following admonition to highlight the importance of joining with others who share your interests:

> If you think that you alone cannot do much to improve your school, you are probably right. You're more likely to get what you want for children if you work with others. If you collaborate with other parents and organizations, you can make a bigger difference than if you make requests on your own. There is strength and power in numbers.
>
> 1 person = A fruitcake
> 2 people = A fruitcake and a friend
> 3 people = Troublemakers
> 5 people = "Let's have a meeting."
> 10 people = "We'd better listen."
> 25 people = "Our dear friends"
> 50 people = "A powerful organization" (Henderson et al., 2004, p. 40)

Although this saying may make you smile, this description of the numbers required to move from a fruitcake to a powerful organization rings true.

Just as numbers count, so do relationships. You need to know the people who are in decision-making positions. That is not hard to do at the school level, but it is very important at the district level as well. Of course, decisions also are made at the state level, both by members of the legislature and by the state school board. Don't hesitate to provide them with information. After all, they represent you, and decisions they make will have a long-term impact on the children you know—in your family and/or in your classroom, district, and state. It is easier to influence a decision before it is final than to change one after the decision is made and established in policy.

The important thing is for you to be well informed about gifted children and their needs and willing to speak out on their behalf. It is also essential to help parents understand why their children must be learning at appropriately high levels.

Parents must be informed so they can be advocates for excellence. After all, your future and the future of your community depend on doing just that.

Conclusion

The need exists for teachers, parents, policymakers, and citizens to be advocates, making sure that students' learning needs are met both in and out of the classroom. Parents also should be encouraged to be advocates for their children, as should school and district administrators and policymakers. One of the most important steps in advocacy is the sharing of your knowledge about gifted children—remember that a little information can go a long way toward ensuring the development of our future leaders, thinkers, and innovators.

Survival Tips

- Knowing why you support gifted education will help you communicate those reasons to others.
- Prepare an elevator speech on gifted children and their needs (created by their strengths), ready to share when opportunities arise. Be ready to ask two very important questions when decisions are being made: (1) How will this decision affect our brightest students? and (2) How will this decision help other students begin to achieve at high levels? Most of the time, those questions will add to the discussion in positive ways for all children.

Survival Toolkit

- Gifted Advocacy (http://www.hoagies gifted.org/advocacy.htm) on Hoagies' Gifted Education Page provides a variety of links to tips on advocating for gifted children.
- *Parenting for High Potential* magazine is a great source of information on many topics, including advocacy. The March 2020 issue focuses on advocacy. Julia Link Roberts and Tracy Ford Inman wrote a column on advocacy that covered several years. A summary of those columns is included in this issue of *PHP* and is entitled "The Basics of Advocacy for Parents: Getting Started."
- *Starting and Sustaining a Parent Group to Support Gifted Children* (https://www.nagc.org/sites/default/files/Parent%20CK/Starting%20and%20 Sustaining%20a%20Parent%20Group.pdf) is a free guide from NAGC and Prufrock Press that provides a multitude of tips and resources for parent advocates and for teachers wanting to help the parents of their students be more involved.
- Other resources include:
  - Besnoy, K. (2005). Using public relations strategies to advocate for gifted programming in your school. *Gifted Child Today, 28*(1), 32–37.
  - Roberts, J. L. (2019). The primer for effective advocacy. *TEMPO,* XL(2), 32–37.
  - Roberts, J. L., & Siegle, D. (2012). If not you—who? Teachers as advocates. *Gifted Child Today,* 35(1), 58–61.

Chapter 4

Don't Treat Gifted Children Like Wallpaper or Accessories

"Nothing is more difficult than competing with a myth." —Lao Tzu

Key Questions

- What is fact and what is fiction related to gifted children?

- Who needs information in order to support fact rather than fiction related to gifted children?

Sometimes people assume that gifted children will be okay, so they treat them like wallpaper: They take them for granted. Frankly, the people who assume that gifted children will make it on their own are mistaken. That would be the same as believing that a child with athletic ability will become the same athlete he would become with no coaching. Gifted children and adolescents will not reach their potentials if educators and others make such faulty assumptions. The truth is our communities, states, and nation need for gifted children to reach their full potentials, as they will be represented in high numbers among our future leaders, innovators, and professionals. Many of them will be the job creators rather than those who fill jobs.

DOI: 10.4324/9781003238553-5

Other times, educators and parents treat children who are gifted and talented as accessories, such as by routinely using them as peer tutors in the classroom. Another example of treating these children as accessories is valuing them for their test scores. Still another example is showcasing these children for something they can do that is precocious. It is shortsighted to value gifted students for peer tutoring, having high test scores, or performing at advanced levels. Instead, valuing a child for positive personal attributes, such as honesty and helpfulness, is important, and doing so reinforces positive values in our communities and creates a promising future for these gifted children as well as for all children.

Educators need to know the facts so that they can counter the myths when they hear them. The following discussion will debunk some of the myths about gifted children, but know there are more.

Myth 1

Isn't proficiency or grade-level learning an admirable goal for teachers to set for their students? Have you experienced being caught on the interstate in traffic that is so heavy that your progress comes to a halt? Compare the feeling you have when you are slowed down or even stopped in traffic with the feeling you have when you are moving right along in the flow of normal driving. That comparison will help you understand the frustration felt by advanced learners when they are "caught in the traffic" of a class that is focused on grade-level learning and bringing all children to proficiency (grade-level achievement). Remember, proficiency is an admirable goal unless you have already reached or exceeded that level; then, proficiency is no goal at all, but rather it becomes a barrier to learning. Always remember that grade-level achievement is a mile marker rather than the end of the journey! For all children, including advanced learners, continuous progress is key to creating lifelong learners.

Myth 2

Aren't all children gifted? If the question refers to all children being special, then they certainly are. However, if "all children are gifted" refers to children performing at advanced levels in comparison to children their age, the answer is definitely not. All fifth or eighth graders do not perform at the same level in mathematics, reading, or science any more than they are all able to shoot free throws, swim laps, or kick goals at exceptionally skilled levels. Some athletes are exceptional just as some children have exceptional abilities as writers, mathematicians, and scientists. It is the level at which they can achieve that denotes that children are gifted in specific content areas, their performance in the visual and/or performing arts, their creative or innovative thinking, or their leadership potential.

Myth 3

Don't gifted children come from middle- or high-income families? Gifted children represent all economic backgrounds. The challenge is that all gifted children need support developing their potential and to develop skills and enhance the knowledge to perform at the highest levels. Characteristics of gifted children from lower income families will look different from those of other gifted children unless these children are afforded opportunities to develop their potential at high levels. Children with gifts and talents from lower income families may not be recognized for their exceptional potential for numerous reasons, including low expectations of educators and parents, and they are frequently underrepresented in gifted programming. Of course, that situation needs to be remedied. Children who are gifted and from low-socioeconomic backgrounds need to know about opportunities, but also about where to find financial support to participate in opportunities that have a cost. Otherwise, an opportunity gap likely already exists and then grows wider. Likewise, gifted children come from a variety of cultural and ethnic backgrounds; speak many languages; live in rural, suburban, and urban areas; and have a mixture of abilities (they may be twice-exceptional with gifted abilities as well as one or more disability).

Myth 4

Aren't children who are gifted and talented outstanding in all areas? Differences are evident among gifted children. A child may be advanced in reading, math, or any other subject, yet perform at grade level in another area. Or, the young person may be above grade level and ready for accelerated learning in several content areas. Still another child may be exceptional in creative thinking and need ongoing opportunities to use those creative thinking skills in various content areas. Further, some students who are gifted also have disabilities—for example, a gifted reader may have a handwriting disability that precludes them from doing well on written assignments. Remember, gifted children are diverse. They don't all exhibit the same profiles of strengths or areas of giftedness. There is no set of characteristics that all children with gifts and talents exhibit.

The public seems to understand that not all athletes are gifted at running, throwing, or shooting baskets, yet they expect someone labeled as academically gifted to be gifted in all areas. Much like gifted athletes, gifted children usually do not display the same level of ability and interest in everything they do.

Myth 5

Don't all gifted children make top grades? The answer is a resounding no. All gifted children do not make outstanding grades; in fact, some of them are under-achievers. Some make high grades when the subject is of interest to them and don't perform at high levels when they aren't interested or when the material being studied is already known and understood. The key to engaging all children in learning is to assess where they are in their learning on that topic or concept and start there, rather than assuming that all fifth graders are at the same point and all need to learn the fifth-grade content. Preassessing students to determine what they know about a concept can make a world of difference in matching learning experiences to what the student knows and is able to do with the specific topic being studied. (Chapter 11 provides a discussion of preassessment.) It is hard to stay motivated when you know most or all of the content. Remember the feeling you have when you are stuck in traffic? That's a feeling you don't want to repeat if you can avoid it, and students don't want to experience that frustrating situation either.

Myth 6

Isn't it a good idea to use gifted children as peer tutors? The answer to that question may depend on how often a child is asked to tutor a classmate, if they enjoy peer tutoring, and whether they are effective as a peer tutor. The goal for each child is to learn every day they are in school or to make continuous progress. Occasionally, it is fine for a child to tutor another; however, it is inappropriate for peer tutoring to interfere with a child's own learning. Also keep in mind that a child who learns something so quickly and effortlessly will often not be effective as a teacher (another name for the tutor) working one-on-one with a student who is struggling to learn the content. Sometimes the peer tutoring is used to occupy the time of children who have mastered the assigned work, and tutoring is not differentiating to address the learning needs of a student. Instead, grouping for instructional purposes (see Chapter 13) can facilitate ongoing learning for children who have already mastered course objectives.

Myth 7

You don't need to worry about gifted kids because they will "get it" on their own. This myth is dangerous, as it leads to benign neglect as the assumption is made that it is okay to concentrate differentiation strategies on children who need support to reach proficiency. Of course, those children are important, too; however, no children should be left out of opportunities to learn on an ongoing basis. Believing this myth leads to young people underachieving and not developing the knowledge or skills to meet an academic challenge when they face one—which is bound to happen. These young people don't develop study skills because they have never needed them. What a loss!

Myth 8

Accelerating a child is harmful, especially to their social-emotional development. Quite the contrary, the various types of acceleration can be very helpful in addressing the learning needs of children and adolescents. The one-size-fits-all approach doesn't work well; some children need to start earlier (kindergarten, middle school, college, etc.), others need the curriculum to be more challenging, and a few others need several types of acceleration in order to accommodate their learning needs (remember, needs for gifted children are created by their strengths). Social-emotional development isn't harmed by acceleration if the decisions are made carefully. In fact, many times the children find idea-mates who are older and, consequently, they are happier than in previous learning situations.

Myth 9

That teachers will challenge all students is something nice to believe; however, it is difficult (if not impossible) to challenge every student in a class when the wide range of learner needs is represented in the classroom. Many teachers have little or no preparation with knowledge or strategies for understanding and then challenging children with gifts and talents. Teacher preparation can provide that important information for teachers to address the learning needs of gifted students, and graduate programs and various types of professional learning can add to the understanding of advanced learners and introduce differentiation strategies to ensure that they are learning every day they are in school, as all children should have the opportunity to do.

Myth 10

Gifted children cannot be both gifted and have special learning needs requiring special education services. Quite the contrary, children can be twice-exceptional; and these children need services of the special education and the gifted education specialists if they are to develop their potential. Overlooking either type of service puts the child in jeopardy of not learning what they are capable of learning. Twice-exceptional learners only may be recognized for their giftedness or the disability, which puts them in jeopardy.

Conclusion

Myths about gifted children and best practices for addressing their needs are prevalent and often believed to be accurate. In fact, the mythology about gifted students is so widely believed that many outstanding educators are influenced by myths such as "Don't worry about gifted children, as they will 'get it' on their own." Teachers need to debunk these myths and work toward spreading accurate information about their gifted students and services to address their needs. Only when the myths are squashed can gifted children thrive in school and become lifelong learners.

Survival Tips

- Use your new expertise to correct myths that many experienced educators and the public in general believe to be true. Gifted children will benefit when you do. This tip is for everyone—parents as well as educators.
- Share resources you have to help others, including decision makers, be well informed about gifted children.
- Ensure that professional learning about gifted children and gifted education is offered annually for educators and parents. This professional learning could be a workshop, but it could also include sending out short articles intermittently, offering discussion groups, conducting a book study (perhaps with this book) with a PLC, hosting a library of materials on gifted education, and serving as a resource to educators and parents.

Survival Toolkit

- *Gifted Child Quarterly* (http://gcq.sage pub.com) dedicated its Fall 2009 issue to the topic of demythologizing gifted education. It provides valuable information for learning what is and isn't true about gifted education. Sadly, the myths persist and are thought to be truths by many.
- "Top 10 Myths in Gifted Education" (https://www.youtube.com/watch?v= MDJst-y_ptI) by GTAMoCo is an effective video on myths about gifted children. This video can be educational for you and useful when sharing information to educate parents, fellow educators, and your students. Perhaps you have young people who would enjoy staging a similar video and sharing it on YouTube.
- NAGC's resource on myths (https://www.nagc.org/myths-about-gifted-stu dents) is available to share with others. Not all lists of myths will include the same ones, as there are so many myths about gifted children.

Chapter 5

Recognizing Differences Among Gifted Children

"We look for differences not to label but to address the differences."
—Margaret Sutherland

Key Questions

- In what ways can you help fellow educators distinguish among characteristics that are typical of young people who are high achieving, gifted, talented, or creative?

- What students have you had that you believe are gifted in various ways, and what characteristics did they have that made that connection for you?

If you know characteristics that are typical of gifted and talented children, you will be prepared to recognize these students in your classroom and among your family and friends. Remember, gifted children are a diverse group, so no set of characteristics will describe all of them, and no child will be characterized by every descriptor in a list.

DOI: 10.4324/9781003238553-6

One way to think about intellectually gifted children is that they learn at a faster pace and a more complex level than their age-peers. Think of the differences between high-speed and dial-up Internet connections. The processing time is quite different, and those different capabilities create very different expectations. The child who is intellectually gifted could be compared to high-speed Internet. This child who has experienced appropriately challenging opportunities knows the joy of learning (just as you have enjoyed the speed of the Internet once you switched from dial-up connections). People who have experienced both types of Internet connection—dial-up and high-speed—are quite impatient with the slower mode of connecting. Likewise, gifted children are likely not easy to engage in grade-level instruction if what they know and are able to do is beyond that level; in fact, for some gifted students, they are well beyond the level of instruction that is appropriate for most children their age. This comparison is offered to help you understand one difference in how children who are gifted and talented experience the world.

Gifted children have different abilities, talents, and interests, making them a very diverse group of individuals. What they share in common are advanced development and an intense interest in a particular content or talent area. Some children will show evidence of talent in numerous areas, but some will be advanced in one particular area. Gifted children won't look alike in a classroom either. You will miss many of them if you don't look for characteristics and behaviors that evidence themselves in multiple ways.

Gifted Children as a Diverse Population

Gifted children are a very diverse population. They share many, but not all, characteristics. On some characteristics, they tend to be at the extremes. For example, they tend to be very well organized or not very well organized at all. Whereas all children are curious, gifted children may exhibit a curiosity that seems like nonstop questioning. Intensities are fairly typical among gifted young people.

Children who are gifted and talented often develop very specific interests at an early age. Zach becomes so interested in dinosaurs that everything he wants to read or to have you read relates to dinosaurs. Caroline develops her interest in history by playing with her American Girl doll Felicity and wanting to read all of the books that are available about Felicity and the historical time period she represents. Jose is very, very interested in playing chess before anyone else in his class shares that interest. Or Claire wants to learn all about butterflies, even though no one knows where she got that fascination. The key is for students to find others who share the interest (idea-mates who may be older students) to keep gifted students learning about a topic that they find so very interesting. Do not worry—the interest will likely shift to a new topic about which they will have a similar intensity to learn.

Examples of Gifted Children

The following vignettes provide a few examples of children who are gifted and talented but have gifts and talents in different areas. As you read these, we hope you'll recognize that not all gifted children look alike and perhaps think about children you know who may be gifted and or talented.

James has had an insatiable curiosity since he was very young; you might say he was born curious. He frequently takes things apart. He uses objects intended for one purpose for another because he tinkers with the pieces to see if it will work or he immediately sees that it will work to do so. Adults worry that something is "wrong" with him, as his constant questioning seems bothersome. The adults in his life need to realize that asking good questions is more important than having the right answers. A positive situation results when a teacher recognizes James's creative thinking abilities and provides opportunities for him to channel his thinking in productive ways.

Maria is very interested in sketching and spends time drawing as the teacher talks to the class. She is a willing learner, and she excels when her class projects allow her to incorporate her artistic abilities. If the teacher recognizes her interests and capitalizes on them, Maria will thrive in school. On the other hand, she is not likely to thrive if she is constantly reminded to put down her sketchbook and listen as though her artistic abilities are mainly an interference.

Ariana is advanced in all core content areas—social studies, math, science, and language arts—and she is also quite accomplished at playing the violin. Sometimes she does not want to go to school and would prefer learning at home, where she can select the books and other resources to learn about topics at the level at which she is ready to learn, and therefore interested. She is happiest in school when she has open-ended projects or other opportunities to make continuous progress.

Chad has been a leader among his age-peers since he entered school—even before then, too. He gets others to do whatever he asks, and usually his goals are good ones. Other young people are eager to hear what Chad has to say and are likely to follow his directions. Chad benefits from services that develop his leadership skills. Without leadership training and chances to develop his skills, he may lose sight of positive ways to advance his leadership capabilities.

Elizabeth is an outstanding reader, comprehending reading materials several levels above her current grade. She is especially interested in history and other social studies topics. In math, Elizabeth is at grade level. She thrives in school when she is clustered with other advanced readers who motivate each other as they discuss their reading choices that usually are different from age-mates'. She is unhappy when she is required to work on grade-level reading materials by a teacher who is afraid that she may have missed a reading skill or two, yet she is fine working at grade level in math class.

The young people described are gifted children, but advanced in different ways. In order for them to thrive in school, they must be grouped for instructional purposes, and assignments must be differentiated in order to capitalize on what they do well and encourage their interests. Chapters 12 and 13 will describe strategies for differentiating assignments. A one-size-fits-all curriculum will not bring out the best in gifted children, nor will that type of curriculum be in the best interest of other children either. Teachers must know their students' interests, needs (remember, needs for them are created by their strengths so they may not look needy), and abilities well in order for all of them to make continuous progress. The best way to address the needs of all types of gifted children is to provide instruction that removes the learning ceiling.

Comparing Characteristics of High Achievers, Gifted Learners, and Creative Thinkers

One way to look at the behaviors of children who are high achievers in comparison with those who are gifted learners is through a chart created by Kingore (2004) and shown in Table 1. The third column of this chart adds the behaviors of

Table 1

High Achiever, Gifted Learner, Creative Thinker

A High Achiever . . .	A Gifted Learner . . .	A Creative Thinker . . .
Remembers the answers.	Poses unforeseen questions.	Sees exceptions.
Is interested.	Is curious.	Wonders.
Is attentive.	Is selectively mentally engaged	Daydreams; may seem off task.
Generates advanced ideas.	Generates complex, abstract ideas.	Overflows with ideas, many of which will never be developed.
Works hard to achieve.	Knows without working hard.	Plays with ideas and concepts
Answers the questions in detail.	Ponders with depth and multiple perspectives.	Injects new possibilities.
Performs at the top of the group.	Is beyond the group.	Is in own group.
Responds with interest and opinions.	Exhibits feelings and opinions from multiple perspectives.	Shares bizarre, sometimes conflicting opinions.
Learns with ease.	Already knows.	Questions: What if...
Needs 6 to 8 repetitions to master.	Needs 1 to 3 repetitions to master.	Questions the need for mastery.
Comprehends at a high level.	Comprehends in-depth, complex ideas.	Abstracts beyond original ideas.
Enjoys the company of age peers.	Prefers the company of intellectual peers.	Prefers the company of creative peers but often works alone.
Understands complex, abstract humor.	Creates complex, abstract humor.	Relishes wild, off-the-wall humor.
Grasps the meaning.	Infers and connects concepts.	Makes mental leaps: Aha!
Completes assignments on time.	Initiates projects and extensions of assignments.	Initiates more projects than will ever be completed.
Is receptive.	Is intense.	Is independent and unconventional.
Is accurate and complete.	Is original and continually developing.	Is original, ever changing, and misunderstood.
Enjoys school often.	Enjoys self-directed learning.	Enjoys creating.
Absorbs information.	Manipulates information.	Improvises.

Table 1, continued

A High Achiever . . .	A Gifted Learner . . .	A Creative Thinker . . .
Is a technician with expertise in a field.	Is an expert, abstracts beyond the field.	Is an inventor and idea generator.
Memorizes well.	Guesses and infers well.	Creates and brainstorms well.
Is highly alert and observant.	Anticipates and relates observations.	Is intuitive.
Is pleased with own learning.	Is self-critical.	Is never finished with possibilities.
Gets A's.	May not be motivated by grades.	May not be motivated by grades.
Is able.	Is intellectual.	Is idiosyncratic.

Note. From *Differentiation: Simplified, Realistic, and Effective,* by B. Kingore, 2004, Figure 4.2, Professional Associates Publishing. Copyright 2004 Professional Associates Publishing. Reprinted with permission.

creative thinkers. This chart provides a good way to recognize differences among high-achieving, gifted, and creative children. The chart is a basic reference to use when helping colleagues understand that high-achieving students do not have the needs that gifted children do and how creative thinkers differ from other gifted children. Keep in mind that all children in each of those categories will not display all of the characteristics but rather some of them.

You may want to adapt Table 1 and cut it into two strips—one for high-achieving students and one for gifted students. Then cut the characteristics into separate descriptors on individual strips and mix them up. The next step is to test your knowledge of the differences between high-achieving and gifted learners. If you can match these descriptors, then add the ones for children who are creative thinkers and test your ability to determine which descriptors are characteristic of each of the three types of learners.

Conclusion

Recognizing the strengths of all children is important, and it is necessary for educators to know the strengths of gifted children in particular. Remember, strengths are relative. For gifted children, their strengths are likely to manifest in achievement one or more grade levels above others in their class. Yet some gifted young people may perform several grades above their age-mates. The strengths of gifted children determine the areas in which they need advanced instruction if they are to make continuous progress. Matching learning experiences to the strengths that children have is the best way to ensure that they have the ongoing opportunity to learn at high levels. Continuous progress or learning on an ongoing basis is the goal of schools, and differentiating instruction is the means to make continuous progress a reality for all children, including those who are gifted and talented.

Survival Tips

- Learn to distinguish among the characteristics of children who are high achievers, gifted learners, and creative thinkers because their needs (based on their strengths) differ one from another.
- Parents often are the first to point out their children's learning needs to teachers and administrators, and they can provide insight into children's strengths and interests outside of school. What does the child enjoy doing when not in school?
- Make sure that parents and educators know there is no one set of characteristics that a teacher can check off in a list that will signal that a child is gifted and talented.
- Check out the mission statement for the school. Likely, it speaks to developing the potential of all students. Know what the mission statement says as you interact with educators at the school.

Survival Toolkit

- The Gifted Development Center (https://www.gifteddevelopment.com/quiz/is-your-child-gifted) shares a list of the common characteristics of gifted children.
- *Identifying Gifted Students* (3rd ed.), edited by S. K. Johnsen (2019, Prufrock Press), provides an overview of characteristics children in various categories of giftedness demonstrate.
- See also *The Kingore Observation Inventory* (3rd ed.), by B. Kingore (2016), Professional Associates Publishing.

Chapter 6

Identifying Gifted Students

"Cast a wide net to identify all types of talents and to nurture potential in all demographics of students. To this end, we must develop and implement appropriate talent assessments at multiple grade levels and prepare educators to recognize potential, particularly among those individuals who have not been given adequate opportunities to transform their potential into academic achievement." (National Science Board, 2010, p. 3)

Key Question

- What are the regulations for identifying children who are gifted and talented in your school, district, and state?

The purpose of identification is to provide assessment data in order to match gifted services to the needs of the child. Teachers need to home in on each student's level of readiness, interests, abilities, and talents. After all, educators must always be interested in ensuring that students have the most appropriate opportunities to

 DOI: 10.4324/9781003238553-7

learn at challenging levels, as well as to recognize and develop their talents. Data gathered during the identification process provide that important information.

Identification is a very important process, and one that must be taken seriously. After all, information gathered during the identification process contributes to their educational trajectory. Educators need to acknowledge that identification is not an exact science, so they must use best practices to guide the identification process.

> On an airplane trip, a woman across the aisle noticed what I was reading and asked if I was a teacher. After I responded yes, she identified herself as a teacher and followed up with questions, eagerly telling about two gifted children in her classroom the previous year. She remarked that she was so glad that they had gone on to a teacher who wasn't overwhelmed by the paperwork for recommending them to be assessed for the gifted program. She said that lots of teachers didn't want to bother with the paperwork. Of course, that may be the case for educators who don't see gifted children as having real needs. They miss the point that gifted children have needs emanating from their strengths rather than from deficiencies. A gifted child is every bit as needy as other exceptional learners if you examine how different they are from the average learner.

If paperwork keeps educators from sharing information to begin the identification process, children who may need advanced learning opportunities will be denied learning experiences that will allow them to reach their academic potential.

Basic Points About Identification

There are a few basic points for you to remember when identifying children as gifted and talented:
1. **Identification must be defensible.** Educators need to know what procedures are to be followed and what assessments are to be used. They need to be well informed, as do parents.
2. **Services must be matched to the area of identification.** That match is very important; in fact, it is the match that makes services defensible. For example, if the assessment is to identify young people who are exceptionally creative in their thinking, the services to be offered must acknowledge creative thinking ability and provide learning experiences to further develop their creative thinking capabilities.

3. **Identification is a two-step process with screening as the first step.** Universal screening must precede identification.

4. **Universal screening is best practice to ensure that all students have opportunities to demonstrate what they know and are able to do.** Without universal screening, exceptional thinking and achievement may not be recognized by teachers when the first step in identifying is a teacher recommendation.

5. **The identification process must be ongoing, as talent emerges at different points in a school career.** It is never too late to recognize that a young person's ability is advanced when compared with their age-peers. Sometimes such abilities show up early, but not always. Various opportunities may increase interest in learning in a specific content area and spark the development of skills and the increase of knowledge and understanding.

6. **Procedures must be followed.** Identification must follow the guidelines that the state and local school district have established. Educators can locate these guidelines by talking to gifted coordinators and school administrators and by searching their state department of education's website.

7. **Services must provide continuous progress.** The purpose of identifying children in some area of giftedness and/or talent is to recognize the need for appropriate services to develop that area of talent or high interest. Continuous progress in an area of strength is necessary if talent is to develop or interest in an academic area is to flourish. Perhaps a talent development plan would be a good way to ensure continuity in a talent or an advanced area.

8. **Multiple measures must be used.** No single assessment should determine giftedness, nor should one score exclude a child from being in consideration to be identified as gifted. These measures might include assessments of aptitude and achievement, rating scales (for teachers and parents to fill out), work samples, and portfolios.

9. **Use assessments to identify giftedness in diverse populations.** Assessments must be selected to maximize the opportunity for children who represent diverse populations to be identified as gifted in one or more categories of giftedness. For that reason, tests must be free of culture bias, and nonverbal measures may need to be used to identify students.

10. **Offer professional learning opportunities on identification.** If children from diverse backgrounds are underrepresented in the school and/or district, professional learning must be provided that will help teachers recognize giftedness and potential giftedness in these populations.

11. **The use of local norms provides the opportunity to recognize children who are performing above their classmates, although not at the level set for identifying gifted children in the district.** Local norms constitute best practice and offer opportunities for ensuring that children from diverse

backgrounds have ongoing opportunities to learn at increasingly challenging levels.

Type of Assessment for Various Categories of Giftedness

Different types of assessments are used to identify children as gifted in various categories. Assessments of aptitude may be administered to a group of students or to individual students, and they provide the means of identifying children as intellectually gifted. Assessments of achievement are used to identify children as gifted in a specific academic area. Measures of creative thinking and examples of creative thinking are key to identifying children as gifted in creativity. Performances and portfolios provide evidence of giftedness in the visual and performing arts. Leadership is assessed through a portfolio and evidence that the young person is initiating projects at school or in the community.

Defensible is the key word when it comes to identifying gifted children. Of course, the district's or state's definition of giftedness will guide the selection of assessments to be used when gathering data on children. Identification needs to be a two-step process: first screening and then identification. Universal screening casts a wide net, as all children have the opportunity to be included in the identification process.

Expert Susan K. Johnsen provides useful information about the identification process. She highlights information that is important to understand in order to implement defensible identification procedures.

Survival Secrets for Identifying Gifted Students

Susan K. Johnsen

What do educators need to know about identifying gifted and talented students? Educators need to be aware of the characteristics of students with gifts and talents in order to identify them. They need to know that students may be gifted in one area and not another. For example, a student may be achieving above grade level in math, but on grade level in reading. Because other factors, such as cultural background, income level of the family, a disability, or even age, may also influence how students exhibit specific characteristics, educators need to understand how a student's characteristics interact with these factors and produce different behaviors. For example, a student who is twice-exceptional (i.e., is gifted and also identified as having a disability) may show critical thinking during science class, but not be able to read or write at grade level.

Next, educators need to create classroom environments that nurture talents and develop opportunities for students to accelerate and to think deeply about the content. Opportunities might include the use of long-term assignments, open-ended activities, contracting, independent research, compacting, preassessment, mentoring, above-grade-level materials, higher level questions, and activities that emphasize depth or breadth in a specific subject area. Without an environment that is challenging and interesting, students with gifts and talents may not be recognized and may even hide what they already know. For example, kindergarteners may try to fit in and not show that they are able to read or do complex math problems. Educators should, therefore, be observant, focus on a child's strengths, and notice characteristics that might be indicative of high potential.

When selecting assessments for identification, educators need to align these with the characteristics of the students and with the services that they will receive. For example, if programming aims to develop students' abilities in mathematics, then the identification instruments would examine potential in that area. Assessments might include achievement tests in math, observations of students solving math problems, intelligence tests, teacher and parent checklists of characteristics demonstrating mathematical aptitude, and classroom projects involving math. Educators should notice that the assessments should include multiple sources of information (e.g., parents, students, teachers) and both quantitative and qualitative data. The assessments also need to consider the unique characteristics of the school population. If the population is quite different from national norms (e.g., primarily Hispanic or students from poverty), then the school might want to consider developing its own norms. In cases where students are not linguistically fluent, alternative assessments, such as nonverbal tests and performance-based activities, need to be considered.

Assessments also need to be reliable and valid for the purpose of identifying gifted students. Not only do they need to be aligned to the program and the student, but they also need to show they are not biased against any group, they will predict student performance in the gifted program, and they will discriminate between gifted and other students (e.g., validity issues). Moreover, they need to be consistent or reliable. A student's performance should not vary dramatically from one testing to the next. Those involved in selecting assessments need to be familiar with the technical aspects of tests and with books or websites that review tests (e.g., Buros Center for Testing [https://buros.org]; Johnsen, 2018). Once the assessments are selected, all staff need to understand the importance of following specific administration instructions and know how to interpret the results (e.g., what scores and performance variations mean).

Finally, schools need to examine how closely their identification procedures follow local, state, and national policies and standards (e.g., NAGC, 2019b). All individuals (e.g., teachers, parents, administrators, counselors, psychologists) who will be involved in identifying students with gifts and talents need to be aware of these policies, procedures, and standards so that the entire identification process is equitable and the students who need services are identified.

—Susan K. Johnsen, Ph.D.
Professor Emerita, Department of Educational Psychology, Baylor University

Who else can help in the identification process? The school psychologist, counselor, and classroom teacher can share responsibility for assessing the students. Special teachers of music, art, and drama are key individuals to assess students for talent in the visual and performing arts. Special education teachers can assist in identifying twice-exceptional students. Parents (who really know the child best) can provide valuable information about developmental milestones as well as interests they see occupying the child's time and attention outside of school.

Expert Geoffrey Moon adds information about the importance of casting a wide net in the identification process. He reminds us not to overlook any child, including those from lower socioeconomic backgrounds, children who are twice-exceptional, those who do not speak English as their first language, as well as children from all ethnic and racial groups.

Survival Secrets for Equitably Identifying Students From Underserved Populations

Geoffrey Moon

Gifted education supports the development of talent, expanding opportunity to match students' abilities. To promote equity, giftedness should be identified in students from all populations so we can develop talents of highly able students across our society. Historically, it has been hard for students with culturally or linguistically diverse backgrounds, economic disadvantages, and disabling conditions, here called CLEDD factors, to access gifted education. How can we overcome these barriers?

Understanding the Problem

Although economic disadvantage and racial/ethnic minority status overlap, they must be understood as distinct factors impacting a student's educational opportunity and situation. English language learner status and learning disabilities pose unique challenges for gifted students' identification.

Economically disadvantaged students often experience less home and school support for advanced academics. These students frequently enter kindergarten having been exposed to less school-type knowledge in early life. They may experience elevated home stressors combined with a lack of resources to help them access enrichment. Higher poverty schools are less likely to push gifted identification.

Being part of a historically disadvantaged minority may magnify or complicate the effects of economic disadvantage. Black students often attend schools with fewer resources and less rigorous curricula. Latinx and Black students are more likely to attend high-poverty schools and are at greater dropout risk. Rates of post-traumatic stress disorder (PTSD) are higher across minority racial and ethnic groups.

Economic disadvantage and disadvantaged minority status negatively impact previous and ongoing opportunity to learn. With depressed opportunity to learn, students are less likely to be referred for gifted education testing and are at a disadvantage on normed tests of reasoning and achievement compared to peers across the nation. To the extent motivation impacts learning, CLEDD students may be further impeded by attending schools that fail to engage.

Students lacking English proficiency face the dual learning challenges of acquiring a new language while missing content others are exposed to. Performance may be hindered because of decreased language processing speed.

Learning disabilities can decrease function in one or more symbol systems like words, numbers, or shapes; slow processing; decrease attention; and make school an unpleasant place to be. Because gifted students are good problem solvers, they may somewhat compensate for a disability, but the combination of gift and disability can make their performance seem average. Consequently, they may not be referred for gifted identification testing, and may not perform well or consistently when tested.

CLEDD factors make it less likely a student will be tested for gifted education and less likely they will perform at the same consistency and level as students without these factors.

Responding to the Need: Growing Equity

To develop equity for gifted students with CLEDD factors, schools should use a systematic response that optimizes administrative goals, school environment, nomination/referral systems, testing, interpretation, planning, and services.

  Set equity goals. Modern information systems allow school officials to easily compare the economic, racial/ethnic, language, and disability characteristics of the whole school or district to those identified as gifted. By dividing the subgroup percent identified gifted by the subgroup percent in a school, one can calculate a representativeness index. With 1 as a perfect score, consider setting a minimum representativeness goal for each subgroup.

- **Optimize school environments.** Students who learn quickly and enjoy complexity will often respond to classrooms that remove limits on pace and developmental expectations. Use gifted education strategies and content in the general education classroom and see who engages. Because minds are highly malleable at early ages, service-before-identification may serve to close gaps in performance.

- **Decrease nomination or referral as barriers to testing.** Many tests of intellectual ability and achievement have been carefully designed to reduce bias, yet large racial/ethnic, language, and economic disparities in identification persist. There are several ways to respond.

  - **Test everyone.** Screening tests performed on all students remove barriers to entry.

  - **Use the data you have.** Many schools already perform universal testing for reading and math.

  - **Ask for observations instead of referrals.** Training teachers to look for specific characteristics instead of referring those likely to qualify can decrease biases.

  - **Use multiple nomination sources.** Teachers may recognize potential for school-type activities. Parents can be good informants about talents less often addressed in school, like building. Tests may reveal what no observation does—high performance in a student who is reluctant to communicate. Because no method is perfectly sensitive to potential or talent in all domains, it may be best to do all of the above.

  - **Test in multiple domains and for talent as well as potential.** Learning speed is important but is more important in early development. Over time, as talent development takes place, achievement and motivation become more important. Assess learning ability, achievement, and motivational characteristics in multiple domains to make sure that the budding engineer, the high-flying writer, and the emerging mathematician are all identified.

  - **Interpret using local or subgroup norms.** Economic disadvantage, racial/ethnic minority status, English language learner status, and disability can each uniquely diminish opportunity and complicate identification. Comparing students to others with the same opportunities control for these differences.

- **Plan to serve students' futures.** Most unique needs of gifted students are either around developing talents or the problems that stem from putting ceilings on growth. Set long-term goals around students' interests and abilities. Realistically assess and plan for what they need to get there, including services to close gaps in opportunity and language development, and build compensatory skills for students with disabilities.

- **Serve them!** Gifted students don't develop their talents without opportunity. Students with CLEDD factors have further to go. Substantial service provided as early as possible helps to maintain potential and develop talent.

An educational system that identifies giftedness and develops talent in all student populations is one we can be proud of. Equitable identification celebrates both our common humanity and our unique potentials.

— Geoffrey Moon
M.A.T. Lead Gifted Education Specialist, Santa Fe Public Schools, NM

Individualized Education Program (IEP)

Once a young person is identified in one or more areas of giftedness and/or talent, some states require an Individualized Education Program, better known as an IEP. An IEP is required in states in which gifted children constitute a category of exceptional children, and it is a written plan designed to ensure that the needs of the special education student are addressed. If that is true in your state, you need to learn as much as possible about the IEP. Please know the IEP may have another name in your state. For example, in Kentucky the IEP is called the Gifted Student Services Plan (although it is the individual education plan in law). No matter the name, the IEP comes with the weight of law. Publications on students with disabilities will help you understand the IEP further, as will your district's gifted and special education coordinators.

Points to Remember to Make Identification Defensible

1. **Match the tools.** Identification tools must match the category being identified. For example, you must use an assessment designed to measure creativity if you are identifying students for creative or productive thinking. Aptitude measures are needed for identification of students as intellectually

gifted, while achievement assessments will be used for identifying students as gifted in a specific academic area. Identification in the visual and performing arts will necessitate using performance measures and portfolios.

2. **Communicate.** Communicate with children, parents, and other educators so they know what the term *gifted* or *advanced learner* means and does not mean. Take the mystery out of identification and out of being gifted. Make sure that all parties understand differences among learners, including why some students are ready for more advanced learning experiences.

3. **Cast a wide net** so as to include children who are from lower socioeconomic backgrounds, who are twice-exceptional, who do not speak English as their first language, as well as children from all ethnic and racial groups.

4. **Encourage teacher observation.** Educators should be vigilant as they observe children for evidence that they are more advanced than their age-mates in one or more areas of giftedness or talent. To be a good observer, the teacher must be familiar with characteristics of gifted learners and know that some of these characteristics may appear to be less than desirable (e.g., asking too many questions to suit the teacher, having lots of energy that needs to be channeled in positive ways through engaging learning experiences).

5. **Hold on to your data.** Keep the tests and assessment data, as you may need them later. The assessments could prove useful in the future, so find a filing cabinet that can be locked in which to keep the results of instruments given to students.

6. **Understand why you identify students.** Remember that identification is not an exact science, but the goal of identification is noble—to recognize strengths among children in order to teach them in ways that will allow their full potentials to develop. Giftedness constitutes a label (not to be confused with a reward) to signal learning needs.

7. **Use local norms.** If your students identified as gifted and talented don't represent the demographics of your student body, look into using local norms.

8. **Make sure that students have ongoing opportunities** to be assessed for potential identification.

9. **Remember that off-level assessments tell you at what level the child can perform.** An off-level assessment is intended for children or young people who are older; therefore, when you administer the off-level assessment and remove the learning ceiling, you can see at what level the child can perform. An example of an off-level assessment is giving the SAT or the ACT to seventh graders as a part of one of the talent searches. That information should be documented and used to plan instruction to match the young person's level of readiness.

Evans and Whaley (n.d.) developed the Jot Downs (see Figures 1 and 2) to help teachers look for behaviors among children in their classes. The teacher sim-

Figure 1
General Intellectual Ability Jot Down

Brief description of
observed activity: _____

Date ___/___/___
Mo.   Day   Yr.

Teacher _____
Grade _____ School _____

1. As students show evidence of the following characteristics in comparison with age peers, jot their names down in the appropriate box/es.
2. When recommending students for gifted services, use this identification jot down as a reminder of student performances in the area of general intellectual ability.

Sees connections/recognizes patterns, may want to know how what is being taught fits in.	Asks many probing questions, sometimes to the point of driving others up the wall.	Able to work one or more years above others in age group.
Widely read or likes to read. May prefer to read rather than be with others.	Knows many things that have not been taught.	Appears to have a deep sense of justice. May correct others when something seems wrong.
	Has a large vocabulary but may choose when to use it.	Benefits from rapid rate of presentation. May refuse to do work seen as busy work.

Figure 1, continued

Displays intensity for learning. Preoccupied and hard to move on to new topic or area of study.	Prefers a few close friends with similar intellect to many friends.	Likes to observe before trying new activities. Thinks through ideas before sharing with others.	Has knowledge about things age peers may not be aware of.
Prefers to work independently with little direction. May be resistant to being the leader of a group.	Displays abstract thinking. Requires time to think before responding.	Shows high energy level (physical, intellectual, and psychological).	Appears to have discrepancies between physical, social, and intellectual development.

Note. From *Jot Downs* [unpublished manuscript], by M. A. Evans and L. Whaley, n.d., The Center for Gifted Studies, Western Kentucky University, Bowling Green, KY. Reprinted with permission of the authors.

Figure 2
Specific Academic Area Jot Down

Brief description of
observed activity: _____

Check One:
- ☐ Language Arts
- ☐ Social Studies
- ☐ Math
- ☐ Science

Date ____/____/____
Mo.   Day   Yr.

Teacher _____
Grade _____ School _____

1. As students show evidence of the following characteristics in comparison with age peers, jot their names down in the appropriate box/es.
2. When recommending students for gifted services, use this identification jot down as a reminder of student performances in this specific academic area.

Sees connections.	Asks many probing questions.	Shares what he or she knows, which may be seen as answering "too often."	Provides many written/oral details.
Is widely read or likes to read about the subject area.	Absorbs information quickly from limited exposure.	Has a large vocabulary in subject area.	Benefits from rapid rate of presentation in subject area.

Figure 2, continued

Displays intensity for learning within subject area.	Requires little or no drill to grasp concepts.	Generates large number of ideas or solutions to problems.	Has knowledge about things age peers may not be aware of.
Prefers to work independently with little direction.	Displays leadership qualities within subject area.	Applies knowledge to unfamiliar situations.	Offers unusual or unique responses.

Note. From *Jot Downs* [unpublished manuscript], by M. A. Evans and L. Whaley, n.d., The Center for Gifted Studies, Western Kentucky University, Bowling Green, KY. Reprinted with permission of the authors.

ply records the name of the child in the square with the specific behavior the child demonstrated. Later the teacher looks for names that were jotted down for patterns among the students in the class.

The first Jot Down included is for general intellectual ability. This type of giftedness is the one people likely think of first when they talk about a gifted child. This type of giftedness is also the one that states designate if they recognize only one category of giftedness.

Giftedness in a specific academic ability (see Figure 2) does not have to accompany general intellectual giftedness, but it may. A child may be gifted in one specific academic area or in two or more. The young person who is gifted in math or language arts may well be on grade level in other subject areas. It is important to understand that a gifted child may be gifted in various ways; thus, being gifted may look different in various individuals.

Remember that all student behaviors that indicate giftedness in any specific category are not positive or endearing to some teachers. It is important for teachers to recognize when characteristics of gifted students (like asking many questions or developing areas of deep passion and interest) can be beneficial, despite whether they sometimes present themselves as negative.

> Wow . . . I wish I had these over the past 18 years. By reading through the "characteristic traits" on the different Jot Downs, I can think back to students in the past who I probably let slip by because I didn't have the correct perspective of what gifted meant. I had a definition in my head from personal experience with my own child, and that narrows the field for students gifted in other areas. The one thing that will help teachers use these efficiently is the teacher-friendly language of the statements that describe what teachers need to look for in students to jot down. I will definitely share these with the teachers at my school to see if they will facilitate more collaboration between them and our Leap teacher.
>
> Kristi Hayes, Teacher
> Jefferson County, KY

Gathering Information

The sole reason for identification is to gather information that will assist educators in providing the services or educational experiences that optimize the development of the gifted student's potential. Teachers are accountable for providing services that enrich and extend learning for the student in the specific area(s) of giftedness in which they are identified.

Identification tools must match the category of giftedness that is being assessed. For example, one does not identify a creative thinker with an intelligence test or a child gifted in science by their leadership activities. The next match must be between the area in which the child was identified and the programming or service provided to ensure continuous progress in this area of strength. In order to have defensible services, both matches must be made.

If the state gifted regulations specify the number of measures required to identify a child in any category of giftedness, that sets the minimum number of assessments that district personnel must use when identifying gifted children. It is perfectly okay to use more measures, just not fewer.

Practical Guidelines for Administering Assessments

1. Make certain that conditions are conducive for the children to perform at optimum levels. Do not give the assessment in lieu of going outside for recess or during a favorite activity.
2. Ensure that the children are familiar with a computer if one is being used in the assessment. Do not use any equipment that is unfamiliar to the children or that does not work well.
3. Provide the optimum time required by the assessment to allow the children to do their very best. Assessments can lead to opportunities (e.g., being identified in one or more categories of giftedness, earning a score that qualifies them for outside opportunities).
4. Control the conditions for the assessment to make sure that children are not distracted. Make certain that others will not be calling or knocking on the door and that there are no disruptions to break the students' concentration.
5. Practice administering the assessment before it really counts for children.

Perhaps you think that such problems do not occur during the identification process, but they actually do. No one plans on these negative conditions, but letting them occur is poor practice and the result of benign negligence.

Conclusion

Appropriately identifying gifted and talented students is key to ensuring that they receive the educations they need and deserve. It is vital for teachers and administrators to use the best practices outlined in this chapter to identify students from a variety of different backgrounds and talent areas for gifted programming. Using the Jot Downs to focus on student behaviors characteristic of giftedness (not all are positive) and remembering the important points to making identification defensible can help you make important decisions about which of your students qualify for gifted programs or services.

Survival Tips

- Cast a wide net when identifying children as gifted and talented.
- In addition to providing one piece of information for identification, the Jot Downs can provide professional learning for teachers as they watch for behaviors that are characteristic of a particular category of giftedness among students in their classes.
- Parents need to have available information about identification so the process is transparent. They also need to know the grievance procedure if they want further steps to be taken in the identification process.

Survival Toolkit

- "Identifying and Supporting Gifted Students in Rural Districts" (https://www.youtube.com/watch?v=avzCgaltw5A) is a video produced by *Education Week*.
- *Identifying Gifted Students* (3rd ed.), edited by S. K. Johnsen (2018, Prufrock Press), provides an overview of identification practices and instruments.
- "The Excellence Gap: Who Is Missing?" (https://www.youtube.com/watch?v=j35UFUBawPs) is a video developed by The Center for Gifted Studies at Western Kentucky University as a partner in a Javits grant, Reaching Academic Potential (Project RAP).

Chapter 7

Educators as Talent Developers

"Talent can be viewed as potential for significant contributions or productivity (in original or creative ways) in any domain of inquiry, expression, or action over an extended period of time. Talent emerges from aptitudes and/or from sustained involvement in areas of strong interest or passion. It is not simply a natural endowment or 'gift.'"—Donald J. Treffinger

Key Question

- As an educator, what will you do in the role of talent scout?

Athletic coaches look for talent among all young people to ensure that they are getting appropriate opportunities to develop their talents; in other words, they serve as talent scouts for this population. That same aggressive search for talent is not often evident in academics. In fact, talent often goes unnoticed in classrooms, in the hope that variations in ability will not cause more work for the teacher. For some time, the focus in many schools has been on getting students to proficiency or grade level. The focus on reaching proficiency in academics is a noble goal if the

DOI: 10.4324/9781003238553-8

child is not there yet, but proficiency is no goal at all for children who are either at the point of proficiency or beyond. Proficiency is grade-level learning. No coach would be satisfied with proficiency or average performance as the goal for the players on a varsity team. Why should educators do anything less than coaches do in talent development? Teachers and educational leaders must launch a search for talent and then work to develop that talent to its full potential.

Talent development depends on first finding evidence of interest in a talent area. As talent scouts, each educator, counselor, and administrator looks for interests and even passions as the early evidence of talent. It is important not to miss the opportunity to talk with the child about their interests and passions. The next step is matching that early sign of interest and/or talent with opportunities. Those opportunities may be contests or competitions, but they may also be putting together a pair or a group of young people who share the interest. It may be cluster grouping children of similar readiness levels so that they can advance as they are ready to do so. Educators may also consider recommending a child for Saturday or summer programming to help the child find peers.

The Schoolwide Enrichment Model for Talent Development

The Schoolwide Enrichment Model (Renzulli & Reis, 2014) divided learning experiences into three types—Type I, Type II, and Type III. Type I experiences are for all children. They may provide a guest speaker, a field trip, a video, or any other opportunity to expose students to a new idea, topic, or career. There is no expectation that all children will be motivated to move on with that topic, but the experience may spark the interest of one or more of the young people. Type II activities build skills. These skills may be critical and creative thinking skills, problem-solving skills, technical skills, research skills, or skills needed for specific products. Type III activities are for students who have an idea that they want to investigate in depth.

Expert Sally M. Reis discusses the importance of passion in developing lifelong interests. Often the topic that develops into a passion begins as a young person engages an independent study, and Dr. Reis shares some examples of this in action through the use of the Schoolwide Enrichment Model.

Survival Secrets on the Role of Passion in Talent Development

Sally M. Reis

I have recently spent some time thinking about passion areas and how students both develop and sustain them. Over the last few years, I have been in contact with several former gifted and talented students from the school district in which I taught and coordinated the gifted program. All of these young people participated in the gifted program in our district that was based on Joseph Renzulli's original Enrichment Triad Model. For example, I received an email from a student who worked with me during elementary school in our Triad gifted and talented program. Sherry emailed and told me that she had recently completed her Ph.D. in science and would be at the University of Connecticut giving a symposium in her area of expertise: pharmaceutical chemistry.

It was the note that she sent that caused me to smile: She wrote indicating that it was the projects she had finished in our Triad program that caused her to want to continue to pursue her Ph.D. She explained that in her years of doing Type III independent studies, she had learned to be passionate about her work from her earliest experiences doing projects and solving problems. In three related instances, I heard from other students from this elementary school who participated in our gifted program and subsequently completed a law degree, a doctoral degree in counseling, and medical school. What did I learn from my former students?

I learned that my students explored their interests and developed their passions over time. In their early years, they explored and developed their childhood interests. As they grew older, their interests and academic talents merged with work and subsequent career interests, enabling them to explore academic paths in areas of passion and finally to help them find work in careers as adult creative producers.

My colleague and friend, Thomas Hébert, and I have talked about this over time, and we believe that our former students developed some of their passion because of their gifted program involvement. For example, their in-depth Type III interests often affected their college majors and their careers. In a favorite example, Tom followed up on four students who had worked on a Type III project in an elementary school Triad program he called "Bobby Bones." These students built a skeletal model of the human body and created a video-based learning module to teach anatomy that accompanied the skeleton when it visited various classrooms. The students who worked on this project were all interested in anatomy, and Tom later learned that three of these four students finished medical school. Tom interviewed these students, who told him that they believed that their Type III project served as important training for later productivity. I have heard from many of my former students who said that their Type III projects served as life-shaping influences on college and their careers, and also as the basis of their subsequent motivation and continued desire for creative outlets throughout their education and life. They also told me that these interest-based projects consistently enhanced very special non-intellectual characteristics such as task commitment, curiosity, and creativity.

So, in my experience, passion develops from involvement in creative projects, the opportunity to explore and play with early interests, the chance to become creative producers, and the opportunity to solve problems in areas of personal interest. Imagine the world we could have if talented and gifted students from across the globe were able to choose important problems and issues, a goal of Type III enrichment, and try to solve them in their life work. I believe that these things are possible if students are able to identify, develop, and explore their interests, and subsequently to find work that is based on their passions.

— Sally M. Reis, Ph.D.
Board of Trustees Distinguished Professor, University of Connecticut

Other Avenues for Talent Development

Educators play a huge role in talent development, and parents do as well. Parents need to share information about their child's interests with teachers and seek opportunities for their child to be with others who share their interests. For example, an 8-year-old chess player may not find other age-mates who love chess in their class or school, and a budding artist may need to find classes after school or on Saturdays to see that they have opportunities for continuing to develop their artistic talent. It is difficult for a child to be the only one of their peers with a particular interest. It is worth the extra effort for parents to find idea-mates for their children, so they can continue to pursue their interests and realize that other young people love doing what they also love. Summer camps for academics and the arts afford opportunities for students to find other young people who share their interests and goals.

Expert Rena F. Subotnik sets the stage for you to see talent development as something that doesn't just happen, but rather it is the result of persistence and dedication.

Survival Secrets for Psychological Strength Training and Talent Development

Rena F. Subotnik

In 1962, Abraham Tannenbaum discovered that students admired "brilliant" classmates as long as they were also athletic and not studious. That is, they didn't show signs of actually having to put in effort to achieve their brilliance. Even 50 years later, this notion of spontaneous brilliance leads many capable children to avoid taking on challenges that require extra work so as to avoid looking dumb. My colleagues and I have derived some solutions to this conundrum from the worlds of elite music and sport. Both domains have invested attention into ensuring that the children and youth who have potential to excel receive not only good physical skills and technique training, but also practice in mental skills. Athletes and musicians strive for the appearance of effortlessness, yet know that the way they get there is through guided practice and persistent effort. Unfortunately, these lessons have not yet been widely adopted in classrooms with elite academic performers.

What are some of the mental skills that coaches share with athletes and musicians? A central message is to view adversity as part of the "game" and part of life—you can't allow setbacks to rattle you too much, and each setback provides an insight into improvement for next time. Second, athletes and musicians are more productive if they compare their current efforts with their own past performance, rather than making comparisons to others, and always strive to reach aspired personal goals.

At music conservatories, mental skills training varies with students' levels of expertise. For example, in the early stages of professional training, it's important to support novice musicians' willingness to practice what their teachers identify as their weaknesses, even when they've been praised effusively for how they already performed when they entered the conservatory. After students acquire a degree of expertise, teachers expect their students to take on more responsibility for identifying and addressing their own strengths and weaknesses. At the most advanced stages of talent development, emerging musical artists capitalize primarily on their strengths while shoring up weaknesses as needed. With each advancing stage, students must exercise increasing amounts of responsibility and risk-taking in order to develop abilities into competencies, expertise, and then artistry.

At sport and music institutions, specialized coaches and teachers provide instruction in these mental skills, or what we call "psychological strength training." Classroom teachers can fulfill some of this role by carefully considering their use of praise. You can compliment students for taking a risk intellectually, tackling their weak skills with vigor, accepting successes gracefully, and being a good sport about other people's accomplishments. Most important is for teachers to model how to handle the fact that most days involve setbacks as well as accomplishment.

The principles of psychological strength training are based on good science. They work to improve students' productivity and yours, too.

—Rena F. Subotnik, Ph.D.
Director, Center for Psychology in Schools and Education, and Associate Executive Director, Education Directorate, American Psychological Association

Benjamin Bloom on Talent Development

In talent development, it is important to capture interest and then to continue the talent development process on an ongoing basis. Bloom (1985) conducted his retrospective study of talent development among internationally eminent people who had achieved the highest level of recognition in science, mathematics, athletics, and the arts. In regard to talent development, he made the following statement:

> No matter how precocious one is at age ten or eleven, if the individual doesn't stay with the talent development process over many years, he or she will soon be outdistanced by others who do continue. A long-term commitment to the talent field and an increasing passion for talent development are essential if the individual is to attain the highest levels of capability in the field. Natural talent or high interest may be the starting places in talent development, but it is the long-term commitment that will sustain progress in an area of talent. (p. 538)

Bloom clearly made the point that a young person must have ongoing opportunities to develop any talent that they have, or they will not develop their talent at the same levels as others who stay involved. In other words, unless a student sticks with the talent area, they will not develop their full potential.

Malcolm Gladwell on Talent Development

Malcolm Gladwell (2008) noted in his popular book *Outliers: The Story of Success* that it takes 10,000 hours of practice in a talent area in order to perform at a truly outstanding level. Discovering talent is only the starting point in talent development. As Gladwell stated, "But what truly distinguishes their histories is not their extraordinary talent but their extraordinary opportunities" (p. 11). Teachers can help gifted young people access the opportunities needed to develop their talents. Parents also can help their children learn about opportunities that can further interest and develop skills to the next level. The catch is that anyone sharing information about opportunities also needs to provide information about how to access financial support if costs are involved.

NAGC's Redefining Giftedness

NAGC (2010) issued a statement entitled "Redefining Giftedness for a New Century: Shifting the Paradigm." It added a talent development focus to terminology in gifted education:

> The development of ability or talent is a lifelong process. It can be evident in young children as exceptional performance on tests and/or other measures of ability, or as a rapid rate of learning, compared to other students of the same age, or in actual achievement in a domain. As individuals mature through childhood to adolescence, however, achievement and high levels of motivation in the domain become the primary characteristics of their giftedness. Various factors can either enhance or inhibit the development and expression of abilities. (para. 2)

Talent Development as a Framework for Gifted Education

Olszewski-Kubilius et al. (2018) provided the rationale for using talent development as a framework for gifted education. A few of the points they offered include:

63

- Giftedness that emphasizes domains of talent rather than general cognitive ability is more easily understood and appreciated by the public. Adults can readily observe, appreciate, and support the need for special services for dance, sports, writing, or science talent development as opposed to IQ.
- Looking for children with domain-specific abilities will result in more children having their talents identified and nurtured.
- The role of education is to develop students' gifts or talents in a specific domain. There are no educational programs to develop IQ.
- In adulthood, giftedness is determined by actual accomplishments. Thus, ability is less important than what one is using the ability to *do*. (pp. 7–8)

The best advice for educators and parents is to be talent developers rather than "deficit detectors" (Siegle, 2018). Recognizing interest and building on strengths in a talent area are essential steps in talent development. At the same time, areas that need support can receive that support while focusing on the strengths.

Conclusion

So why should you be interested in talent development? The reasons are numerous, but let's start out with a very important one. You create your future when you ensure that children who are gifted and talented are appropriately challenged. Educating your students to actualize their potentials will build a promising future for you and for everyone in your community.

Survival Tips

- Educators must see being a talent scout as an important role.
- Parents need to know that academic and artistic talents follow a similar pattern as athletic talent. Interest may be sparked early, often before their children's age-mates have that interest. Then, their children need teachers who develop their skills at the next higher level on an ongoing basis. Levels of learning and performance are not limited by the age of the young person.
- Know what you believe about talent development and be ready to share that with others.

Survival Toolkit

Valuable resources include:

- Bloom, B. S. (Ed.). (1985). *Developing talent in young people.* Ballantine Books.
- Csikszentmihalyi, M., Rathunde, K., & Whalen, S. (1996). *Talented teenagers: The roots of success and failure.* Cambridge University Press.
- Jarvin, L., & Subotnik, R. F. (2005). Understanding elite talent in academic domains: A developmental trajectory from basic abilities to scholarly productivity/artistry. In F. Dixon & S. Moon (Eds.), *The handbook of secondary gifted education* (pp. 203–220). Prufrock Press.
- Neihart, M. (2008). *Peak performance for smart kids: Strategies and tips for ensuring school success.* Prufrock Press.
- Olszewski-Kubilius, P., Subotnik, R. F., & Worrell, F. C. (Eds.). (2018). *Talent development as a framework for gifted education: Implications for best practices and applications in schools.* Prufrock Press.
- Van Yperen, N. W. (2009). Why some make it and others do not: Identifying psychological factors that predict career success in professional adult soccer. *The Sport Psychologist, 23,* 317–329.

Chapter 8

Maximizing Potential Through Social and Emotional Understanding and Support

"The most common counseling need of this [gifted] population is assistance in coping with stressors related to growing up as a gifted child in a society that does not always recognize, understand, or welcome giftedness."—Sidney M. Moon

Key Questions

- How can educators provide social and emotional support for gifted children?

- How can you work with parents to support them as they interact with their children in ways that build social and emotional well-being?

Many people have the misperception that gifted children must be as socially awkward as Sheldon Cooper on the television show *The Big Bang Theory*. Not true. When young people who are gifted and talented have opportunities to interact with others who share their interests, they are remarkably social. It is when they

DOI: 10.4324/9781003238553-9

cannot find others who have mutual interests that they may appear less than social. That, however, is a problem for most people who find it difficult to appear social when they have little to talk about with others—nothing of mutual interest. Just consider what it is like for someone who has no interest in the Super Bowl when it is Super Bowl Sunday and that sporting event is the topic of conversation in many, if not most, circles. The social-emotional development of gifted children is nurtured or stunted by so many things in their lives. You must learn about their social-emotional development in order to support the development of their potential.

Gifted Children's Bill of Rights

A way to establish a classroom and a school in which all children who are gifted and talented thrive is to understand what it takes for them to do so. In 2007, Del Siegle, then president of the National Association for Gifted Children, presented the organization's membership with the Gifted Children's Bill of Rights (see Figure 3). Each statement provides sage guidance to you as an educator or a parent, whether you have one gifted child or an entire classroom of gifted children. Posting the Bill of Rights in your classroom is a good reminder of key tenets that create a positive classroom and school environment. The Bill of Rights is also important for students themselves. When educators and parents convey similar messages to children, young people are the winners.

Two Sets of Peers for Gifted Children

Understanding the needs of gifted children includes knowing that they have two sets of peers—their age-mates and their intellectual peers (those with whom they share an interest or a passion). The intellectual peers may also be referred to as idea-mates, as ideas and interests are what they have in common. Intellectual peers are often, but not always, older children. Gifted children find that because they share interests with their intellectual peers, it is easy to talk with them and create friendships. One reason to provide grouping for instructional purposes is to allow children to find age-mates who are also intellectual peers. Every person needs someone with whom they relate easily, and gifted children are no exception. It is very lonely for a child to be in a classroom in which they can't find anyone else who is interested in anything about which they are passionate. "What's wrong with me?" can be the concern when a child feels isolated. Of course, being different can

Figure 3
Gifted Children's Bill of Rights

Gifted Children's Bill of Rights

You have a right . . .

1 . . . to know about your giftedness.

2 . . . to learn something new every day.

3 . . . to be passionate about your talent area without apologies.

4 . . . to have an identity beyond your talent area.

5 . . . to feel good about your accomplishments.

6 . . . to make mistakes.

7 . . . to seek guidance in the development of your talent.

8 . . . to have multiple peer groups and a variety of friends.

9 . . . to choose which of your talent areas you wish to pursue.

10 . . . not to be gifted at everything.

—Del Siegle
2007–2009 NAGC President

NATIONAL ASSOCIATION FOR
Gifted Children
http://www.nagc.org

Provided as a service of
the National Association for Gifted Children & Taylor & Francis group
Copies are available online at http://www.nagc.org

ROUTLEDGE
Routledge
Taylor & Francis Group
www.routledge.com

Note. From National Association for Gifted Children (http://www.nagc.org). Reprinted with permission.

be positive, but to many children and adolescents, being different does not generate positive feelings.

Grouping for instructional purposes can go a long way toward ensuring that children have peers for discussion, intellectual stimulation, and encouragement. Those potential groupings can focus on interests, readiness, or needs. They can be short term for a project or flexible groupings by assignments. They can be cluster groups or homogeneous classes with young people with similar levels of readiness. A cluster would be four to six (could be more) students who are grouped together, while a homogeneous class would have the entire class grouped likely by readiness.

Sometimes children find kindred spirits in activities outside the school. Musical and sporting opportunities, as well as organizations of various types, can lead to finding peers who share interests. Saturday and summer programs also provide opportunities for children to find others with whom they can easily relate. Author Barbara Kingsolver (2002) wrote that her daughter's experience at a summer program for gifted young people "helped her understand the potential rewards of belonging to a peer group that's more interested in Jane Austen and Shakespeare than Calvin Klein and Tommy Hilfiger" (p. 9).

Asynchronous Development

One of the most important understandings to have in regard to children who are gifted and talented is that asynchronous development must be understood. Drew may talk like an older child, yet she may react to a disappointment as the 8-year-old that she is. It is often problematic for adults when they get used to Sean discussing an ethical issue as an adult yet having a reaction that would be expected of a much younger child. That is what asynchronous development is all about, and educators and parents need to know that asynchronous development is to be expected of children who are gifted and talented.

Overexcitabilities

The research of Kazimierz Dabrowski (Lind, 2011) highlighted characteristics of gifted and talented children that he called overexcitabilities. The various overexcitabilities reveal themselves as intensities—psychomotor, sensual, intellectual, imaginational, and emotional. Likely, it would be very unusual for all of these intensities to characterize a particular gifted child, yet one or more of these intensities are often key attributes of various children. Knowing about overexcitabilities helps educators and parents understand children with whom they interact.

Expert Thomas P. Hébert shares his thoughts and strategies for addressing the social and emotional needs of children who are gifted and talented. He describes strategies that you will find both enjoyable and useful to implement.

Survival Secrets on Meeting the Social and Emotional Needs of Gifted Students

Thomas P. Hébert

Meg's parents were facing a divorce, and she appreciated my spending time after school listening to her express her fears about how her family would change. Molly, an elementary student, released the bees trapped in her jelly jar following our trip to a beekeeper's farm because she could not emotionally deal with seeing them trapped. Andrew joined me for brown bag lunches and important man-to-man conversations about his struggles to find other middle school boys who appreciated his intelligence, sensitivity, and creativity. As an educator, I have been blessed with opportunities to teach a variety of student populations, and through my experiences with students like Meg, Molly, and Andrew, I have learned how important it is to understand what is happening in young people's lives beyond my classroom. The more I worked with highly intelligent students, the more I realized the importance of understanding their social and emotional lives.

Today, in my university classroom, I work with graduate students and educators to pay close attention to particular social and emotional characteristics and behaviors evidenced in gifted learners. I call attention to the following characteristics to assist them in understanding gifted students (Hébert, 2020):

- high expectations of self and others (perfectionism);
- internal motivation, inner locus of control;
- emotional sensitivity, intensity, and depth;
- empathy;
- advanced levels of moral maturity with consistency between values and actions;
- strong need for self-actualization;
- highly developed sense of humor; and
- resilience.

With an understanding that gifted students often display these characteristics, educators realize that these characteristics may influence their childhood and adolescent development in different ways. To assist gifted students in their developmental journey, it is critical that educators create supportive classroom cultures. In my work with graduate students and teachers in gifted education, I spend much time addressing how to create a healthy emotional climate in a classroom. My goal is to have teachers design environments that enable young people to feel valued for their intelligence and creativity, and respected as individuals by both their teacher and classmates. The following strategies are three favorites that I implemented in my classroom. My hope is that my readers will consider incorporating them in their own classroom practice.

Business Cards

During the first week of school, I facilitated an activity I called "Business Cards." I explained to my students how professionals have business cards that present an image to the world of what they are all about. I then shared with them my collection of business cards and pointed out how many of them send a clear message. I have collected cards from all over the country and have enjoyed showing students how Ann Marie McGranaghan's card from "The Courtesy Cleaning Company" in Bowling Green, OH, speaks to me with its clean crisp lines that say Ann Marie offers a house-cleaning service that is thorough and fussy—the kind of woman I would want taking care of my home. My card from "Cakes Extraordinaire" in Portland, ME, is a simple and elegant-looking card. I decided to order my parents' 50th wedding anniversary cake from this bakery because I wanted a cake that was simple and elegant looking. It was a smart decision. The cake I ordered was perfect and made a big hit on my parents' special day.

After the introduction of my card collection, I had students reflect on the question "What does a business card say about you?" I distributed large sheets of construction paper and provided them time to design their personal business cards. My objective behind this activity was to have gifted students find a friend. I wanted the science fiction buffs to find each other. I wanted the Boston Red Sox fans to find other sports enthusiasts. I wanted the girls who designed step dance routines to find other dancers and to have the computer experts discover each other. The business cards were prominently displayed on the walls of my classroom, common interests were recognized, and children were able to make friendship connections. This nonthreatening activity was what I needed to begin building community and supportive relationships.

Photo Elicitation

Realizing that students are tech-savvy and have mobile phones, I enjoyed utilizing their favorite technology to implement a strategy known as photo elicitation—using visual images to begin conversation. I provided my students with the following prompt: *Using your cell phone camera, shoot five pictures that represent your identity as a gifted individual.* I asked them to write a descriptive paragraph to accompany each image and had them submit their work via email.

I explained that their photographs could not include any individuals that were identifiable, helping to ensure that the focus remained centered on their identity. I wanted to give them ample time for introspection and provided them one week to submit their responses.

Kip, a highly creative student, shared a photo of himself wearing a hat that covered his face, and attached to the hat was a large sketch of Wile E. Coyote, the well-known cartoon figure. He explained, "Wile E. Coyote is important to me because he represents the ideas that travel so fast through my head, my hyperactivity, and my creativity applied to my life." Shanika included a photo of a tall ladder pointed toward a high ceiling and explained, "I took a picture of a ladder because I'm very hard on myself. I want to go very far and high. This photo is of the bottom of the ladder. I feel you can always strive to climb higher." I enjoyed infusing photo elicitation into creative writing as well as crafting autobiographies with my students. I acquired helpful information through this technique, enabling me to develop supportive relationships.

Guiding Students to Self-Understanding Through Literature

I have long been a proponent of using literature to facilitate discussions with students about their issues or concerns. I believe that authentic interactions with literature contribute to affective growth. In facilitating good discussions with young people about good books, teachers can help them draw parallels between their experiences and those of the main characters in the books. During such discussions, the students have an opportunity to listen to their classroom peers as they share their feelings about personal experiences related to the focus of the lesson. Such an approach is an attempt to help gifted students understand themselves and cope with problems by providing literature relevant to their developmental needs at appropriate times. In any discussion of high-quality literature with young people, the goal is to have participants share their feelings and listen closely to each other as well as to themselves. In such a conversation, it is important that students leave the classroom with an awareness that others have experienced the same feelings. With the guidance of an empathic teacher, a group discussion can bring about an understanding that "we are in this together." After discussing the book, teachers then incorporate meaningful and enjoyable follow-up activities, such as artistic responses, creative writing, journaling, writing song lyrics, writing raps, designing television commercials, or other self-selected options for students to pursue individually or collaboratively. As students engage in these activities, conversations continue and students provide each other with supportive feedback.

Through these three classroom strategies, I gained many important insights about my students. These simple and nonthreatening methods enabled me to come to know them as gifted young people, and in our work together I was better prepared to support their social and emotional development. I encourage my readers to do the same.

—Thomas P. Hébert, Ph.D.
Professor of Gifted and Talented Education, University of South Carolina

A Few Strategies That Address Social-Emotional Development

There are many ideas you can implement to provide a positive classroom environment for all children. One such strategy is to have a place in the classroom for children to go to "escape" for some quiet time. That place could be a rug in the corner of the room, a beanbag, or a pillow on the floor. Although those suggestions sound more applicable to an elementary classroom, it is also appropriate for older students to have a quiet space. Perhaps a pass to the library could offer a few minutes to escape if such time were needed.

Choice is also a strategy that recognizes the strengths, interests, and passions of gifted young people. Of course, choice is not always appropriate, but occasionally students can be offered choice of a topic (the content), the way they will pursue the topic cognitively (the process), and the way they will demonstrate what they have learned (the product). Think of the positive social-emotional climate that is created when students have opportunities for differentiated learning experiences. There is an important tie between the social-emotional development of children and the opportunities they have or do not have to learn new content and develop their thinking on a day-to-day basis. The following poem by a gifted young person can help you to see her wishes for learning.

Stop Holding Us Back

You wouldn't tell a bird
Not to fly
You wouldn't tell a baby
Not to cry
So why

Do you keep holding
Me back?

You wouldn't tell
The wind not to blow
Or a river not to flow
Or the waves in the ocean
Not to crash
But you keep telling me
That you don't believe in my potential
Oh why
Do you keep holding me back?

You wouldn't tell a star
Not to shine
Or the sun not to rise
Don't you realize
You're holding me back?

You're resisting what should be
And it's not hurting just me
So I'm asking you please
Just see what you're doing

Here in us lies such great potential
Such potential for so many great things

And I say to you
We ARE the future
That's what I'm trying to make you see

And you, yes you
Are building your future
And I know you hope
It will be a great one
But the future is only ensured by the present
And presently, let's look
At all that you've done

Raise us up
For we are the next leaders
Don't stifle us
Hear what we must say
Push us
Because we are tomorrow's thinkers
Don't hold us back
That's not the way
To ensure your bright future
That you hope for
Yes, I know you want one

But for tomorrow's bright future
Today you must teach us
You must let us learn
You must hear us
And believe in us
And I promise
We WILL get more done

—Elizabeth Gatten
Ninth grader from Union County, KY

75

Bullying

A problem that often touches gifted children is bullying. Gifted children are vulnerable to bullying for a couple of reasons. One reason is that many gifted children are especially sensitive. Another reason is that they are often different from their age-mates in their interests and may not have others who share their interests. Being different can make a gifted child the target for a bully. Expert Brad Tassell discusses bullying with young people who are gifted and talented.

Survival Secrets for Dealing With Bullying
The Discussion You Must Have With Your Gifted Student Leaders About Creating a Culture of Support

Brad Tassell

I forced my daughter to join the middle school cross country team. She was highly gifted, the star of the academic team, and already a champion of the speech team, but physically she was not gifted, to say the least, and she did not enjoy exercise, especially running. So, my Faustian bargain was to give her many wishes if she competed for the junior high cross country team. I have always been a distance runner—one of those deluded humans who likes a couple hours of trotting with worn shoes down a lonely trail. I thought I could indoctrinate her into the fold with a semester of team training. Suffice it to say, it didn't work, but she and I both learned a great deal about how student leaders can affect everyone as it relates to bullying and success.

As a seasoned runner I was asked to be a parent assistant coach by the head coach. She was a kind and gentle new teacher who liked to run and was willing to sponsor the team for the school. Her training experience did a nice job warming them up and giving running assignments for a day's practice, but she had no experience creating leaders or molding character in youth. Like most teams and many companies, classrooms, dorms, and most of the Earth, she chose her captains by their level of giftedness and personality, in relationship to how they treated her and not with respect to any correlation of how they would treat those below them.

Within the first few practices I started to notice a pattern with the runners. First, some were very gifted runners, and some were very weak runners. My daughter was one of the very new runners along with three other girls with similar dads with similar philosophies as mine. The coach had already made her choices known as to who would get the bulk of her attention. The gifted runners were extroverted and jumping in with both feet, while the weak runners were introverted and trying to follow along as best they could with a new skill set. The coach had immediately started to heap attention on the strong runners and gave them all the power to run the practice. She was a new coach and figured that she could use the help of the grade 7 and 8 boys who already knew the lay of the land. Because both teams trained and competed together, it seemed a natural choice. In the first week of practice, I was in the background. No one except the coach and my daughter knew who I was. To the rest of the team I was just another guy running around the public trail they used for training, which is why I got to see the true face of middle school's lack of emotional empathy and leadership gone wrong (which I have also witnessed in hundreds of schools during the years). The captains and their friends were brutal to the new weak runners. I heard them lap after lap saying:

"You suck!"

"Why not just walk, Loser."

"You need to quit so we don't lose every meet."

And these were the lighter attacks they tossed out as my daughter and a few of the other grade 6 and 7 girls struggled around the track with less and less motivation. Humiliation has a pronounced negative effect on performance and the will of the performer.

Those choosing leaders without investigating the relationship between their gifted leaders and their peers are creating an almost surefire recipe for increased bullying. Those who do not continually monitor their leaders' effectiveness as positive role models will create a clique atmosphere where those with the least power and skill will be the most hurt. Most gifted students who become leaders are very good at "teacher pleasing," and some are so good that the authority figure is so flattered by the attention that unchecked power is granted to their chosen leader, which can be used to literally terrorize the most vulnerable of their peers. Rarely do teachers/coaches make sure their leaders fulfill the most important leadership role, which is supporting every person, showing endless empathy, and stopping any other person in the group from showing any lack of support. The student is perceived as helpful and nice to the teacher, so the student must be a popular and friendly person to their peers, right? Sadly, this is not always the case. We often forget they are still children and need to be mentored and monitored to become effective leaders.

There are good reasons that gifted kids become leaders. They are usually the strongest performer at the skills they are asked to lead, which itself is not a bad choice. However, this can sometimes lead to an increase in bullying as these new leaders suddenly are not just more talented but have power over the other members of the group and have been recognized as superior. Plus, one trait of most leaders is an enhanced self-esteem, and that can often come with a lack of emotional empathy.

The most important role of all student leaders is that they are supportive of every member of their team or group at all times, and the surest way to end their tenure of power is to degrade, belittle, or show a lack of empathy to those they are leading. The discussion that you must have with your chosen leaders is a clear one: You will treat every person with honor and support and demand that all around you do the same, or you will not be a leader here, and I will be watching.

After a few days watching the cross country team captains and their friends degrade, mock, and belittle the newer young runners, who were miserable and dying to quit, I met with the coach and asked to be introduced to the team. (Many had already read my book on bullying in their class a few years before, so the name rang a bell.) She and I discussed beforehand what I would say and what was going on. She was horrified and nonplussed to say the least. She knew the new girls were having a hard time but had no idea what the boys were doing. She thought it was just that the running was tough that had made the girls withdrawn.

My talk was a simple and direct one. The coach and I agreed that if you were on this team you would always be supportive. Every word out of your mouth would be one that would build up and never tear down. It didn't matter your skill level; no win was worth bullying, and that extended off the track to school. You bully; you don't run. We spoke separately with the team captains as I shared their comments back to them. They were speechless as we outlined their jobs—100% positive support always or they would not be on this team, plus they were to make sure every other person on the team showed the same support or they would also not lead this team. The actions of every member of the team reflected on them. Plus, we monitored their progress and interviewed the team on a regular basis to see how it was going, but it didn't matter because once there was 100% support you could feel it in the air. My daughter even became a pretty strong runner as the high fives replaced the taunts. The captains stood at the finish line clapping for every member of their team and even some of the struggling runners from other teams. The culture had changed, and everybody had a positive experience.

The steps to take:
1. Compliment your leaders on their amazing abilities.
2. Be clear that their most important role is empathy and support. Any hint of negativity, bullying, favoritism, etc., will be the end of their leadership role and maybe the end of their participation at all.
3. Be clear they are responsible for every other member of the group. All members will be supportive.

They will take to it quickly as you create a culture of support, and even gifted students with a history of bullying behavior will soon be on board and enjoying their new role, although sometimes they will need your support and supervision to stay on track. My story is sports-related, but it translates to classroom, debate team, dorm floor, etc. When you choose leaders, you are not handing the reins to a gifted person so you can hand over the responsibility of the work at hand. You are creating a bigger job for yourself. Gifted student leaders need to be molded, and being clear that the perks of leadership come with a responsibility to be 100% supportive always is a lifelong lesson in obtaining core values. Lastly, as the instructor, you are responsible for the physical and mental health of every student your leader leads. You must constantly monitor that every member is receiving support and empathy.

My daughter improved greatly after our cross country experience, and she had a decent year. She improved her time each race. She liked being cheered on as she ran, but most importantly, the entire team walked away enhanced personally and as a group. She wasn't ever going to win, and the winners don't really spend much time remembering a sixth-grade triumph on the course. However, every one of those captains found out the real power of true empathetic leadership, and that will last forever. My daughter hasn't run one step since, but not because anyone hurt her. She just really hates running.

—Brad Tassell
Author of Don't Feed the Bully, *Llessat Publishing, Bowling Green, KY*

Counseling Gifted Students

Bullying is only one of the issues that young people face at all levels of schooling. Teachers, counselors, and principals can work together to create a positive climate in schools, including helping students see the dangers in bullying and working with students to build self-esteem. People with positive self-concepts have little need to take advantage of others.

In order to have social-emotional needs addressed, the counselor plays a key role. Counselors need to have accurate information about gifted children and their needs in order to facilitate the development of their potentials. Expert Jean S. Peterson describes the counselor's responsibilities with young people who are gifted and talented.

Survival Secrets on the Role of Counselors for Gifted Children and Teens

Jean S. Peterson

Counseling focuses largely on normal developmental challenges. Counseling recognizes pathology, but typically focuses instead on empowering people to use personal strengths to make changes, resolve problems, cope with transitions, or explore complex feelings.

Giftedness does not preclude social and emotional difficulties, and counselors should not only validate and normalize feelings, but also help gifted youth make sense of themselves, feel heard, and develop effective coping strategies. All students face developmental challenges; however, how gifted students *experience* development may differ from how others experience it. Nevertheless, educators may not consider developmental challenges when organizing services for gifted students. Educators and even parents may believe that academic rigor is the only need. If academic performance or nonperformance is the only focus at home or in school, "normal development" might not be discussed much. Gifted students themselves tend to be reluctant to ask for help, according to several of my studies. Therefore, when social and emotional development is not an overt program focus, gifted students may not consider talking with a school counselor other than for assistance with schedules and college applications during high school.

The asset side of giftedness can help highly able youth cope with difficulties. In fact, intelligence is often on lists of factors of resilience. In contrast, the burden side may be reflected in expressed or unexpressed emotional reactivity, unrelentingly rapid processing of environmental information, lack of support from adults or peers, heavy responsibilities, unreasonable expectations from self and others, and high stress. Adults, peers, and even family may assume that giftedness means being able to cope with anything.

Characteristics associated with giftedness, such as sensitivity, overexcitability, and intensity, may be pathologized by professionals and dismissed by peers as simply "weird." When school and community counselors understand how giftedness can potentially exacerbate challenges related to developmental and other transitions, gifted students are likely to feel understood and make sense of confusing feelings and behaviors. When counselors are respectful of the asset-burden paradox, they likely can build a therapeutic alliance with gifted children and teens.

School counselors, in small-group discussion about development-oriented topics, can help high academic achievers and bright underachievers connect meaningfully, develop social skills, learn to express emotions effectively and appropriately, and find support. Counselors can attend to career development, including with young gifted children, who often are precociously concerned about having too many realistic options for future direction. Perfectionism, procrastination, anxiety, fears, self-image, and concerns about college life are among topics that can be discussed in small groups, as well as concerns related to identity, relationships, and differentiating from and within family. Counselors can offer a nonjudgmental presence, poised and thoughtful reflection, validation of humanness, and crucial respite in a competitive school environment.

School counselors are capable of conducting in-depth individual sessions, but typically are responsible for several hundred students, with limited time for regular, extended clinical work. When a gifted student's feelings or behaviors are significantly affecting relationships, well-being, and learning, a school counselor can offer suggestions for community resources, including professionals especially trained to work with children, teens, and families.

—Jean S. Peterson, Ph.D.
Professor Emerita, Former Director of School Counseling, Purdue University

Questions arise about the social-emotional well-being of young people, and perfectionism is sometimes linked with giftedness. Expert Kristie Speirs Neumeister discusses perfectionism in the following piece.

Survival Secrets for Perfectionism

Kristie Speirs Neumeister

Perfectionism is a characteristic often cited of gifted individuals. In order to understand how to facilitate adaptive attitudes toward achievement in these students, we first must understand what perfectionism is and what it is not. Contrary to what some may think, perfectionism is *not* striving for excellence—that is a goal we would openly support for all students! Rather, perfectionism comprises two factors that occur together: *excessively* high standards coupled with a high degree of concern for making mistakes. Because high levels of perfectionism may be associated with stress, anxiety, and depression, and, ironically, inhibit students' ability to perform to their potential, parents and educators need strategies to both prevent perfectionism from developing and help diminish it in those who are already exhibiting these tendencies.

Before any strategies can be implemented, the first step is to determine whose unrealistic expectations the student is trying to reach. In the early 1990s two researchers, Paul Hewitt and Gordon Flett, published their Multidimensional Theory of Perfectionism. They observed that the source for the unrealistic expectations may come from within the individual (self-oriented perfectionism) or from others such as parents, teachers, or coaches (socially prescribed perfectionism). An honest discussion with the gifted child is necessary to determine the origin of these unrealistic expectations. If children perceive that others in their lives are putting the pressure to be perfect on their shoulders, then discussions and possible counseling are needed with both the children and the adults to change behaviors and expectations. Ideally, counseling will open healthier channels of communication for the future.

If, on the other hand, the unrealistic expectations for performance are coming from the children themselves, then steps need to be taken to help students modify their own expectations. For example, students with self-oriented perfectionism often panic if they experience a "failure" (which may be only an A-, a 98%, second place, etc.) because they overgeneralize the implications of not meeting their expectations. In this situation, one simple but effective strategy to use with students following a perceived "failure" is to ask them to write down 10 ways their lives will be different because of the failure. In nearly every case, they will not be able to think of anything to write and seeing the blank list can offer immediate reassurance. A second strategy is for parents and teachers to model effective coping strategies to deal with mistakes. In general, adults are not in the habit of showcasing their mistakes. Consequently, students erroneously may conclude that adults do not make mistakes and, therefore, assume they should not make any either. If parents and teachers make an effort to share their mistakes openly, students will benefit from observing how adults handle these mistakes and see that life goes on, regardless. So, the next time you forget to proofread a newsletter and send it out with a couple of grammatical errors, burn an apple pie, forget to attend a meeting, or get a speeding ticket, share these experiences and how you handled them with your students. Additionally, students may also benefit from hearing about famous individuals and their "failures" as well (for example, J. K. Rowling was rejected by 12 publishers before Scholastic accepted her Harry Potter manuscript, Michael Jordan did not make the varsity basketball team during his first tryout, and Steve Jobs was fired from Apple, the company he created). Students will benefit from hearing firsthand about how the adults they admire in their personal lives as well as famous adults make mistakes and learn from them, and the world doesn't end when they do!

Parents and educators also play an instrumental role in preventing perfectionism from developing within gifted children. One of the most significant things they can do is ensure that gifted children experience the appropriate level of challenge beginning in kindergarten, so they never develop the expectation that they will always earn perfect scores without effort. When challenged appropriately from the beginning, students learn that feeling challenged and making mistakes are normal parts of the learning process rather than something to be feared. When giving feedback, parents and educators should strive to give specific comments pertaining to factors within the child's control rather than global comments pertaining to traits the child may perceive as fixed. For example, instead of praising a child for being "so creative!" a teacher may say, "I like how you tried to think of ideas that no one else would consider" or "I love how much detail you included when describing the scene-I felt like I was there!" These comments place the control for future performance back on the child—they will know that they should try hard to come up with original ideas or include descriptive words in their writing to improve performance rather than just worrying about "being creative" without knowing what that means.

As parents and educators, we also need to be careful not to demonstrate affection to our children only when they have performed well (earned a good grade, qualified for the next level of an academic competition, etc.) because students can easily make the assumption that they are only loveable and worthy when they perform well. If they equate their self-worth with their achievements, it is no wonder they would fear making a mistake, as that would mean they were no longer worthy or loveable. We need to make a conscious effort to demonstrate our acceptance and affection for our students at all times and especially when they fail, as they need the reassurance then the most.

Parents and educators play a significant role in shaping gifted students' expectations for performance and responses to failure. By establishing open channels of communication, modeling the normalcy of mistakes, and demonstrating unconditional acceptance, parents and educators can mitigate perfectionistic tendencies and facilitate healthy attitudes toward achievement within gifted students.

—Kristie Speirs Neumeister, Ph.D.
Ball State University

Conclusion

Understanding the social and emotional development of gifted children is so important for parents and educators. It is essential for gifted young people to find idea-mates who may or may not be their age-peers. Finding others who share their interests is most likely to happen when students are grouped for instructional purposes as well as in Saturday and summer programs. Teachers and counselors need to understand that gifted young people constitute a diverse group and that removing the learning ceiling is the best way for these exceptional young people to develop their interests and make continuous progress.

Survival Tips

- Never miss an opportunity to tell a student about a strength they have, something that they do well, or a kindness they have displayed. Your comments may inspire your students to soar, and you may be the only one noticing and saying something.
- Parents and educators need resources to better understand the social-emotional development of their children.
- Young people who are gifted and talented need to know what that means. In fact, the Gifted Children's Bill of Rights should be available with opportunities to question and discuss.

You may want to share this chapter with counselors at your school and then follow-up to discuss questions they may have. Having counselors on board with gifted students will help the young people and provide support for the work you do.

Survival Tips, continued

Survival Toolkit

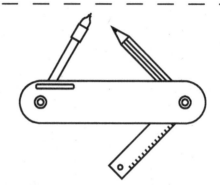

- "I Am Gifted" (https://www.youtube.com/watch?v=YcuCJ9EZu9U) is a video that you might want to discuss with your students who have been identified as gifted.
- Supporting Emotional Needs of the Gifted (SENG; https://www.sengifted.org) has lots of articles on topics related to the social and emotional development of children who are gifted and talented.
- The Whole Gifted Child Task Force: Report to the NAGC Board of Directors (https://www.nagc.org/sites/default/files/key%20reports/4.1%20WGC%20Task%20Force%20Report.pdf) offers points that could guide a discussion with colleagues.
- Serving the Whole Gifted Child (https://www.nagc.org/sites/default/files/Publication%20PHP/NAGC-TIP%20Sheet-Whole%20Gifted%20Child.pdf) is a valuable resource for educators and parents.
- Useful resources on this topic include:
  - Cross, T. L. (2018). *On the social and emotional lives of gifted children* (5th ed.). Prufrock Press.
  - Fonseca, C. (2016). *Emotional intensity in gifted students: Helping kids cope with explosive feelings* (2nd ed.). Prufrock Press.
  - Fonseca, C. (2020). *101 success secrets for gifted kids: Advice, quizzes, and activities for dealing with stress, expectations, friendships, and more* (2nd ed.). Prufrock Press.
  - Galbraith, J. (2009). *The gifted kids' survival guide: For ages 10 & under* (3rd ed.). Free Spirit.
  - Galbraith, J., & Delisle, J. (2011). *The gifted teen survival guide: Smart, sharp, and ready for (almost) anything* (4th ed.). Free Spirit.
  - Hébert, T. P. (2020). *Understanding the social and emotional lives of gifted students* (2nd ed.). Prufrock Press.

Lind, S. (2011). *Overexcitabilities and the gifted.* https://www.sengifted.org/post/overexcitability-and-the-gifted

Peterson, J. S. (2008). *The essential guide to talking with gifted teens: Ready-to-use discussions about identity, stress, relationships, and more.* Free Spirit.

Survival Toolkit, continued

Chapter 9

Acceleration
Accommodating a Different Pace for Learning

"Schools pay lip-service to the proposition that students should learn at their own pace; in reality, for countless highly able children the pace of their progress through school is determined by the rate of progress of their classmates." (Colangelo et al., 2004, p. 1)

Key Questions

- What must be in place to make various types of acceleration successful?

- What are the types of acceleration that would be possible to use at the school at which you teach?

The 20-Plus Types of Acceleration

Acceleration has many forms, only one of which is grade acceleration. Strange as it may seem, most people think that a reference to acceleration automatically means grade-skipping. However, the full range of acceleration includes many

 DOI: 10.4324/9781003238553-10

options (see Figure 4). The key for all forms of acceleration is to make a match between the needs of the child and the acceleration option. Acceleration advances students academically and supports their social-emotional needs as well. After all, the goal is for each child to learn new things every day in school or make continuous progress.

A Nation Deceived: How Schools Hold Back America's Brightest Students (Colangelo et al., 2004) defined acceleration as "an educational intervention that moves students through an educational program at a faster-than-usual rate or younger-than-typical age" (p. 1). The authors presented a strong case for acceleration, reporting that "(1) the research on acceleration is expansive and consistent; and (2) we are not aware of any other educational practice that is so well researched yet so rarely implemented" (p. 11). Please note that this two-volume series is available at https://www.nationdeceived.org, and within it readers can find a plethora of information on various types of acceleration shown in Figure 4.

These 20 types of acceleration can be divided into two categories—one involves timing of when the child is accelerated or grade based, and the other relates to the curriculum or is content based. Acceleration options that relate to timing include early entry into kindergarten, first grade, middle school, high school, or college. Acceleration options that focus on curricular interventions include self-paced instruction, subject-matter acceleration, mentoring, Advanced Placement classes, and curriculum compacting. Acceleration should be matched to the individual, addressing the needs of the student, so it is important for you to be familiar with all of the options for acceleration.

Acceleration: Opportunities and Barriers

A major barrier to offering appropriate acceleration options is lack of information that well-meaning people have about accelerating students. So many people knew a person, or perhaps knew a person who knew a person, who experienced some type of acceleration and say that it was not a good experience for that person. What parents and educators need to know is that research supports all types of acceleration if the decisions are made carefully by considering the child and matching the opportunity for acceleration to the child.

Another barrier is the fact that many educators and parents think specifically about whole-grade acceleration (or grade-skipping) when the term *acceleration* is used. Whole-grade acceleration can work well, but it is not the only way to accelerate. Other acceleration options should be tried before moving a child up in grade

Figure 4

Types of Acceleration

- Early admission to kindergarten
- Early admission to first grade
- Grade skipping
- Continuous progress
- Self-paced instruction
- Subject-matter acceleration/partial acceleration
- Combined classes
- Curriculum compacting
- Telescoping the curriculum
- Mentoring
- Extracurricular programs
- Correspondence courses/distance learning programs
- Early graduation
- Concurrent/dual enrollment
- Advanced Placement
- Credit by examination
- Acceleration in college
- Early entrance into middle school, high school, or college

Note. From Southern and Jones (2004).

levels; in fact, it is best to implement the least unusual options for acceleration before suggesting skipping a grade.

A young person who is gifted in a specific academic area will need single-subject acceleration. This type of acceleration could involve the child being placed in a cluster group with other children who are similarly advanced in mathematics or by having the child go to a higher grade for math instruction. At the middle school and high school levels, the young person who is ready to progress in math at a faster pace than their age-mates needs opportunities to take more challenging mathematics classes. Perhaps they will be taking Algebra I in seventh grade rather than eighth grade. Please remember that there is plenty of math to learn, so don't be discouraged when a well-meaning person remarks, "What will we do when she is a senior or when he runs out of math classes?" A far more important question is "How can we be sure that she has every opportunity to learn in math on a continuous basis?" Possibilities for extending learning include virtual math classes or college classes. It is also possible for the high school to add more advanced math options to the curriculum.

The acceleration option that a particular child needs may be offered solely at another building. In that case, who is responsible for providing transportation when the child needs to take a class at the middle school but is still in the elementary grades, or is in middle school but needs to go to the high school for one or more classes? Often a parent takes the child to the class (which hopefully has been arranged to be during the first or last period slot so that time is not used for transportation on both sides of the class). The preferable solution for transporting children to classes in other buildings is for the district to assume the responsibility. That way, more children can participate when they demonstrate readiness for the more advanced opportunities. If the district assumes responsibility for transporting students to a different school, children whose parents could not provide rides would not be kept from learning at an accelerated pace. It will be important to find out what the policies are in your school district.

Another way to accelerate is to have children start school at a younger age. In cases in which the child demonstrates readiness to enter kindergarten early, doing so may or may not be possible. The answer would depend on the law in the state and/or policy in the school district. In some states, a child who demonstrates readiness to move to a higher grade will be easy to accelerate, while other states throw up a barrier by requiring that a child must be 5 years old by August 1 or September 15. With deadlines for starting school, it is very desirable to have an option for assessing the readiness of individual children whose birthdays do not fall within the published deadline.

Still another way to accelerate students is for them to enter a level of schooling earlier than their age-mates. For example, early entrance to college is one way to move through school at a faster pace than anticipated. This option includes matriculating into college ahead of schedule. It could also mean going to a residential school that specializes in mathematics and science in which the students complete high school while they are earning 2 years of college credit. The Carol Martin Gatton Academy of Mathematics and Science in Kentucky (http://www.wku.edu/academy) is one example of this acceleration possibility.

Making Whole-Grade Acceleration the Right Choice

When a full-grade skip is thought to be the best way to meet a child's academic needs, assessment is in order. The child and the receiving teacher must be on board for a grade acceleration to work. The third edition of the Iowa Acceleration Scale (Assouline et al., 2009) is a useful tool to guide your decision making. A point to remember about a grade skip is that advancing the child will only solve the problem for a short time, and differentiation and other acceleration strategies often will be needed. After all, a child who is grade accelerated is usually achieving at two or more levels above their current grade, so skipping a grade may be a temporary solution that will need various adjustments if the child is to make continuous progress.

Have an Acceleration Policy in Place

Having policy in place is very important for addressing children's needs for any type of acceleration. *Developing Academic Acceleration Policies: Whole Grade, Early Entrance & Single Subject* (Lupkowski-Shoplik et al., 2018) provides information, guidelines, and sample policy for acceleration (see https://www.accelerationinstitute. org/Resources/Policy_Guidelines). It is always good to have a policy adopted before it is needed, so do not wait to put policy in place until there is a critical need for one or more types of acceleration.

One positive point about acceleration options is that generally there is no expense to implementing them. Not accelerating has a different kind of cost—a personal loss of learning time and potential. That is a loss that is difficult to recoup!

Conclusion

One characteristic of gifted children is that they often learn at a faster pace and at a more complex level than many other young people their age. Using the various forms of acceleration, teachers and administrators can accommodate students' needs for a faster pace in learning. The forms of acceleration must be matched to the children, selecting the type that will allow for continuous progress, beginning with the least disruptive option. All parents and educators who are considering any acceleration option should be well informed about the research on this topic. It is recommended to read *A Nation Deceived: How Schools Hold Back America's Brightest Students* and *A Nation Empowered: Evidence Trumps the Excuses Holding Back America's Brightest Students* and to have copies in the school library so they are accessible to parents as well as educators.

Survival Tips

- Start with the form of acceleration that makes the least change for the child. Check out the results and then move on to the next form of acceleration if the first one is not enough. Don't hold a student back from learning experiences because others of the same age are not ready for those experiences.
- There are many ways to accommodate a child's need to move at a different pace in learning, and there is a strong research base supporting all of them. Encourage parents to learn about acceleration options if their child may benefit from one or more forms of acceleration.
- Broaden educators' and parents' views of acceleration to go beyond grade-skipping.
- Remember that it is a myth that there is social-emotional harm when a child is accelerated. When decisions are made thoughtfully, acceleration can have positive results for children with gifts and talents.

Survival Toolkit

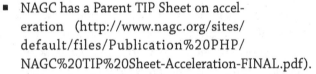

- The Acceleration Institute (https://www. accelerationinstitute.org) is dedicated to the study of curricular acceleration for academically talented children. The website provides lots of information about the procedure and policy development related to acceleration.
- NAGC has a Parent TIP Sheet on acceleration (http://www.nagc.org/sites/default/files/Publication%20PHP/NAGC%20TIP%20Sheet-Acceleration-FINAL.pdf).
- Both volumes of *A Nation Deceived: How Schools Hold Back America's Brightest Students* (https://www.accelerationinstitute.org/nation_deceived) are key resources for anyone (parent or educator) who is considering any type of acceleration and would make a good book study for a PLC. Start with Volume I and then proceed to Volume II, which has the research support for acceleration.
- This tool guides decisions for whole-grade acceleration: Assouline, S. G., Colangelo, N., Lupkowski-Shoplik, A., Forstadt, L, & Lipscomb, J. (2009). *The Iowa Acceleration Scale* (3rd ed.). Great Potential Press.

- "What I Learned As An Ex-Gifted Kid | Caroline Cannistra | TEDxAshburnSalon" (https://www.youtube.com/watch?v=5Kkf-6o1q4Q) shares one young woman's experience with radical acceleration.
- Other resources include:
  - Assouline, S. G., Colangelo, N., VanTassel-Baska, J., & Lupkowski-Shoplik, A. (Eds.). (2015). *A nation empowered: Evidence trumps the excuses holding back America's brightest students* (Vol. 2). The University of Iowa, The Connie Belin & Jacqueline N. Blank International Center for Gifted Education and Talent Development.
  - Lupkowski-Shoplik, A., Behrens, W. A., & Assouline, S. G. (2018). *Developing academic acceleration policies: Whole grade, early entrance & single subject.* The University of Iowa, The Connie Belin & Jacqueline N. Blank International Center for Gifted Education and Talent Development, National Association for Gifted Children, the Council of State Directors of Programs for the Gifted.
  - Smutny, J. F., Walker, S. Y., & Meckstroth, E. A. (2007). *Acceleration for gifted learners, K–5.* Corwin Press.

Survival Toolkit, continued

Chapter 10

Making Differentiation Defensible

"The 'pressure for coverage' is the greatest enemy of understanding." (Gardner, 1993, p. 22)

Key Question

- What elements must be in place for differentiation to be defensible?

The Importance of Challenge

When should challenge first be a part of a child's learning? That answer is easy to find. Challenge begins at home with a child learning new things on an ongoing basis. Then, challenge must continue in school from the time the child enrolls in preschool or kindergarten. Teachers in all classes and in all grades should be committed to every child learning new things in school and making achievement gains on an ongoing basis. For the well-being of the child, the community, and the country, challenge is essential for all children. And challenge doesn't mean following the

DOI: 10.4324/9781003238553-11

grade-level content if the child demonstrates on a preassessment that they have met the standard. That is the signal for differentiating the curriculum.

What is challenging to one child may be too difficult or too easy for others, even though they are in the same grade—this is why differentiation strategies are incredibly important for all teachers to master. Teachers must remember that one doesn't start differentiating on a full-time basis when one has not been accustomed to using differentiation strategies (see Chapter 13). The key is to start with one differentiation strategy and then to build a repertoire of strategies. That takes time, yet it cannot happen until you get started.

The Essentials of Differentiation

When a teacher begins to differentiate, the place to start is planning for instruction. The first question to answer is: What do you want everyone in the class to know and/or be able to do? Of course, that question leads to preassessing and raises a second question: Who already knows the information and/or can demonstrate the requite skills? It is only after the teacher plans the unit/lesson and then preassesses the concepts and skills, as well as interests in the topic being studied in the unit/lesson, that defensible differentiation can occur. The third question is: What do you plan for the child or children who already know or can do what is planned? It is this last question that leads to differentiation that is defensible.

Without preassessment data, different learning experiences are just that—different. Simply offering a choice of learning experiences without matching the opportunity to levels of readiness, interests in the content being studied, and learning preferences is different, but not differentiated in a defensible way. Information gleaned from the preassessment informs the teachers as they match learning experiences to what the student or students already know. Preassessment is essential to ensure that each student is learning concepts and honing skills at an appropriately challenging level. It is not possible to learn what one already knows, and it is not appropriate to expect children to learn what is beyond their reach at that moment. Differentiation is a bit like the tale of Goldilocks and the three bears—the learning tasks can't be too difficult or too easy, but they must be just right.

Perhaps the main reason teachers do not plan for a wide range of learners is that they do not understand the need to differentiate for students who are advanced. They think gifted children will "make it on their own." The second reason, a close second, is that strategies to differentiate just have not become a natural part of their teaching routine. *Routine* is an important word, as differentiation will only be ongoing if it fits into the way that the educator teaches on an everyday basis. The third reason for not differentiating is the emphasis schools place on proficiency or grade-level learning. The problem with setting proficiency as a goal is that minimum

Figure 5
Tied to the Proficiency Post

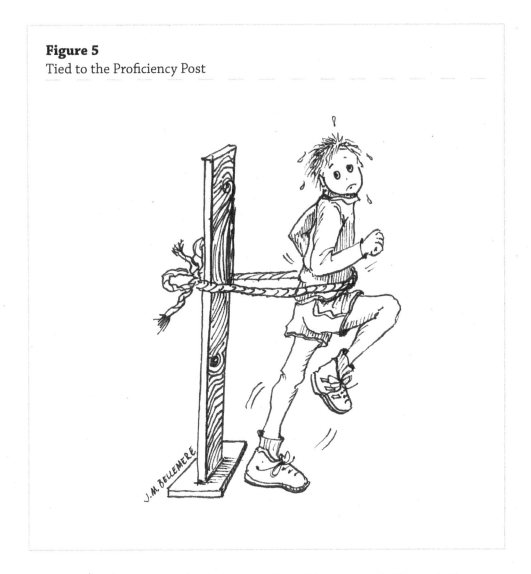

competencies become maximum expectations. The cartoon in Figure 5 illustrates the problem of a child who is struggling to run but is tied to the proficiency post.

Basic strategies to differentiate instruction start with questioning strategies, writing assignments, and reading options. Recognizing that students in the class are different in their levels of readiness, interests, and skills is the first step in figuring out why differentiating is essential.

PLAN

A simple formula for differentiating is PLAN—Preassessment, Learning Experiences, Assessment, and using the assessment data for planning the Next

Figure 6
PLAN Model

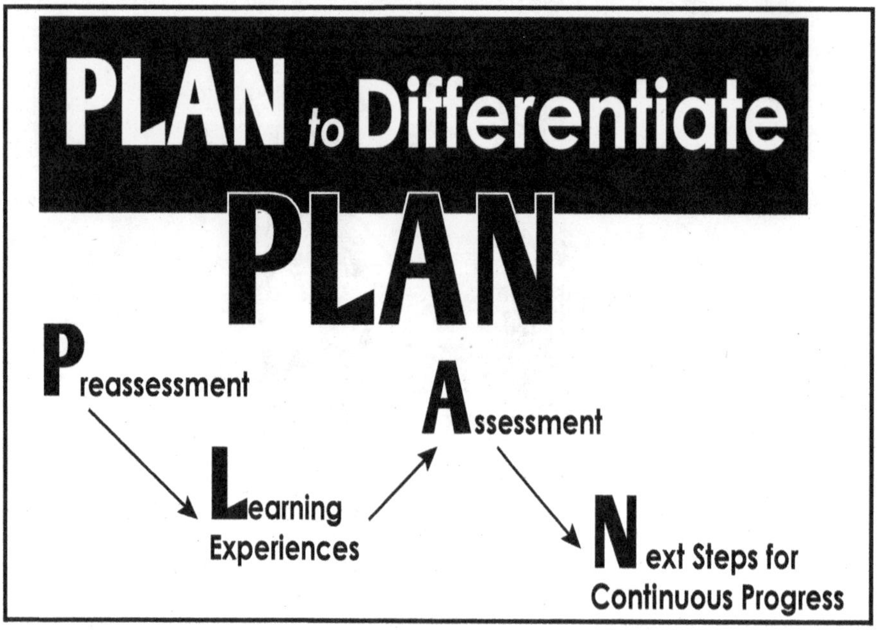

Note. From *The PLAN Model* [unpublished manuscript], by J. L. Roberts, n.d., The Center for Gifted Education, Western Kentucky University, Bowling Green, KY. Reprinted with permission.

Learning Experience (see Figure 6). This approach is recommended for educators beginning to differentiate instruction.

The Principles of a Differentiated Classroom

Appropriate expectations must be in place in a classroom in order for differentiation to occur on an ongoing basis. Roberts and Inman (2015b) offered the following principles to set the stage:

- A differentiated classroom respects diversity.
- A differentiated classroom maintains high expectations.
- A differentiated classroom generates openness. (p. 20)

Data must be used to make differentiated instructional decisions. Expert Jan Lanham provides information on how to use data to make defensible decisions about differentiation.

Survival Secrets for Gathering and Using Data as the Key to Effective Differentiation

Jan Lanham

Effective instruction requires balancing the instructional needs and readiness of the student and the skills and concepts identified as the objectives for student learning by unit and curriculum planning. Just as students must possess the background skills and experiences to be ready to learn, students cannot be taught something they already know. Yet many teachers spend time trying to do just that! The use of performance data empowers teachers to improve the match between what is taught and student readiness in order to assure continuous progress. Performance data provide measures of student levels of mastery through the analysis of anecdotal information (notes and observations based on actual student performance, skills, preferences, learning preferences, etc.), work samples (student products, individual and group tasks, assigned and voluntary extensions, etc.), performance on teacher-made tests, any relevant assessment data (including student IEPs, universal screening data, content testing, etc.), and specific preassessment data (KWL charts, THC charts, schema charts, conversations, journals, etc.). Those data are then used to inform basic decisions about instructional groupings and pacing within a content area or unit, as well as decisions about specific instructional delivery on a weekly and daily basis.

Effective use of data is built around clear objectives that address three key questions:

1. What do I want the students to know or be able to do? (*Content and skills*)
2. What activities will be provided to explore and practice those skills? (*Guided and independent practice*)
3. What are the mastery criteria that will show that the student has achieved the objective? (*Product or performance*)

Performance data prompt differentiation decisions around adjustments in content and skills, the process by which students will take in and/or practice with the content and skills, and the product(s) by which students will demonstrate mastery.

By clearly answering each of these questions in planning, differentiation becomes purposeful and matched to the needs and readiness of students. For example, a basic objective might be: Students will demonstrate understanding of the steps in the water cycle by defining each term and placing each term correctly on a student-generated, illustrated flowchart.

Once the objective and levels of individual accountability are identified, the teacher can ask, "Who will need extra support (and what kind of support) to successfully complete the task?" and "Who can already do this?" Data are used to answer both questions and to refine instruction to ensure continuous progress. For those students needing extra support, definitions for the steps of the water cycle might be made available on file folder labels or as a part of a word bank, or a flowchart schematic might be provided so that students only have to provide additional details and add in the terms.

Remembering that the goal is to facilitate the students' ability to identify and use the terms, differentiation adjusts the manner in which the students practice their learning.

Based on the preassessment data, it is important to think about the students who can already do the stated task in the same way in order to ensure new learning. Typically, students would be asked to work with the skills/concepts at a more advanced level. For example, students who can already identify and sequence the scientific terms in the water cycle may be asked to use synthesis and analysis skills by illustrating and captioning the importance of each water cycle phase to the biome they have illustrated, or they may be asked to compare and contrast the phases of the water cycle in different seasons, or they may be asked to illustrate and explain the impact of humans on each phase of the cycle. The goal is to provide applications of the concepts at a higher level that reflects new learning for the students.

—Jan W. Lanham, Ph.D.
Consultant Recognized in the Kentucky Teacher Hall of Fame

Conclusion

Each child deserves to make continuous progress, making at least a month's achievement gain for a month in school. Differentiation makes continuous progress possible. Differentiation must accommodate the various paces of learning, interests, and academic possibilities within a group of children, even a class of gifted children.

A very effective way to begin a discussion of differentiation in a faculty meeting, a PLC, or with a parent group is to read and then discuss the book *Mrs. Spitzer's Garden*. As Mrs. Spitzer differentiates for plants in her garden, it is easy to make connections to doing so within a classroom.

Survival Tips

Children who learn differently must be taught differently in order to make continuous progress.

All children need to be learning on an ongoing basis. Consequently, not all 10-year-olds are ready for the same level of math, music, writing, literature, or soccer on the same time schedule. Different learning experiences on the same concepts or skills must be matched to readiness, learning preferences, and interests if all children are to make continuous progress.

Survival Toolkit

- "Mini-Course: The Musts of a Differentiated Classroom" (https://nagc.org/mini-course-musts-differentiated-classroom) includes an overview of differentiation and a list of resources.
- Other resources include:
  - Pattou, E. (2001). *Mrs. Spitzer's garden*. Harcourt.
  - Roberts, J. L., & Boggess, J. R. (Eds.). (2012). *Differentiating instruction through centers in the gifted classroom*. Prufrock Press.
  - Roberts, J. L., & Inman, T. F. (2015). *Strategies for differentiating instruction: Best practices for the classroom* (3rd ed.). Prufrock Press.
  - Winebrenner, S. (with Brulles, D.). (2018). *Teaching gifted kids in today's classroom: Strategies and techniques every teacher can use* (4th ed.). Free Spirit.

Chapter 11

Preassessing in Order to Teach What Students Don't Already Know

"Diagnostic assessment is as important to teaching as a physical exam is to prescribing an appropriate medical regiment." (McTighe & O'Connor, 2005, p. 14)

Key Questions

- What preassessment tools are both easy to administer and quick to use to garner student information?

- What are the advantages of preassessing with new learning experiences throughout the school year?

In 2000, Julian Stanley wrote an article entitled "Helping Students Learn Only What They Don't Already Know"—the title alone tells us why preassessment is the natural and necessary step that follows planning a unit (you can't preassess until you have planned what the students are to know and to be able to do). After all, if the student already knows or can do what you want the unit to accomplish, it presents a wonderful opportunity to allow them to learn about the same topic but at a more complex and in-depth level. Do you remember all of the times you have said,

 DOI: 10.4324/9781003238553-12

"I wish I had more time to teach this topic or concept"? Preassessment allows you to find that desired time for one student, a few students, or all students. Of course, preassessment guides your decision about matching learning experiences to the interests, needs, and readiness of the learners.

Just think of what your perception would be if you went to see your physician, and they prescribed the same drugs to you that all patients got that particular day—after all, it was Tuesday, and that was what was planned for Tuesday. Of course, that makes no sense at all, yet the one-lesson-fits-all-students approach to teaching follows the same logic. It doesn't work for all of the patients, and it doesn't work for all students. In fact, Reis and colleagues (1993) found that gifted elementary children knew more than half of the content when they started the year, leading the subtitle of their study on content to be "Why Not Let High Ability Students Start School in January?"

Preassessment information, including interest and learning preference inventories, proves to be important for knowing which questions, writing assignments, and reading options will allow each student to make continuous progress.

Types of Preassessment

There are many ways to preassess what students know before teaching a unit. To do this routinely, the preassessment must be easy to use. That is, it must be easy in terms of creating the preassessment and tabulating the results. Here are examples of ways to try to gather information about what your students already know and are able to do.

The T-W-H Chart

Let's start with a familiar way to preassess—the K-W-L Chart, but in this case it is called the T-W-H Chart (see Figure 7). The T column lets students tell you what they think about the topic (not quite so specific as knowing about a topic). The W column allows them to tell you what they want to know about the topic, and the H column provides the opportunity for students to let you know how they would like to learn about the topic.

The T-W-H Chart garners a lot of information about each student's knowledge on the topic of study, as well as what about the topic interests them and how they would like to learn about the topic. Can you use all of the students' suggestions? Of course not! However, when you can use a suggestion about instruction from a reluctant learner, you have made an important connection that can motivate the child. Information you learn from the completed T-W-H charts can help you group

Figure 7
T-W-H Chart

T – W – H CHART

Topic/Unit _____   **Name** _____

What do you **T**hink about this topic?	What do you **W**ant to learn about this topic?	**H**ow do you want to learn about this topic?

children of like interests and similar levels of readiness. The charts can be sorted easily into three piles—those who know quite a bit about the topic, those who know a little, and those who are new to the topic. If you find out that none of the students are familiar with the topic, it is fair game to plan the same learning experiences for all children. You may find out that all or most students know a lot about the subject. However, it is far more likely that some students will have interests in the topic that vary from "very interested" to "unaware."

Open-Ended Writing

Another easy way to preassess is to give the class 5 minutes to write about the topic they are to study. Open-ended writing can reveal a lot about what each student knows or does not know about the topic. A quick read of their responses tells you what each student brings to the new unit of study. It will take little time to sort the responses into three piles—knows quite a bit, knows some, and new to the topic or concept.

End-of-the-Unit Assessment or End-of-the-Previous-Unit Assessment

Using assessments given at the conclusion of the unit or at the end of the previous unit can be informative as preassessments. The assessment given at the end of the previous unit works well as a preassessment (and takes no extra time) if the material to be learned is sequential. If the learning is not sequential, another type of preassessment other than the end-of-the-previous-unit needs to be your choice for information about what students know and are able to do in relation to the topic/concept they will be studying.

Punnett Square/Frayer Model

The Punnett Square or the Frayer Model is a graphic organizer that provides a quick way to see what the students in your class already know about a concept. In the four quadrants the students provide their understanding of the definition of the concept, characteristics or attributes of the concept, an example of the concept, and a nonexample of the concept. Jerome Bruner in the 1950s highlighted the need to know if a student can recognize nonexamples as well as examples of the content. Recognizing the attributes of the concept that are essential for understanding the concept can reveal the level of understanding the student has before embarking on a study of that topic.

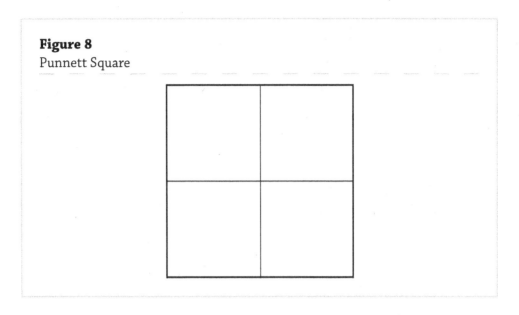

Figure 8
Punnett Square

Preassessing for Learning Preferences

Preassessments can also be used to determine the learners' preferred ways of learning or their interests concerning a topic to be studied. The preassessment for a project on COVID-19 shown in Figure 9 is an example of this type of preassessment. Asking a few questions and getting student responses provide a great starting point for putting students in small groups or in planning for specific topics for projects when pursuing a specific topic of study.

Stoplight Questions

You can give young students the opportunity to color-code their answers using the colors found in a traffic light. Green means a student definitely knows it, yellow says that they think it is correct but guessed, and red tells you that they have no idea. This coloring system works with young students and can be used with older ones as well.

Five Most Difficult Questions

If you provide the students with the opportunity to answer the five most difficult questions in the unit and the student(s) can answer them with at least 80% accuracy, you have strong evidence that the student doesn't need to study the unit in the same way as students who don't have that level of understanding of the content or the demonstration of skills. Winebrenner (2018) provided this guidance for

Figure 9
Preassessment for a Project on COVID-19

The coronavirus changed lives dramatically in 2020. A pandemic had been predicted and written about previously; however, the preparation for such a pandemic varied a lot from country to country. This time was a defining moment for individuals across the globe—a time to remember and share with your children.

In preparation for conducting a study of one aspect of the pandemic, please respond to the following.

Circle all that apply:
1. I was most interested in the statistical projections related to the spread of the coronavirus.
2. I was very interested in the social distancing required to slow the pandemic and the changes to life that social distancing required.
3. I was most interested in the approach to handling the coronavirus in another country (name one or more countries).
4. My time and attention during the pandemic was focused on learning remotely.
5. I didn't pay much attention to COVID-19.

Circle the response that best applies to you.
1. I enjoy interviewing to learn.
2. I have no experience interviewing for a project, but think I would like to give it a try.
3. I have interviewed for a project but would prefer getting information another way.

I would prefer to show my results in a:
1. Video
2. Series of illustrations or charts to accompany a report
3. Project of my choice (with teacher approval)

preassessing and then planning opportunities for engaging in learning experiences on the same topic the class is studying but at a more complex level. That learning can be shared with the class and extend the learning of all in the class.

Words From Students

Sometimes you can glean important information about what the child knows about a topic from their conversation. Jane Ann, a new first grader who tells her teacher, "I really don't want to hurt your feelings, but we are doing kindergarten work," and Luke, who is in kindergarten and correctly explains negative numbers, are providing information about what they already know and can do. Priya, a middle school student who discusses a book that the English teacher is surprised that anyone in her class has read, provides information that she has advanced literacy skills. Clues appear all of the time, and teachers must be paying attention to what they hear from young people or observe them doing in order for this informal information to be useful and inform instructional decisions.

Would-Could-Should Test

Passow (1982) presented three questions to guide teachers in deciding whether learning experiences would be appropriate for all or some students in a classroom.
   * *Would* all children want to be involved in such learning experiences?
   * *Could* all children participate in such learning experiences?
   * *Should* all children be expected to succeed in such learning experiences?

Answers to these questions help teachers decide what learning experiences should be offered for which students. No students should be denied opportunities to learn what they are ready to learn just because everyone isn't ready. Think of sports in your school. Some students are ready to play with the varsity and need the opportunity to do so, while other students are appropriately acquiring skills that are typical of age-mates.

Jan W. Lanham describes important points that increase the effectiveness of preassessment.

Survival Secrets for Preassessing

Jan W. Lanham

The use of student performance data is pivotal for appropriate instructional planning and differentiation for all students. Although it is only one type of performance data, a topic or unit pretest commonly administered in order to group students for instruction within the unit is a cornerstone. After watching the administration of pretests across countless classrooms, some important practices to ensure effectiveness emerge:

1. **Identify unit/lesson skills and concepts.** (What do I want the students to know?) Identify specific skills and concepts for the unit and design a pretest that looks similar to the posttest in order to identify student levels of awareness and mastery relative to those target skills and concepts. Select pretest items that will inform instruction (e.g., If students miss this question, what instruction is needed to make sure they can answer other questions like this?). The pretest should provide instructional insights on each student.

2. **Preteach.** (Who just needs refreshing on this content?) It is important to spend some time "priming the pump" to ensure that the pretest data are accurate. For many content-related vocabulary terms and concepts, students may not have used those terms or procedures since the same unit last year. However, they did master it when it was taught, so they do not need to go back to the very beginning. Spending a class period or two preteaching the skills, vocabulary, and concepts in the unit proves valuable to generating the most accurate data for grouping students relative to their content readiness. For students who need multiple repetitions, preteaching is one more repetition. For students who were just "rusty," preteaching refreshes their memories, increases motivation, and allows them to more accurately show what they know and save valuable instructional time.

3. **Minimize the pretest threat.** (Why are we doing this?) Help students understand that the pretest is a strategy to validate what students know and to save instructional time. Projecting a message that student time is valued is often a powerful motivator. Make sure students know that the pretest is not related to a grade, but is a single piece of information to help inform instruction. Pretest data can be used for pre-post comparisons to help students see how much they have improved, but they should not ever be used to negatively impact grades.

4. **Administer pretest/conduct preassessment activities early enough to allow for instructional design adjustments.** (Will my timing allow me to use these data to improve instruction?) Formal and informal preassessments given the first day of a unit do not allow for meaningful adjustment of grouping and pacing. Purposeful scheduling of pretest activities must allow enough lead time to promote meaningful adjustments to instructional delivery.

5. **Use the data for instructional groupings and differentiation.** (How can I use these data to assure continuous progress for every student?) Analysis of pretest data should be conducted in order to identify students with common instructional needs, to identify unit concepts that are already mastered by most of the group, and to create purposeful targeted groupings that provide for appropriate access to the level and pace of instruction needed for each student. The data can then be used to adjust the depth and

complexity of instruction, of activities, and of student products based on that data analysis.

Pretesting is one of the most important tools for diagnostic differentiation of instruction.

—Jan W. Lanham, Ph.D.
Consultant Recognized in the Kentucky Teacher Hall of Fame

Conclusion

One further recommendation about preassessment is to keep the students' individual preassessments to document what they knew prior to studying the topic. These records give teachers a way to talk with the students about their growth in learning over time, and they also are useful to show parents why their children are doing specific assignments. Teachers can discuss the match between the assignments and the interests, needs, and readiness of the child. Overall, preassessment is a valuable tool in planning and differentiating instruction for gifted learners.

Survival Tips

- Learn as much as you can about your students. It will make your students feel valued, and it will help you match instruction to the student to enhance learning.
- The preassessment sets the starting point, but the outstanding teacher establishes the final destination.
- The teacher needs to inform parents that the purpose of preassessment is to see what the child already knows so time isn't wasted teaching those concepts and/or skills. Teachers need to know that students are not expected to answer all of the questions correctly on a preassessment; rather, it is a way to plan learning experiences that will match the students' readiness to learn certain skills and about particular topics. Otherwise, parents may be anxious when they hear that their children had an assessment (test) and that they didn't know the answers to most of the questions that were asked.
- Remember, teaching without preassessing is like going bowling with the pins covered!

Survival Toolkit

Useful resources on this topic include:

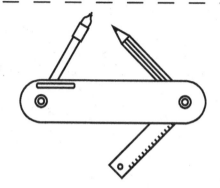

- Black, P., & Wilian, D. (1998). Inside the black box: Raising standards through classroom assessment. *Phi Delta Kappan, 80,* 130–148.
- Kirchner, J., & Inman, T. (2005, Winter). Differentiation tips for teachers: Practical strategies for the classroom. *The Challenge, 14,* 10–11. https://www.david songifted.org/search-database/entry/a10331
- Tomlinson, C. A., & Moon, T. R. (2013). *Assessment and student success in a differentiated classroom.* ASCD.

Chapter 12

Strategies to Light the Fire of Learning

"Education is not the filling of a pail, but the lighting of a fire."
—Unknown

Key Question

- When many teachers first heard about 21st-century skills, that century had not arrived; however, we now live in the third decade of that new century. Now you need to prepare students for tomorrow's world. What do students need to know and be able to do to be successful in the 21st century?

Interdisciplinary learning is important in setting the stage for lifelong learning. Expert Sandra N. Kaplan provides information as to why it is so important to make interdisciplinary connections.

 DOI: 10.4324/9781003238553-13

Sandra N. Kaplan

Rationale for Interdisciplinary Learning

"In what ways are these related?" is a basic question that stimulates both the interest and ability to observe, create, and/or state the relationships or connections that are within or between areas of study. This process is called interdisciplinary learning. Theorists have discussed the natural ways that children make sense of something by identifying how they share within and between group commonalities and/or differences. Early in the description of child development, Piaget stated that the ability to sort within and among items is an integral feature of the learning process (Singer & Ravenson, 1996). Examinations of curriculum and pedagogical designs do not consistently reveal the importance or presence of the feature of interdisciplinary learning. Although interdisciplinary learning often is referenced as a viable feature to be included in a differentiated curriculum for the gifted, it is not consistently present in the curriculum available to gifted students. Several issues appear to inhibit the inclusion of interdisciplinary learning:

- a belief that the contained presentation of a subject or skill provides better preparation for significant learning and retention and that relating subjects across disciplines diffuses understanding of a given subject or skill;
- the scope of teacher background knowledge and the unavailability of resources presenting subject matter or disciplines that are not familiar to the teacher can create academic dissonance that subsequently making connections within and between disciplines is not a natural or comfortable process for the teacher; and
- national and state assessments primarily focus on the understanding of a single content area; thus it is assumed that interdisciplinary learning minimizes the opportunity to be successful on some measures of achievement.

Although these factors appear to be prohibitors to the implementation of interdisciplinary learning, there is a set of alternative factors that promote and support the concept and implementation of interdisciplinary learning:

1. *Interdisciplinary learning reinforces many of the traits of giftedness.* Renzulli (2007) described the traits of abstract thinking, automatization of information processing, and rapid, accurate, and selected retrieval of information. These characteristics underscore the process of interdisciplinary learning and indicate a "readiness" for interdisciplinary thinking.

2. *Interdisciplinary learning provides a means to accelerate and enrich the understanding of a subject or discipline.* Replete in the descriptions to differentiate curriculum for gifted learners is the reference to acceleration or providing gifted learners with subject matter and/or skills that are responsive to their abilities as advanced learners and provide the opportunity for learning beyond the age/grade boundaries.

3. *Interdisciplinary learning promotes creative productive thinking and problem solving.* Perhaps the most valuable support for the relationships of creativity and problem solving to interdisciplinary learning is providing students with the study of noted recipients of awards for their scientific and artistic accomplishments. Biographical and autobiographical studies reveal that the process of interdisciplinary thinking has contributed to creative expressions and the solving of problems.

4. *Interdisciplinary learning stimulates broader perspectives of a subject and initiates interests that could otherwise remain dormant.* The development and pursuit of individual interests as an integral feature in the education of gifted students is often discussed as an element included in a planned differentiated curriculum. Interdisciplinary learning affords gifted learners multiple opportunities to reveal and analyze branches of a regular or basic study that can become new and dedicated interests.

Initiating Interdisciplinary Learning

Introducing the value of interdisciplinary learning to gifted students is an important feature in initiating differentiated curriculum and instruction. A study of well-noted disciplinarians is the first step to illustrate the purposes and consequences of interdisciplinary learning and to reinforce the importance of interdisciplinary thinking as the stimulus for an invention by an inventor, a remedy by a doctor, and literary publication by an author. "What knowledge from different fields of study were important to Einstein's achievements?" is an example of introducing the importance of the study of the disciplines from a disciplinarian's perspective.

Introducing Interdisciplinary Learning

The curriculum and pedagogical practices incorporating interdisciplinary learning require understanding of the features of subject matter: facts, concepts, principles, generalizations, theories, laws. These features are the stimuli to activate interdisciplinary relationships. The following examples illustrate how the features of subject matter that are identified within the basic, core, or advanced or differen-

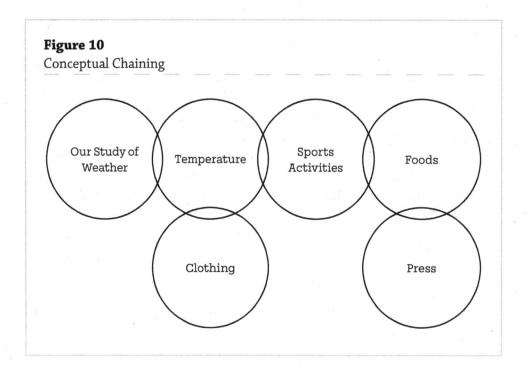

Figure 10
Conceptual Chaining

tiated curriculum can be utilized to introduce and integrate interdisciplinary thinking and learning.

Conceptual Chaining. The teacher identifies a significant concept from the subject matter to be taught and demonstrates to students how the selected concept can initiate a chain of related concepts (see Figure 10). This learning experience introduces the concept of relating or associate ideas to form a more profound or advanced understanding of a subject. An important factor associated with this learning experience is to inform students that there is no one correct link to be made and that the only "requirement" is that the student describe their thinking that motivated the connection.

Disciplinary Chaining. This learning experience requires a preliminary introduction to the nature and structure of a discipline (see Figure 11). Basically, disciplines are the formal structure of subject matter that include goals, language, tools, significant outcomes, people with accompanying roles and responsibilities and levels of expertise. A simple introduction to the disciplines is to describe how the content studied in a given subject, such as social studies, is a composite of disciplines: geography, anthropology, sociology, history, economics, political science. In some instances, teachers have initiated a "Discipline Treasure Hunt" so students can become familiar with the range of disciplines that are within the familiar subjects of literature, mathematics, science, physical education, and art that they currently study.

Disciplinary Support. The introduction to the "Disciplinary Support" learning experience is dependent on students' awareness of the formal discipline that represent or are included in the concept they are learning in a given subject (see

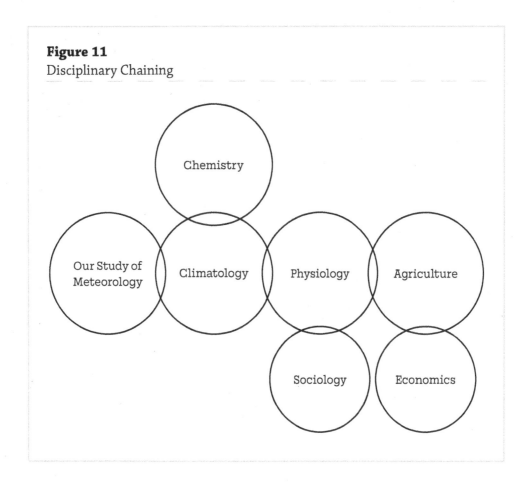

Figure 11
Disciplinary Chaining

Figure 12). Another important variable is the need for students to become aware of the fact that all studies include many and varied disciplines to some degree of relative importance (see Figure 13). The Disciplinary Support learning experience provides greater depth of understanding, introduces a different perspective or orientation to the topic, and initiates new areas of study and possible personal interests. Broadening the scope of the learning expectations from this type of interdisciplinary learning experiences sometimes creates a new perspective for students to determine what it means to be "accomplished or a good student."

Conclusion

The elements that constitute the "best" or most appropriate differentiated curriculum for gifted learners will be a continuous point of discussion among educators. It is important to recognize that interdisciplinary learning has many important benefits for gifted learners beyond being included in a differentiated curriculum. Interdisciplinary learning is a personal introduction to the many and varied options for advanced study and, thus, it can be considered as a segment

Figure 12

Disciplinary Support

Concept	Subject	Disciplines
Colonization	Social Studies	History Geography Economics Philosophy Sociology Politics

Figure 13

Examples of Varied Disciplines in a Subject

Concept	Subject	Disciplines	Degree of Emphasis for Discipline Inclusion
Colonization	Social Studies	Geography Sociology Politics	Landforms Community development Leadership

of a "college readiness" curriculum as well as preparation for future professional decisions.

—Sandra N. Kaplan
Professor of Clinical Education, University of Southern California

Top 20 Principles From Psychology

The Center for Psychology in Schools and Education of the American Psychological Association (2017) published *Top 20 Principles From Psychology for PreK–12 Creative, Talented, and Gifted Students' Teaching and Learning*. This document includes key information to guide educators as they work with children and young people with gifts and talents. The principles are listed in the Appendix.

The Higher Education Opportunity Act and Gifted Learners

The Higher Education Opportunity Act (2008) included specific language about gifted children and the need to tailor instruction to address their needs. The Higher Education Opportunity Act (HEOA) included gifted children for the first time in 2008. Specifically, the HEOA included the following language:

(23) TEACHING SKILLS—The term "teaching skills" means skills that enable a teacher to—
A: increase student learning, achievement, and the ability to apply knowledge;
B: effectively convey and explain academic subject matter;
C: effectively teach higher-order analytical, evaluation, problem solving, and communication skills;
D: employ strategies grounded in the disciplines or teaching and learning that—
   a. are based on empirically-based practice and scientifically valid research, where applicable, related to teaching and learning;
   b. are specific to academic subject matter; and
   c. focus on the identification of students' specific learning needs, particularly students with disabilities, students who are limited English proficient, **students who are gifted and talented**, and students with low literacy levels, and the tailoring of academic instruction to such needs. (3132–3133; emphasis added)

The inclusion of gifted children in the Higher Education Opportunity Act is worth noting and sharing as you advocate and plan instruction for gifted and talented students.

A single chapter cannot begin to be comprehensive of the many strategies available for teaching gifted kids. Consequently, a few important strategies are highlighted—ones to engage students in learning and hopefully light the fire of their lifelong learning.

119

Continuous Learning Opportunities

Allow students to learn on an ongoing basis. If every child in the class is capable of doing the activity, they should all have the opportunity to do so. If everyone isn't ready for that learning experience, children who are ready should be given the opportunity.

Encourage Higher Level Thinking

The Partnership for 21st Century Learning (2019) published the Framework for 21st Century Learning. Under Learning & Innovation Skills are (1) critical thinking, (2) communication, (3) collaboration, and (4) creativity.

Twenty-first century skills require thinking at high levels, just as gifted education has for several decades. Critical and creative thinking are very important skills that should be required and developed in all classes, no matter the content. Problem-based learning (PBL) begins with a discrepant situation or problem. Then the students use their thinking and collaboration skills to provide solutions to the problem. Remember that the world's biggest problems have no magic bullet solutions or solutions that are known and students need to find, so students need strategies to solve problems and experience doing so.

Choose strategies that encourage higher level thinking in your classes. Remember that if you or the students can find the answer using a simple Internet search, then it isn't a higher level question. Here are some tips for making sure the questions you ask are at a higher level:

1. Ask who, what, when, and where questions, but then move on to questions that ask students to combine ideas in new ways.
2. Ask if-then questions—questions that require speculating as to what could happen.
3. Carry a card with the higher level questions you have planned. Planning questions in advance will spark your thinking, especially if you are used to asking lower level questions.

Engage Students

Select strategies that actively engage students in the learning experiences. Engagement may relate to the topic, the skills required to learn at high levels, and/ or the product. When young people are engaged in learning, it is hard to separate work from play. Engagement usually is the result of hands-on, minds-on learning experiences. Just hands-on activities are not enough, as real learning experiences must also be minds-on. What are students engaged in cognitively? That is the important question to ask to ensure that students are thinking at high levels.

Also make sure to provide resources that engage students in learning. Advanced readers need resources at their challenge levels—neither too easy nor too difficult. De Wet et al. (2005) described the Schoolwide Enrichment Model in Reading (SEM-R) and offered strategies for engaging advanced readers using appropriately challenging, rather than grade-level, reading materials. Downloadable materials are available from the Renzulli Center for Creativity, Gifted Education, and Talent Development (https://gifted.uconn.edu/semr-about) that provide questions on characters, nonfiction, biography, reading attitudes, and other literary topics. These questions can stimulate discussions on any high-interest books you select for your classroom.

You can also use data to engage students in learning. Renzulli et al. (2010) described strategies to involve students in hands-on investigations using data-gathering skills (see Table 2 for a suggestion of instruments teachers can use in their classrooms). Their book, *Think Data: Getting Kids Involved in Hands-On Investigations With Data-Gathering Instruments*, is a useful resource for teachers interested in using data collection to engage students in learning.

Teachers can offer technology to engage learners, particularly reluctant learners who are eager to use the classroom technology tools but dread written or paper-based assignments. One way to do this is to offer students a choice of products to demonstrate what has been learned. Technology can be used in many ways, one of which is to engage students in projects based on their interest in the technology involved in creating the product; some students may have little interest in a topic, but if technology is involved in the learning, they become engaged. For example, creating a podcast or developing a blog or video may catch the interest of students who are weary of writing another report about what they have learned on a topic.

Table 2

Instruments for Data Collection

Name of Instrument	What It Measures
Digital sound level meter	Sound wave amplitude in decibels
Protractor	Angles
Caliper	Distance between opposite sides
Kitchen scale	Mass in grams
Walking tape measurer	Distance traveled by a wheel
Clap-o-meter	Volume of applause
Odometer	Distance
Glo-germ kit	"Germ" residue
Salt check monitor	Salt level in substance
pH meter or pH level indicator strips	pH levels (1–14) of a substance
Tally counter	Counting units
Digital thermometer	Temperature
Instant ocean hydrometer	Specific gravity (density) of water
Barometer	Air pressure
Soil meter	Soil pH
Blood pressure monitor	Systolic and diastolic blood pressure
Stopwatch, egg timer, sundial	Time
Planimeter	Area
Accelerometer	Acceleration
Pedometer	Number of steps
Speedometer	Speed, velocity
Wattmeter	Electrical power

Note. Adapted from *Think Data: Getting Kids Involved in Hands-on Investigations With Data-Gathering Instruments,* by J. S. Renzulli, N. N. Heilbronner, and D. Siegle, 2010, Taylor & Francis. Copyright 2010 by Taylor & Francis. Adapted with permission.

Provide Problem-Based Learning Experiences

Create situations for students to become scientists, mathematicians, archeologists, and other professionals. When your students don the lab coat and engage in the thinking process that a scientist uses, learning is more engaging than when reading a science text and discussing the topic in the chapter. The Center for Gifted Education at William & Mary (see http://www. cfge.wm.edu) has developed science units to engage children in the act of being young scientists. Each unit requires students to develop their own answers and thoughts about a real-life problem. The units can be purchased from Routledge (https://www.routledge.com). At the University of Connecticut, a federally funded project called Project M³ has developed mathematics materials that lead students to think like mathematicians (see https://gifted.uconn.edu/projectm3). Such thinking has positive implications for creating lifelong learners.

Provide Mentors

Real-life experiences also include various types of mentoring. The first level is shadowing. A student spends a day with a veterinarian to check out what a day in the career of a vet is like, or goes to the state capitol to follow a senator to learn about the business of creating legislation. Mentoring that is a long-term relation-ship focuses on an interest shared by the mentor and mentee. Often that interest is a research area the student wishes to pursue. Successful mentorships depend on mutual benefits for both partners.

Implement Project-Based Learning

Involve students in project-based learning. Project-based learning provides a great way to engage students in high-level learning, and this type of application of knowledge is in tune with 21st-century learning goals. Students often put forth their best effort when working on a project, especially when they have an element of choice in the project. Perhaps a student gets to pose the specific question to be addressed about a topic the class is studying. Perhaps they have the choice of which product they'll create to communicate what they discovered as they learned about the specific topic. Either way, choice is often a motivator for young people in a classroom.

Conclusion

Make sure you are providing assignments or learning tasks that are worthy of the students' time and energy. Busy work is never a winner in the eyes of students, and such assignments waste the teacher's valuable teaching time as well. Effectively differentiating assignments ensures that students aren't running in place but are learning on an ongoing basis. Remember, differentiation allows students to not be bound by age or grade in their learning.

Survival Toolkit

- Project M³ has curriculum units for a variety of grade levels (https://gifted.uconn.edu/projectm3/m3_teachers).
- *Gifted Child Today* (https://journals.sagepub.com/home/gct) is filled with practical strategies for teachers. It also reviews new products for teachers of gifted students.
- This video discusses concepts and the probing of thinking about concepts: https://www.youtube.com/watch?v=3IMUAOhuO78.
- *Methods and Materials for Teaching the Gifted* (5th ed.), edited by J. H. Robins, J. L. Jolly, F. A. Karnes, and S. M. Bean (Prufrock Press, 2020), provides many strategies for enhancing learning for all children, including those who are gifted and talented.
- *Teaching for High Potential*, a publication of NAGC, offers practical strategies for teachers of gifted children and young people.

Chapter 13

Strategies to Differentiate Instruction

"In the United States, differentiation was a way of life in the one-room schoolhouse. There, the teacher knew students would vary greatly in age, experience, motivation to learn, and proficiency. To effectively instruct the range of students, teachers had to be flexible in their use of time, space, materials, student groupings, and instructional contact with learners." (Tomlinson, 2005, p. 8)

Key Question

- What are all of the things you can do to ensure that all students understand increasingly complex concepts, engage in learning that challenges, and develop a work ethic—important ingredients for successful learners?

Differentiation allows students to move beyond learning boundaries imposed by age and grade. That a one-size-fits-all lesson does not allow all students to make continuous progress is clear. Teachers know they must modify content and strategies for children who need more time and more basic explanations to grasp the

 DOI: 10.4324/9781003238553-14

concept. Likewise, children who learn at a faster pace and already understand the concept being taught need modifications in order to continue to learn and not just mark time. Remember the drawing of a learner tied to the proficiency or grade-level post on page 97? Proficiency is grade-level achievement, a worthy goal indeed unless the student is already there or has exceeded that level. This chapter will provide examples of various ways to modify the curriculum to provide challenging learning opportunities for all young people. Of course, the starting point is the preassessment of what the students know and are able to do in relation to the topic of the unit and skills required to reach the learning goals. Information gained from inventories of learning preferences and interests will also help you tailor differentiated learning experiences to make them motivating and appropriately challenging to the students.

The Revised Cognitive Taxonomy

The revised Taxonomy of Cognitive Objectives (Anderson & Krathwohl, 2001) provides a means of differentiating the level of thinking in learning experiences. Figure 14 describes the six categories in the revised taxonomy.

Differentiating learning experiences using this model means keeping the content/concept the same for all six cognitive levels but varying the process (the verb) and offering a choice of product when possible. An example of a planning chart for differentiating learning experiences with the revised taxonomy can be found in Figure 15.

Not all students will do all six of the learning experiences, but the preassessment will guide the learning experiences offered to students, offering two of the three learning options that will require them to think in order to complete the tasks. Otherwise, some advanced students will choose the easier options in order to speed through the assignment and miss the opportunity to think at a challenging level in order to complete the task.

One caution for the teacher in planning learning experiences at the create level: Designing a poem or a poster about the concept does not qualify the learning activity for the top level (creating) unless students are charged with thinking about the content or concept in a new way or from a different perspective. Instead the student must be required to think creatively about the content or concept that was the reason for designing this set of differentiated learning experiences. In this example, students had to think creatively about fractions.

Figure 14
The Six Categories of the Cognitive Process Dimension

1. REMEMBER: Retrieve relevant knowledge from long-term memory.

2. UNDERSTAND: Construct meaning from instructional messages, including oral, written, and graphic communication.

3. APPLY: Carry out or use a procedure in a given situation.

4. ANALYZE: Break material into constituent parts and determine how parts relate to one another and to an overall structure or purpose.

5. EVALUATE: Make judgments based on criteria and standards.

6. CREATE: Put elements together to form a coherent or functional whole, reorganize elements into a new pattern or structure.

Note. Adapted from *A Taxonomy for Learning, Teaching, and Assessing: A Revision of Bloom's Taxonomy of Educational Objectives* (Complete ed., p. 31), by L. W. Anderson and D. R. Krathwohl (Eds.), 2001, Longman. Copyright 2001 by Longman.

Venn Diagrams

All teachers use Venn diagrams, but not all use the Venn diagram to differentiate learning experiences for their students. Kanevsky (2003) described this strategy, and Roberts and Inman (2015b) developed examples for using Venn diagrams to differentiate learning experiences. Very simply, differentiating using the Venn diagram allows the teacher to match the challenge of a learning experience to the students' levels of readiness based on preassessment results. All students are engaged in the same task, whether it is examining characters in a short story or novel, different colonies in U.S. history, or types of severe weather. The difference is that some students will be doing that task with one, two, three, or even four characters or colonies, altering the complexity of the task. The templates that Roberts and Inman provided are ovals rather than circles, as they offer more space on which the student can record their thoughts.

Figure 16 shows an example of a differentiated learning experience using the Venn diagram. All students list adjectives to describe one or more characters in the book. Some will work with one character, while others will compare and contrast two characters. Still others will work with three characters, and a small number may be ready to look at four characters in relation to each other. The key to successful differentiation is to match the level of challenge to the readiness of the student

Figure 15
Bloom Chart for Fractions

	PROCESS	CONTENT	PRODUCT
CREATE	*Create*	*Fractions*	*Open Product/ Your Choice*
	Create examples of an interesting, unusual way to use fractions or to teach someone else about fractions. Select the product to present your ideas.		
EVALUATE	*Justify*	*Fractions*	*Persuasive Essay or Debate*
	Justify learning about fractions in a persuasive essay or debate.		
ANALYZE	*Compare*	*Fractions*	*Venn Diagram or Poster*
	Compare fractions and decimals on a Venn diagram or poster.		
APPLY	*Organize*	*Fractions*	*Number Line*
	Organize fractions on a number line.		
UNDERSTAND	*Explain*	*Fractions*	*Discussion or Role Play*
	Explain fractions in a discussion or a role play.		
REMEMBER	*Identify*	*Fractions*	*Chart or Pictures*
	Identify fractions on a chart or with pictures.		

Note. Adapted from *Enrichment Opportunities for Gifted Learners* (p. 24), by J. L. Roberts, 2005, Taylor & Francis. Copyright 2005 by Taylor & Francis. Adapted with permission.

Figure 16
Venn Diagrams for Lemony Snicket's *A Series of Unfortunate Events*

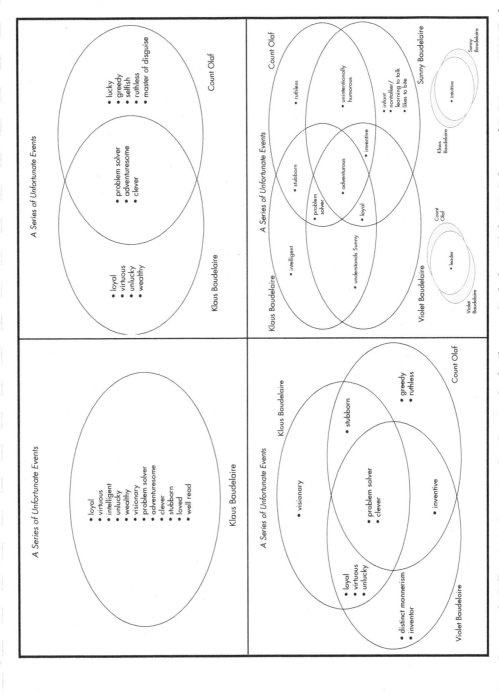

Note. From *Strategies for Differentiating Instruction: Best Practices for the Classroom* (2nd ed., p. 87), by J. L. Roberts and T. F. Inman, 2009, Taylor & Francis. Copyright 2009 by Taylor & Francis. Reprinted with permission.

to complete the learning experience. Once again, preassessment data provide the rationale for the match between the learning experience and the student.

Think-Tac-Toe Model

Another way to differentiate learning experiences to provide challenge and spark interest for students is the think-tac-toe model. Students do not try to do learning experiences to get Xs in a straight line on the think-tac-toe board but rather to complete ones that allow them to demonstrate what they have learned in a unit of study and to extend their learning.

Usually the students are asked to complete learning experiences on various levels, highlighting the important concepts that are being studied in a unit.

An example of a think-tac-toe chart is found in Figure 17. Students choose one learning experience to complete on each row, which ensures that they have learned important concepts during the course of the unit study. The think-tac-toe allows students an element of choice as they demonstrate what they have learned using a variety of products.

Another level of differentiation with the think-tac-toe model of differentiation is to have two different think-tac-toe charts, with one more challenging than the other. The two think-tac-toe charts look very similar, but the teacher ensures that each student has specific choices on the think-tac-toe that will make sure all students work at an appropriate level of challenge. A tremendous advantage of this level of differentiation, as well as with using one basic think-tac-toe, is that all students can discuss what they have learned together because all are focusing on the same concepts as they complete different products. The more challenging level ensures that a student who knows a lot about the topic doesn't have easy options that take little time or thought.

Preassessment data inform you as to which students receive which chart. All students have choices, and all need to work at challenging levels. Remember, the one-size-fits-all approach does not prepare lifelong learners.

Figure 17
Think-Tac-Toe

Directions: Choose one activity to complete from each category (3 activities total).

Think-Tac-Toe #1

Plot	Create a movie poster to represent the events in the story. Include a title, subtitle, and short description.	Congratulations! You have been asked to write a sequel to the story. Write the first paragraph of your sequel.	Create a card game using events from the story.
Character	Make a diagram of a character from the story that shows the character's personality and traits.	Think of a song that you feel represents the main character and the challenges he/she/it faces in some way. Why did you choose this song?	Choose four adjectives to describe the main character. Provide examples from the story to support your choices.
Setting	Imagine the setting in your story had a temperature drop of 50 degrees. Rewrite one scene at this new temperature.	Draw an Instagram picture of the story's setting. Use captions and hashtags to describe the picture.	Make a model of your favorite scene from the story using materials in class. Be prepared to tell why the scene is your favorite.

Think-Tac-Toe #2

Plot	Write a poem based on the events in the story. Challenge: Try to use rhyme scheme or alliteration.	Use Pixton (Google's comic maker) to develop a digital storyboard of a sequel of the story.	Create a digital "Breakout" game in Google Sites using events from the story.
Character	Rewrite a part of the book from a different character's point of view.	Pick a character to interview. Write questions to ask and answers you think the character would provide.	Write 5 "tweets" (limited to 30 words each) of the main character's thoughts.
Setting	Add or subtract 100 years to the setting of the story. Draw how the setting might look. Support your illustration with research.	Rewrite the story as if it took place where you live. Write an "Author's Note" at the end of your story explaining how the setting affected your version.	Write a news article informing the public of a hypothetical environmental, economic, or social issue for the story's setting.

Note. Developed by Samuel Northern, NBCT, Simpson County, KY.

Tiering

Tiering lessons means that all students are studying the same subject; however, they are all doing so at a level that challenges them academically. Adams and Pierce (2006) offered examples of tiered lessons. Lessons may be tiered based on readiness, interests, or learning preferences. An example of a tiered lesson is shown in Figure 18. Once again, all students are studying the same topic or concept but learning at a level that presents challenge.

Another example of a tiered lesson focuses on the concepts of force and motion. After all students go to the lab and conduct experiments on force and motion, the teacher passes out follow-up assignments. The determining factor in which students get which assignments is information the teacher has about how the students prefer to learn and their strengths. The assignments are to write a description of a car coming down a mountain road using the concepts of force and motion, to design an experiment using these concepts, or to describe three to five examples in everyday life that utilize the concepts of force and motion at work. These different prompts are distributed based on what the teacher knows about the individual student's interests in the topics and strengths (i.e., writing, designing an experiment, etc.). You are interested in what they are learning, in this case, rather than how they demonstrate what they have learned.

Choice of Products

Often students having a choice of product to demonstrate what they have learned results in the students doing their best work. After all, they are motivated to do so, as they have likely selected a product that interests them and that relies on their strengths. A list of products (see Table 3) can be lengthy. Categorizing the products will let the teacher offer choices of products to students. Roberts and Inman (2015a) categorized products into the following five categories: kinesthetic, oral, technological, visual, and written.

Although students should not always have product options that match their learning preferences, occasionally each student should have the opportunity to do so. Sometimes the teacher will not care how the students show what they have learned, and then it is appropriate to offer a choice of products. For example, students may be able to show what they learned about the Civil War in a monologue that is written and performed, a video, or a series of illustrations. The key is to provide choices that will appeal to students with different learning preferences and interests and not to offer three different written products.

Figure 18
Sample Tiered Lesson

Sample Tiered Lesson 4
Needs of Plants: Grade 2

Subject: Science
Grade: Second
Standard: Content Standard C: All students should develop understanding of the characteristics of organisms.
Key Concept: Organisms have basic needs and can survive only in environments in which their needs can be met.
Essential Understanding: Plants need soil, sunlight, and water in order to grow.
Background: The students have already studied the needs of animals as part of their work with living things. The activity introduces a lesson that allows students to discover what is necessary for plants to grow. Students will use guided discovery to learn the needs of plants. Students who need step-by-step directions and more structure should work in Tier I. Tier II is less structured, and Tier III is the least structured.
All groups will be investigating the needs of plants. Available materials should include soil, water, cups, milk cartons or pots, seeds (some seeds that work well are radish, beans, or the Wisconsin FastPlants available from Carolina Biological Supply), metric ruler, metric measuring cup, and markers.
Tier I:
These students will be given step-by-step directions to perform an investigation that will assist them in determining what plants need in order to grow. Students will use the variables of soil, water, and sunlight to determine what plants need to live. Most science books will have a detailed step-by-step experiment with plants that can be used or you may choose to write out the directions.
Tier II:
These students will investigate the needs of plants by varying the amount of water given to the plants while keeping the amount of soil and sunlight constant. Provide directions for the students to begin the investigation (materials, how to plant, amount of soil to use, number of seeds per cup, etc.), but have them determine the number of cups they will use and how to vary the water in each cup.
Tier III:
These students will read *The Empty Pot* by Demi (1996) or another story that deals with the needs of plants. Students will design and carry out an investigation based on the story. Students should include their research question, hypothesis, materials, procedure, data collection, results, and conclusion. As students carry out their investigation, provide assistance as needed.
Assessment: The teacher will use a flip card chart to assess students' progress during the design and implementation of the investigations for formative assessment. Science journals and activity sheets that include the information necessary to replicate the investigation, as well as the data tables and conclusions serve as summative assessment. Appropriate results (e.g., plants grew, plants didn't grow) based on experimental conditions also serve as summative evaluation.

Note. From *Differentiating Instruction: A Practical Guide to Tiered Lessons in the Elementary Grades* (pp. 51–52), by C. M. Adams and R. L. Pierce, 2006, Taylor & Francis. Copyright 2006 by Taylor & Francis. Reprinted with permission

Table 3

Possible Products

Products List		
Advertisement (print)	Feature Article	Photo
Advertisement (radio)	Film	Photo Essay
Advertisement (television)	Game	Picture
Application	Graph	Plan
Article	Graphic Organizer	Play
Audiotape	Greeting Card	Podcast
Biography	Illustrated Story	Poem
Blog	Illustration	Political Cartoon
Blueprint	Interview (live)	Poster
Book	Interview (recorded)	PowerPoint
Book Cover	Interview (written)	Presentation
Brochure	Invention	Project
Bulletin Board	Journal	Public Service Announcement
Cartoon	Lesson	(radio)
Case Study	Letter (business)	Public Service Announcement
Chart	Letter (friendly)	(television)
Choral Reading	Letter to Editor	Puppet
Collage	Mask	Puppet Show
Collection	Matrix	Questionnaire
Column	Mathematical Formula	Research Report
Commercial	Mentorship	Review
Computer Graphic	Mime	Science Fair Project
Computer Program	Mock Court	Sculpture
Costume	Mock Trial (attorney)	Scrapbook
Creative Writing	Mock Trial (defendant)	Script
Dance	Mock Trial (judge)	Service Learning Project
Debate	Mock Trial (plaintiff)	Simulation
Demonstration	Model	Skit
Diagram	Monologue	Song
Dialogue	Movie	Speech (oral)
Diary	Mural	Speech (written)
Diorama	Museum	Story
Display	Museum Exhibit	Story Telling
Document-Based	Musical	Survey
Question	Newscast	Technical Report
Documentary	Newsletter	Technical Writing
Dramatic Presentation	Newspaper Story	Timeline
Drawing	Open Response	Transparency
Editorial	Oral History	Venn Diagram
Essay	Oral Report	Video
Exhibit/Display	Outline	Video Game

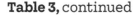

Table 3, continued

Products List, *continued*		
Experiment	Painting	Volunteer Activity
Evaluation Form	Peer Evaluation	Webpage
	Pamphlet	Wiki
		Written Report

Note. Adapted from *Assessing Differentiated Student Products: A Protocol for Development and Evaluation* (2nd ed., p. 12), by J. L. Roberts and T. F. Inman, 2015, Taylor & Francis. Copyright 2015 by Taylor & Francis. Adapted with permission.

It is very important that you provide guidance on how to complete the product so that it is of high quality. A rubric can provide the standards that need to be addressed with each product. Another way to guide the development of products is using the DAP Tool (the Developing and Assessing Product Tool; Roberts & Inman, 2015a). The advantage the DAP Tool offers is that you can provide a choice of products without needing to write new rubrics, as the DAP Tool is a protocol to be used with products again and again. In a nutshell, the DAP Tool is:

1. consistent in its components (content, presentation, creativity, and reflection);
2. ready for differentiation, as each DAP Tool has three tiers that provide varying levels of difficulty; and
3. of high level in that the scoring goes two levels above proficient with the highest one being a professional level, one that few, if any, students will be expected to reach.

Differentiation with products allows teachers to offer students opportunities to learn as they engage in developing products that offer choice and often may be in their preferred way of learning. Of course, sometimes students will need to complete products for other reasons. For example, all students may be expected to write a research paper or to conduct an experiment for a science fair. When that is the expectations, all students will work with the same DAP Tool although they may use different tiers of that DAP Tool based on their experience and expertise in writing research papers or planning and conducting experiments.

Grouping for Instructional Purposes

Grouping for instructional purposes can be done in many ways, with the goal always being to allow students to make continuous progress; therefore, grouping options must be linked with differentiation strategies. Some types of grouping are the result of acceleration and were discussed in Chapter 9. However, it is difficult to have a discussion of differentiation without looking at various grouping possibilities. Experts Karen B. Rogers and Peta Hay present different grouping options with a chart describing each (see Table 4).

Survival Secrets for Grouping Gifted Children for Talent Development and Socialization

Karen B. Rogers and Peta Hay

Grouping has suffered a long uphill battle with people in general education, not because it is damaging for gifted learners, but more because the benefits it provides gifted learners cannot be matched when it is used with other groups of differing ability or performance levels. Since 2000, nine published research syntheses (literature reviews, meta-analyses, meta-syntheses) concerning the academic, social, and psychological effects of grouping have been conducted; before these last 2 decades, there were also major literature/research reviews that offered similar findings. My colleague Dr. Peta Hay and I have just completed an exhaustive meta-analysis of all research studies concerned with the academic, social, and emotional outcomes of gifted and talented learners from 1990 through 2018. Although we assumed there would not be much new since the last meta-analysis completed in 2007 (Rogers, 2007), we discovered that the topic has been "touched upon" by approximately 500 pieces of literature and/or research. So, what does this "newer" research say? Basically, the opponents are correct about its effects on learners *not* identified as gifted: We found that when these *nonidentified students* were the control group (i.e., were grouped due to similar performance levels), their outcomes were very close to what would be expected for spending a year at a specific grade level, with little to no additional growth beyond these expectations. Recent research, however, has found that for these nonidentified learners there are some self-efficacy and socialization benefits to be gained when they are placed with others who are capable of performing at their respective levels.

As previous research reported, we found that the academic, social, and psychological effects for *learners with gifts and talents* are substantial: We can expect, on average, about an additional half year's academic achievement jump (beyond the one year the children make by just being in school) when compared to equally capable learners who have been placed in mixed-ability classes or mixed-ability learning groups. Socialization is also improved, not so much in terms of the social skills they exhibit, but in terms of their ability to work with others like themselves and learn from these intellectual or academic peers. Attitudes toward what they are learning

Table 4
Glossary of Grouping Option Terms

Ability-Grouped Options	Any strategy that identifies and sorts students into learning groups by their ability level (usually involving a test of ability or IQ as the measure used).
Gifted magnet school; governor's school	High-ability students attend a specialized school for all academic learning at differentiated, accelerated level.
Full-time gifted program; school-within-a school program	High-ability students attend a special school either as a separate school or a specialized school within a neighborhood school for all academic learning at differentiated, accelerated level.
Cluster grouping	The top five to eight high-ability students at each grade level are "clustered" within an otherwise heterogeneous class so that the teacher can differentiate for this group for a proportionate amount of classroom time in all academic subjects.
Like-ability cooperative learning groups	Each teacher creates a high-ability cooperative group (top three to four students in a classroom) and differentiates the learning task and expectations for this group in a specific academic subject area.
Performance-Grouped Options	Any strategy that identifies and sorts students into learning groups by their current performance/achievement levels (usually involving standardized or curriculum-based measure of performance).
Regrouping for specific instruction	The highest performing students at a grade level are placed in a separate class for their instruction, with concomitant curriculum at their current performance levels, regardless of actual grade placement; can be done at all building levels.
Honors or advanced classes (could also include Advanced Placement and International Baccalaureate programs)	The highest performing students are placed in separate classes for their instruction, with concomitant curriculum beyond what is offered as "regular" curriculum outcomes; usually found at middle and high school levels.

Table 4, continued

Performance-Grouped Options, *continued*	Any strategy that identifies and sorts students into learning groups by their current performance/achievement levels (usually involving standardized or curriculum-based measure of performance), *continued*
Performance cluster grouping	The top five to eight high-performing students in a specific subject, such as reading or mathematics, are "clustered" with one otherwise heterogeneous class so that the teacher can differentiate in that academic area. At the elementary level, this usually means two cluster classrooms—one for reading/language arts and one for mathematics. Students who are in the top performance groups of each area can usually take part in both classrooms when the two teachers coordinate their differentiation schedules.
Within-class grouping	Each teacher sorts students by their readiness (and perhaps interest) for each unit within an academic area, such that there might be three groups being differentiated accordingly in reading units, social studies, science, and math. This is sometimes referred to as *flexible* grouping.
Performance cooperative learning groups	Each teacher creates a high-performance cooperative group (top three to four students in a classroom) and differentiates the learning task and expectations for this group in specific academic subject area.
Cross-graded classes	Students are "sent" to the appropriate grade level for specific subject instruction according to their current performance level (e.g., fourth-grade student goes to sixth-grade classroom for math).

also improve remarkably. Self-efficacy remains fairly constant: If these learners felt good about what they were capable of doing before they were grouped, it remains so, as does the converse.

In looking more closely at the "instructional management" strategy of grouping, there are basically two forms of placing children together: (1) ability grouping, for which learners of the same intellectual or ability level are placed together for their learning; and (2) performance grouping, for which learners are placed with others performing at the same high level (usually beyond grade level). In the last 3 decades, the research has covered a broader spectrum of forms of grouping than in earlier decades, and the impacts measured with these differentiated forms of grouping have been reported in new ways. As the NAGC position on grouping tends to favor the idea of talent development or extraordinary academic performance, we will share what our recent research has told us about the impact of achievement grouping or performance grouping.

To be more specific, Table 5 defines the forms of grouping currently under study, as well as the measured impact for academic, social, and/or emotional growth. The effect sizes we have tentatively calculated tell us how great an impact each form of grouping has on gifted learners who have been grouped for at least one year (i.e., how much additional academic growth they made beyond the one expected year's growth, and how much additional growth they made socially or emotionally beyond the normal psychosocial development expectations).

In summing up what these estimated effects (impact) tell us, we have many good choices for developing the talents and skills we see in the classroom. At the elementary level, (1) we can allow a pair of like-performing students to pursue a topic or area in science, (2) we can build in more depth or breadth with a differentiated outcome (dyad cooperative learning), (3) we can put our four top-performing students in a classroom to pursue a task or project that has more complexity or depth, (4) we can pull our highest performing students out at a grade level and extend their learning in a specific talent area (pull-out), or (5) we can provide a single advanced class across all classrooms at a specific grade to extend and deepen learning in a talent area. All of these grouping arrangements will allow students to go well beyond grade level learning in their respective areas of talent, be it math, reading, science, or social studies.

At the middle school level, these same options show gains well beyond participating in a heterogeneous class, but we also have the options of performance grouping, summer enrichment via Talent Search programs held on university campuses, and special schools within a school (SWAS) programs for students with special talents. For high school, most of these options have proven to extend the specific talents for the highest performers, and the additional choices are rich: (1) advanced classes, (2) honors classes, (3) Advanced Placement classes, and (4) International Baccalaureate programs.

Any way we look at it, there is a menu of grouping options that provide substantial, positive outcomes for learners with gifts and talents, and we haven't even touched on what will be offered in the grouped setting or how instruction will be delivered. But the research is clear: If we group high-talent students in any form to extend the depth, breadth, and complexity of their learning, they will thrive, improve in their motivation, and form social relationships that result from the sharing of their interests and talents. Grouping becomes an effective vehicle that is the starting point for teachers to begin their differentiation for talent development. We can certainly allow students to learn independently, but their chances of learning about a subject with others with similar interests and skills are less likely in a mixed ability context.

Table 5

Grouping Effects 1990–2018 for 12 Forms of Achievement/Performance Grouping

Grouping Type	Definition	Academic Growth Impact	Social Growth Impact	Emotional Growth Impact
Advanced Placement	Teachers deliver college-level curriculum in specific content areas for college credit	Strong	Strong	Small
Cluster Grouping	Highest achieving students are grouped in single classroom for daily differentiated curriculum	Small	Small	Slight
Cooperative Grouping–LP	3–4 high-performing students work together on differentiated task in single academic domain	Moderate	Moderate	Strong
Dyad Grouping–LP	2 high-performing students work together on differentiated task in single academic domain	Strong	Not Studied	Not Studied
Flexible Grouping	Grouping and regrouping within or across classes according to student performance for individual units and/or different subjects	Small	Not Studied	Not Studied
Homogeneous Classrooms	Identified students take all of their advanced classes together	Strong	Slight	Small
Honors Courses	Advanced courses with students grouped by performance level	Small	Small	Small
Performance Grouping	Across-year grouping in different school subjects according to student achievement levels	Strong	Small	Moderate
Pull-Out Classes	High-achieving students are withdrawn from regular classes and grouped together for advanced study for a short duration each week	Small	Slight	Small

Table 5, continued

Grouping Type	Definition	Academic Growth Impact	Social Growth Impact	Emotional Growth Impact
Special Schools	Schools for high-achieving students across country, county, state, or district in a tiered schooling system, where students are sorted into university-bound schools or based on optional entrance examinations	Moderate	Slight	Small
Summer University Programs	High-performing students elect to attend accelerated summer courses at university	Strong	Not Studied	Small
Within-Class/ Cross-Grade Grouping	Achievement grouping by performance levels within a single classroom for specific subject instruction, subject by subject	Small	Not Studied	Small

Perhaps James Kulik said it best all those years ago as he summarized his own meta-analyses on grouping (1992):

> The questions that people ask about grouping are not easy to answer. Do children benefit from it? Who benefits most? Does grouping harm anyone? How? Why? The answers depend on the type of grouping program. Results differ in programs that (a) group students by aptitude but prescribe a common curriculum for all groups; (b) group students by aptitude and prescribe different curricula for the groups; and (c) place highly talented students into special enriched and accelerated classes that differ from other classes in both curricula and other resources. Benefits from the first type of program are positive, but very small. Benefits from the second type are positive and larger. Benefits from the third type of program are positive, large, and important. (pp. xv–xvi)

—Karen B. Rogers, Ph.D.
Professor Emerita of Gifted Studies, University of St. Thomas

—Peta Hay, Ph.D.
Lecturer of Gifted Education, University of New South Wales

141

Conclusion

Teachers must want to differentiate or they won't do it, at least not often or not unless a principal or another supervisor who wants to see differentiation is coming for a visit. Teachers most likely will be motivated by knowing differentiation is best for their students—that differentiating is the only way to engage all students in learning and to ensure that each student makes continuous progress.

No strategy is implemented as easily or as well the first time as it is after repeated use. Teachers must keep up the good work of differentiating and bring more and more strategies into their repertoires, strategies that allow for differentiation. It will be worth the effort and get easier each time the teachers use the differentiation strategies. More students will be engaged in learning, so students win and so does the teacher.

Survival Tips

Parents must be provided with information on differentiation so they will understand that all students will not be completing identical assignments. They can begin to "get it" when you explain that all children in your class don't wear the same size of shoe, and their experiences, interests, and levels of readiness vary as well. The one-size-fits-all curriculum is a misfit just as one size of shoe would be.

When teachers differentiate from the beginning of the year, students in the class won't expect everyone to be on the same page or doing the same learning experiences. After all, doing the same thing will result in some students finding school too easy and some too hard. Each one needs the "just right" level of learning to make continuous progress.

Survival Toolkit

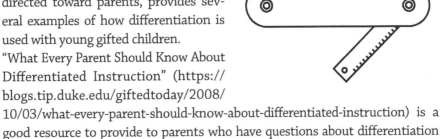

- "Differentiated Instruction for Young Gifted Children: How Parents Can Help" (https://www.davidsongifted.org/search-database/entry/a10465), although directed toward parents, provides several examples of how differentiation is used with young gifted children.
- "What Every Parent Should Know About Differentiated Instruction" (https://blogs.tip.duke.edu/giftedtoday/2008/10/03/what-every-parent-should-know-about-differentiated-instruction) is a good resource to provide to parents who have questions about differentiation in the classroom.
- Other resources include:
  - Karnes, F. A., & Stephens, K. R. (2010). *The ultimate guide for student product development and evaluation* (2nd ed.). Prufrock Press.
  - Tomlinson, C. A. (2017). *How to differentiate instruction in academically diverse classrooms* (3rd ed.). Association for Supervision and Curriculum Development.
  - Westphal, L. E. (2016). *Differentiating instruction with menus: Math (Grades 3–5)* (2nd ed.). Prufrock Press. (*Note.* Westphal has written many books on differentiating with menus.)

Chapter 14

Excellence

An Important Yet Elusive Goal in Schools

"This report is intended to provide some preliminary excellence gap data and kick start the national discussion on the importance of excellence in our national and state K–12 education systems." (Plucker et al., 2010, p. 1)

Key Questions

- What does excellence look like for elementary, middle, and high school students in this age of proficiency?

- Why raise the discussion from proficient to advanced learning levels as goals?

Excellence seems to be much like motherhood and apple pie. How could anyone oppose such a concept? Yet excellence is often supported selectively in our schools, communities, and nation. Frequently, people cheer for excellence in sports of all types. People are likely to support excellence in the arts. Yet it is very important, actually essential, for excellence in levels of learning to be the goal available for chil-

DOI: 10.4324/9781003238553-15

dren at all grade levels, by all educators. Excellence must be the goal of education for children from all backgrounds—including those who are gifted and talented.

Excellence in U.S. Schools

The report *National Excellence: A Case for Developing America's Talent* (U.S. Department of Education, 1993), the second national report on gifted education, stated:

> In a broad range of intellectual and artistic endeavors, America's most talented students often fail to reach their full potential. . . . They are often tenacious in pursuits that interest them. The way in which they learn sets them apart from most other children and challenges educators and parents. (p. 5)

This report described "a silent crisis in educating talented students" in the United States, silent in that the effects of not developing the potential of advanced learners will not be felt for another generation (p. 5). In this silent crisis, "the talents of disadvantaged and minority children have been especially neglected" (p. 5). That silent crisis is not over.

Excellence took a backseat to proficiency with the No Child Left Behind (2001) legislation. Loveless et al. (2008) reported that "teachers are much more likely to indicate that struggling students, not advanced students, are their top priority" (p. 4). With the emphasis on bringing all children to proficiency, Loveless and colleagues found that "while the nation's lowest achieving youngsters made rapid gains from 2000 to 2007, the performance of top students was languid" (p. 2). *Languid* is a word that you would hardly want to be the descriptor of achievement for high-ability children, nor is it a word that you would choose to describe your hoped-for future. Does that situation describe the current situation in your school?

In *Mind the (Other) Gap!*, Plucker et al. (2010) delivered the strong message that there is an excellence gap in the United States, one that is infrequently mentioned. One suggestion in the report is that two questions should be asked when decisions are made for the classroom, school, or district:

1. How will this [decision] affect our brightest students?
2. How will this [decision] help other students begin to achieve at high levels? (p. 30)

These questions would raise the level of awareness of the impact of classroom and school decisions on removing the learning ceiling. Excellence is out of reach for children when the learning ceiling is low, and certainly when the ceiling is placed at grade level, which is the bar for proficiency. As John M. Bridgeland, coauthor of *Achievementrap: How America Is Failing Millions of High-Achieving Students From Lower-Income* Families (Wyner et al., 2007), stated, "These extraordinary students are found in every corner of America and represent the American dream. They defy the stereotype that poverty precludes high achievement. Notwithstanding their talent, our schools are failing them every step of the way" (as cited in Frost, 2017, para. 9).

Survival Secrets for Eliminating Excellence Gaps

Jonathan A. Plucker

Excellence gaps are among our most serious societal problems, and closing them is a critical goal of education. Of course, equity concerns are not solely the concern of education. Many, if not most, aspects of our society, culture, and economy are marked by considerable inequities. Lack of equality in access to healthcare, transportation, mortgages, and museums are among countless examples of important services in which socioeconomic status and race play big roles.

Within education, we often talk about achievement gaps, inequities in student performance and participation based on student race/ethnicity, socioeconomic status, gender, or geographic location. If one believes talent is equally distributed across humans regardless of these demographic characteristics, then a primary goal of education should be to close and eventually eliminate these gaps.

Within gifted education, a particular concern is the closing of excellence gaps, those opportunity gaps that appear at the most advanced levels of achievement. By some measures, racial and socioeconomic excellence gaps have grown considerably over the past generation, with the percentage of European American, Asian, and upper-income students performing at advanced rates increasing steadily each year, in contrast to stagnant rates for African American, Hispanic, Native American, and economically insecure students. For example, 3% of students qualifying for lunch assistance in 2019 scored advanced on the grade 4 mathematics portion of the National Assessment of Educational Progress (NAEP), a small increase from an advanced rate of 0% in 1996. Over that same time period, however, the advanced rate for students *not* qualifying for lunch assistance increased from 3% to 15%.

Researchers have identified several probable causes for excellence gaps, ranging from generational poverty to lower quality education in low-income schools, to low expectations for disadvantaged students. And if we believe gifted education and other advanced learning programs are beneficial for students, we have to acknowledge that inequitable access to these programs is a likely cause of excellence gaps. In nearly every school district, the percentage of European American, Asian, and upper-income students in gifted education programs is considerably higher than the percentage of African American, Hispanic, Native American, and lower income students.

Of course, these issues have been discussed for decades, but our knowledge of effective strategies for closing excellence gaps has advanced by leaps and bounds over the past decade. These strategies include recruitment, universal screening with local norms, ability grouping, professional learning, and, perhaps most importantly, frontloading. Contrary to the conventional wisdom, research suggests psychosocial interventions—those focusing on mindset, grit, stereotype threat reduction, and related concepts—have negligible impacts (both in general and with respect to the closing of excellence gaps).

Recruitment is a key aspect of providing new opportunities to students. Ensuring all students have access to opportunities for advanced learning and that barriers to access and participation are low-to-nonexistent are important, but educators should note that some families may be nervous about these opportunities if they have little family or personal history with them. And sending a flyer home or holding a single evening information session (when a parent may be working a second shift or second job) are often not adequate for recruiting students into our programs.

Universally screening all students in a school or district when identifying talented children is a research-backed strategy for closing excellence gaps. Removing nominations and applications as initial gateways into such systems and using building-level norms during the identification process help level the playing field for many students who otherwise would not even be considered for participation in your programs. The use of local norms involves asking the question, "Who are our most talented students in the school?" versus, "Who are our most talented students in the district, state, or nation?" Given that we are each responsible for teaching the students in our schools, the use of district, state, or national norms to identify gifted students often doesn't match the scope of our services.

Ability grouping is a key survival strategy due to the wide range of student performance in our classrooms. Without some form of grouping, many classrooms have a range of 8 or more grade levels of student performance, providing a daunting challenge even to teachers with significant skill in differentiation. Narrowing the range of student performance within each classroom facilitates differentiation and makes it easier for teachers to help students perform up to their potential.

Many aspects of educator *professional learning* are important for closing excellence gaps, but an important role for teachers to play each day is to help ensure their colleagues have a basic understanding of gifted students, their development, and their unique needs. For example, teachers often confuse performance with potential, believing only high-performing students are gifted and discounting the potential of low-income students who have not had similar opportunities to develop their academic talents. Being an advocate for advanced education, and for advanced students regardless of their current performance levels, is important.

Frontloading prepares students for advanced opportunities by raising the rigor and challenge level of early childhood and early elementary experiences. An example would be providing more rigorous preparation in middle and elementary school for low-income students, so they are ready to thrive when provided with challenging Advanced Placement courses in high school. Without that frontloaded preparation, expecting those students to succeed when they receive those AP opportunities is unrealistic.

Although the problem of excellence gaps has existed for as long as we've had schools, our understanding of interventions to close them is advancing rapidly. Given the current pace of research and implementation, we can be optimistic about our ability to close and eventually eliminate excellence gaps in the future.

—Jonathan A. Plucker, Ph.D.
Julian C. Stanley Professor of Talent Development, Center for Talented
Youth and School of Education, Johns Hopkins University

The first recommendation by the National Science Board (2010) is to "provide opportunities for excellence":

> We cannot assume that our Nation's most talented students will succeed on their own. Instead, we must offer coordinated, proactive, sustained formal and informal interventions to develop their abilities. Students should learn at a pace, depth, and breadth commensurate with their talents and interests and in a fashion that elicits engagement, intellectual curiosity, and creative problem solving—essential skills for future innovation. (p. 2)

Students from low-income families consistently underachieve in schools, regardless of the grade level. One solution offered in *Achievementrap* was that "Educators must raise their expectations for lower income students and implement effective strategies for maintaining and increasing advanced learning within this population" (Wyner et al., 2007, p. 7). Teachers must have high expectations for all of their students regardless of their background.

How important is excellence in your school? Isn't excellence the goal for the basketball and soccer teams in your school? Hopefully, teachers and school leaders have excellence as the desired goal throughout your school. What does excellence look like in science, social studies, language arts, and mathematics, as well as in the visual and performing arts?

Thomas Friedman (2010) implored all of society to get involved in a push for excellence in a *New York Times* article:

> Finally, just when globalization and technology were making the value of higher education greater than ever, and the price for lack-

ing it more punishing than ever, America started slipping behind its peers in high school graduation rates, college graduation, and global test scores in math and critical thinking. . . .

Beyond the recession, this triple whammy is one of the main reasons that middle-class wages have been stagnating. To overcome that, we need to enlist both the U.S.G. [U.S. government] and the P.T.A. We need teachers and principals who are paid better for better performance, but also valued for their long hours and dedication to students and learning. We need better parents ready to hold their kids to higher standards of academic achievement. We need better students who come to school ready to learn, not to text. And to support all of this, we need an all-society effort—from the White House to the classroom to the living room—to nurture a culture of achievement and excellence. (para. 6, 8)

Gaps Leading Up to the Excellence Gap

Three gaps often precede the excellence gap and get in the way of children reaching their potential—the belief gap, the opportunity gap, and the achievement gap. Only after those gaps are eliminated do young people reach the level of excellence.

The belief gap is an obstacle when educators don't believe that children who are often underrepresented in gifted programming or in advanced academic programming can achieve at high levels. What a mistake that is! Educators and parents, too, must be looking for behaviors that children are thinking at high levels and often about complex content.

The opportunity gap becomes a deterrent for the development of potential to high levels when young people are not connected with opportunities for advanced academic classes, summer and Saturday academic programs, and extracurricular activities that would expand their interests and bolster their academic accomplishments. Please remember that it is not enough to know about opportunities if there is a cost for participating, a cost they cannot manage without assistance. Sharing information about how to garner financial assistance is crucial to having the opportunity materialize.

The achievement gap enters the picture when examining grade-level achievement among various groups who are often underrepresented in gifted programming. It is key to note that grade-level achievement is a mile marker rather than an end-goal for students with high potential. Setting high expectations is key to

Figure 19

There's No Heavier Burden Than a Great Potential

Note. Reprinted with permission. Peanuts: 2010 Peanuts Worldwide LLC., dist by UFS, Inc.

developing skills and learning complex content that are necessary for achieving at levels that would be equivalent to playing on the varsity team.

The excellence gap must be a concern in classrooms and schools throughout the United States. In order to eliminate the four gaps, Roberts (2020) made the following recommendations:

1. Remove blinders that get in the way of teachers recognizing the high potential of children.
2. Provide opportunities for children who are ready to learn at higher levels without waiting until all children are ready.
3. Communicate to children and families concerning opportunities in school and out of school, as well as about sources of support that may be needed to take advantage of the opportunity.
4. Examine achievement data in schools in order to know if children who are from lower income families, those who are twice-exceptional, and young people from all ethnic and racial groups are achieving at grade level or, even better, at the advanced level.

Conclusion

Think about the last frame in the Peanuts cartoon in Figure 19. The last frame raises the idea that there is no heavier burden than having a great potential. What a powerful message it includes. It is a message that needs to be kept in mind as you work with children who are gifted and talented. Remember that much of the public and many educators believe firmly that gifted children will make it on their own, so you don't need to worry about them. Of course, giving gifted children opportunities to fulfill their great potentials is the overarching goal of this book. It is a survival guide for parents and educators so that they will have the information and strategies to help children who are gifted and talented thrive—thereby developing their full potentials. The goal is to lighten the burden that having such potential has for some young people. They need to aim for excellence and to have learning opportunities that facilitate reaching that high goal.

Survival Tips

- You must not lose sight of excellence in this age of proficiency.
- Parents need to know that proficiency is grade-level learning and that their children need to have excellence as their goal. They need to advocate for excellence, knowing that a school can bring children to proficiency who are not there yet and also teach children who have already gone beyond proficiency to levels of excellence.

Survival Toolkit

Useful resources on this topic include:
- Davidson, J., Davidson, B., & Vanderkam, L. (2005). *Genius denied: How to stop wasting our brightest young minds.* Simon & Schuster.
- Patrick, K., Socol, A. R., & Morgan, I. (2020). *Inequities in advanced coursework: What's driving them and what leaders can do.* Education Trust.
- Plucker, J., Giacola, J., Healey, G., Arndt, D., & Wang, C. (2015). *Equal talents, unequal opportunities: A report card on state support for academically talented low-income students.* Jack Kent Cook Foundation.
- Plucker, J. A., & Peters, S. J. (2015). *Excellence gaps in education: Expanding opportunities for talented students.* Harvard Education Press.
- Wyner, J. W., Bridgeland, J. M., & DiIulio, J. J. (2007). *Achievement trap: How America is failing millions of high-achieving students from lower-income families.* Jack Kent Cooke Foundation.

Chapter 15

A Tough Choice for Some

An "A" Today or Preparation to Be Successful Tomorrow

"All students need to break an academic sweat on a regular basis. No athlete who only breaks an athletic sweat occasionally will become a champion."—Julia Link Roberts and Julia Roberts Boggess

Remember Friedman's (2010) call for "an all-society effort to nurture a culture of achievement and excellence" (para. 8)? Such a national effort requires teachers, parents, and students to answer the question: Which is more important—all A's today or being successful in postsecondary opportunities and careers tomorrow?

To a parent or teacher who knows the dangers that come from students earning easy A's, making that choice is probably no decision at all. After all, a child's future is more important than any grade; however, many parents sabotage their child's academic future by complaining to the teacher that "You gave my child her first B" or "My child does not have any time for homework, as he is practicing soccer and involved with other afterschool activities every afternoon." Parents need to consider the child's future academic success as they examine family priorities. Messages that are both spoken and implied will have a huge impact on academic preparation for being successful as learning experiences become more challenging.

DOI: 10.4324/9781003238553-16

What Is Academic Success?

One of the biggest problems for children who are gifted and talented is that educators and parents often equate excellence with straight A's or scores of 100. Unless a child works hard to earn the A or 100 (or close to that number), that grade is no move toward excellence, but rather the child gets a reward for exerting little or no effort. Ongoing learning needs to be the goal of school, with the ultimate goal of producing a lifelong learner. Figure 20 displays the levels of learning. The bottom rung is a risky place for a child to stay, at least for very long, because they will get accustomed to "easy" work that often is done quickly. Before long, easy work is expected, and when assignments take time and thought, many gifted students doubt whether they are capable or not. That is when underachievement sets in, and underachievement is difficult to reverse. When the young person is challenged to earn the A, only then can excellence be equated to an A.

What is your personal definition of academic success? Your answer to this question will determine your approach to teaching in general and to differentiation specifically or to your view of learning and grading from a parent's perspective.

A big question: Can you have both equity and excellence? If you think of equity not as everyone doing the same thing, but rather as each student learning in order to make continuous progress, then excellence is a target that can be reached.

When children are not required to engage in challenging learning every day at school, they develop expectations that school may be equated with "easy." Parents who rebuff a teacher for preparing challenging learning experiences, indicating a preference for all A's rather than important learning, often get what they ask for— easier work for their children. Teachers may decide that it is not worth the effort to buck parents' objections to the challenging work that they plan. Who loses when that happens? The child for sure—and, Friedman (2010) argued, the nation as well.

Academic Challenge as the Key for Future Success

What should you know in order to understand why challenging academic work is the foundation of success in postsecondary education?

1. Schools should provide ongoing opportunities for each child to make continuous progress, which translates to learning on an ongoing basis. A child who is reading at a level above their grade should be reading at another year or higher level by the end of the school year. A child should be learning more advanced math each year, no matter what the curriculum is for their grade

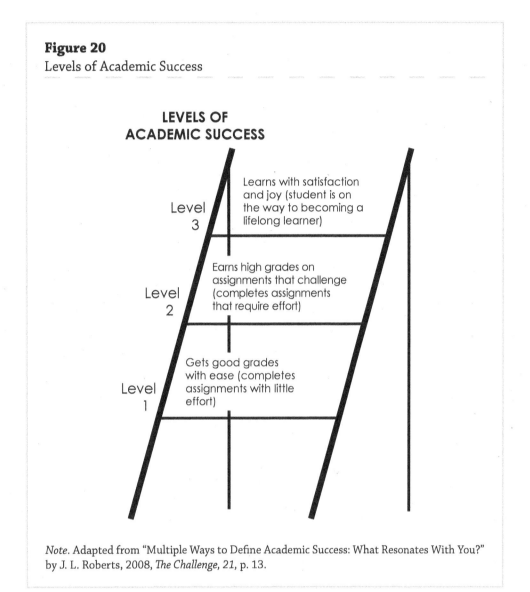

Figure 20
Levels of Academic Success

**LEVELS OF
ACADEMIC SUCCESS**

Level 3 — Learns with satisfaction and joy (student is on the way to becoming a lifelong learner)

Level 2 — Earns high grades on assignments that challenge (completes assignments that require effort)

Level 1 — Gets good grades with ease (completes assignments with little effort)

Note. Adapted from "Multiple Ways to Define Academic Success: What Resonates With You?" by J. L. Roberts, 2008, *The Challenge, 21,* p. 13.

level. Imposing ceilings on what a child who is advanced can learn in school stifles their academic progress and paves the way for underachievement.

2. Children who find A's easy to gain often get into a pattern of underachievement that is hard to reverse. Underachievement is a pervasive problem. (See Chapter 21.)

3. Reports indicate that all students who appear to be ready for college are not ready to be successful. ACT reports (Gewertz, 2010) revealed that only 23% of the graduating seniors taking the ACT had scores that indicated that they were "college ready" in all four content areas that the ACT assesses—math, English, reading, and science. Arriving at college without adequate preparation places a young person in a hazardous position.

Do you know anyone who excels as an adult who does not have a strong work ethic in their area of expertise? A work ethic usually develops during a child's early years. It is very difficult, if not impossible, to work hard at something you already have mastered at the level that instruction is being delivered. Easy schoolwork deprives a child of the opportunity to work hard to accomplish learning goals that are challenging. The child does not learn to be resilient or to set challenging goals. How much better would it be for the student to arrive at college with a strong preparatory background as they embark upon what a parent hopes will be a college career that culminates in graduation?

Barriers to Academic Success

What actions create barriers that prevent children from being prepared for success in postsecondary education?

1. Parents rescue the student when the class seems difficult for fear the child will not have straight A's.
2. Schools are not offering challenging learning experiences in all classes at all levels—kindergarten through the senior year.
3. Students are not choosing the rigorous classes when they are available.
4. Students are not developing a work ethic related to academics. Either classes lack the rigor to require hard work or the student has not devoted both time and energy necessary to develop a strong work ethic.

The country needs to embark on a major public relations campaign that encourages parents and educators to support children in working hard to meet challenging academic goals and to develop talent. A catchy slogan would help carry the message. School newsletters should carry information to help parents understand the great need to support their children as they work hard to reach important goals in their schoolwork. Nothing short of that will turn around the focus on grade-level curriculum as the standard fare for all children in a certain age range. Instead, we need to focus on nurturing lifelong learners who are ready to problem solve and make ethical decisions. All A's on grade-level assignments won't keep our country in a competitive status.

A Very Important Question

A great question to ask in order to get educators and parents thinking about why academic challenge is critical for developing lifelong learners follows:

> If during the first 5 or 6 years of school, a child earns good grades and high praise without having to make much effort, what are all of the things they don't learn that most children learn by third grade?

Take a few minutes to answer that question. Even better, gather together others on your faculty or parents to generate responses to this question. For many educators and parents, this question brings the first realization that children who are advanced are actually hindered in their academic and social development when they don't have academic challenges as a regular part of their learning. Some of the important learning that doesn't happen when school is easy and praise is frequent includes resilience, persistence, problem-solving skills, ability to deal with disappointment (maybe even creating a sense of failure in the student when they receive a B instead of an A), and study skills. To top that list off, the children haven't developed a work ethic either. It isn't possible to build a work ethic without learning opportunities that involve challenge. Then, ask your colleagues to make generalizations based on this discussion. For many educators, the opportunity to discuss what students have not learned will be their first time to consider how bright students are harmed when they are not challenged. What an important realization that is! It is a motivator for teachers to differentiate from the day that children start school. After you have engaged in discussing this very important question, share the article by Tracy Inman in the Survival Toolkit for this chapter on "What a Child Doesn't Learn."

Effort and Motivation Matter!

Reis and Renzulli (2009) highlighted the importance of effort and motivation, adding an exclamation point to their summarization of these two concepts:

> *Effort and motivation matter!* No single non-cognitive trait is more influential on higher levels of performance than effort or motivation, and . . . young people and adults with high potential are most hampered by underchallenging learning or work experiences. High-aptitude students often "coast" through school without having to expend effort, and when they finally do encounter a chal-

lenge, some experience a loss of confidence in their abilities result-ing in diminished achievement levels (Reis & McCoach, 2000). (p. 234)

Carol Dweck (2006/2016) described mindsets in two categories—those that are fixed and those that have a growth mindset. Students with a fixed mindset believe that being smart means they just need to show or demonstrate their abilities. In contrast, those students with a growth mindset know they need to work hard to get the best results. If they aren't successful at something (e.g., they don't do well on a test), they determine what they need to do in order to not have that occur the next time. Successful people have a growth mindset. On the other hand, students with fixed mindsets who do poorly on a test will see themselves as being not as smart as they thought they were. Providing feedback on effort students made or didn't make reinforces for young people that they are in charge of their future. The effort they put into a project makes a huge difference in the assessment of the project. Mindsets are formed early in life, but they can be changed with concentrated effort.

Survival Secrets for Mindset and Advanced and High-Potential Learners

Mary Cay Ricci

Over that last several years in education we have been hearing more and more about the importance of the mindsets of educators and learners. The application to education stems from the work of Carol Dweck, a Stanford University researcher who identifies two belief systems that we apply to a variety of situations: a *growth mindset* belief and a *fixed mindset* belief (Dweck, 2006/2016). When we apply growth mindset thinking, we believe that with perseverance, resiliency, some mistakes along the way, as well as a cadre of strategies, we can understand and accomplish just about anything. With a growth mindset we consider the possibilities, embrace growth, and welcome any perceived challenges. A fixed mindset is the belief that we only have the capacity to understand, accomplish and/or achieve in certain areas. A fixed mindset belief is one where we believe that people are born with intrinsic strengths and weaknesses that cannot be changed. For example, if you are asked to set up a virtual classroom for your students and you do not consider technology a strength, you might immediately feel intimidated, feel that you will not be success-ful, and/or wonder if you can get someone else to set it up for you!

The field of gifted education continually goes through philosophical and instruc-tional shifts. It is important to apply growth mindset thinking and to be ready and open to learn things that might be counter to what you have always believed. More importantly, we need to view children through a growth mindset lens and see the potential and possibilities in all children. We understand that all children should experience some degree of struggle so that we know that they are academically challenged. If a student consistently easily understands concepts and content, and gets good grades without much effort, then they are terribly underchallenged. This can sometimes set up our advanced learners for social and emotional difficulties down the road when they are not accustomed to having to work hard and think critically, are not accustomed to lower grades and anything but positive feedback. (For some students, this may not occur until college when they face a course like organic chemistry.) Deliberate cultivation of academic resiliency is essential when developing growth mindsets in our students.

Gifted, advanced, and high-potential students need to learn about the power of a growth mindset. Specific areas of focus for these students include the importance of reflection, acceptance of struggle and using mistakes, and failures to their advantage. We sometimes find that students who have been identified as gifted try to take the safe or easy way so that they are guaranteed success. They may fear errors due to perfectionistic tendencies or fear that people may not think that they belong in their advanced instructional group. Students may become risk-averse and consistently make choices so that they know they will have success. We need to cultivate learning environments in which mistakes are viewed as data that can be learned from and struggle means that we are giving our brains a good workout.

Building a Conceptual Understanding of Perseverance and Resiliency

I will never forget a visit I had with a first-grade class presenting a session about growth mindsets. At the end of my visit I asked students to share with me something they learned during my time with them. Immediately an energetic student raised his hand in the air and shared that we all must "put forth effort." I thanked him for his response, and then he immediately put his hand in the air again and asked, "What's effort?" What an eye opener for me! We talk with students about things like effort, perseverance and resiliency . . . but do they really have a conceptual understanding of what these mean? Think about ways to build the concepts of perseverance and resiliency so that students understand the value of these skills. Think about the following:

- What are some implications for a highly gifted child who lacks resiliency?
- What are some implications for a nongifted child who has developed academic resiliency?

Traditionally Underserved

Growth mindsets can have a positive effect on students who are often over-looked for advanced learning experiences in school. Consider the following aspects of gifted identification procedures that could be problematic for students from underserved groups:

- No national process for identification of gifted children exists—identification processes vary. Some are more inclusive, some exclusive. A child might be considered "gifted" in one district but go around the corner to another district and not make the cut.
- Teacher checklists/surveys may not include nontraditional characteristics of gifted learners (or may not be used at all—unfortunately, some practices rely solely on one test score).
- Many districts use identification processes that are overly focused on already developed ability.

For these reasons and more, it is critical that both students and educators understand basic brain science; the brain is a malleable structure, and we can all get smarter. Students who do not meet traditional identification guidelines can still work side by side with students who are formally identified as gifted. You don't have to choose one philosophy or the other, you can meet the needs of gifted learn-ers *and* open doors and provide opportunities for students with the motivation and resiliency to take on challenging work. The secret is to build growth mindset princi-ples in our students so that they know what to do when they face challenge or fail.

A learning environment where mistakes are expected, perseverance and resil-iency are valued, and optimism is modeled is a place where all students can learn and feel comfortable taking risks—a growth mindset learning environment.

—Mary Cay Ricci
Educator and Author, Mindsets in the Classroom: Building
a Growth Mindset Learning Community, Nothing You
Can't Do!: The Secret Power of Growth Mindsets

Conclusion

A very important question for teachers to pose and parents to answer is "What do I consider to be academic success for my children?" Educators need to educate parents concerning the critical need for young people to acquire the motivation and skills to be lifelong learners. Educators also need to challenge all children, including those who are gifted and talented, so that they know how to break an academic sweat. Being successful in postsecondary opportunities and later in careers depends on a strong work ethic, perseverance, and lifelong learning skills. Real academic success depends upon having a learning opportunity that the young person isn't quite sure they can accomplish, with the end result of reaching that goal by working hard.

Survival Tips

- Parents and educators need to understand what their children will face when they are not prepared to meet academic challenge. Eventually that challenge will come, and a great grade point average won't help them.
- This message may be the most important one of all for parents: They must understand that making top grades without academic challenge results in young people who are unprepared for success in postsecondary opportunities.

Survival Toolkit

- "What a Child Doesn't Learn" (https://www.wku.edu/gifted/documents/resource_articles/what_a_child_doesnt_learn.pdf) by Tracy Inman discusses the things children who expect to get easy A's don't learn in school, like work ethic, time management, goal setting, and study skills.

Chapter 16

Encourage Creativity
The Edge for the Future

"Creativity is far more than just the generation of new ideas or the production of artistic works. It is a way of thinking and a comprehensive ongoing process that involves multiple types of thinking, working, revising, producing, and evaluating."—Tamara Fisher Alley, a K–12 gifted education specialist for a school district in northwest Montana

Key Question

- What ongoing opportunities for creative thinking do children and young people have in your classroom and school, and how do you encourage creativity?

Creativity is a very important topic, one being discussed by leaders in business and industry. Creative breakthroughs often fuel the economy. Moving forward economically depends on innovation. As Thomas Friedman (2009) stated,

DOI: 10.4324/9781003238553-17

The country that uses this crisis to make its population smarter and more innovative—and endows its people with more tools and basic research to invent new goods and services—is the one that will not just survive but thrive down the road. (para. 3)

What does innovation have to do with gifted education? There are several connections. Individuals who are gifted and talented will not be the only innovators; however, they have exceptional potential to have great ideas that lead to innovations. On the other hand, the potential to innovate is often stifled when creativity is not modeled or encouraged.

Creative thinking and creative problem solving have been at the core of gifted education for decades. Curriculum that highlights high-level thinking includes skills that focus on complexity of content and creativity in process.

Sometimes creativity has not just been ignored but actively discouraged in the race for proficiency testing. Yet the future depends upon creative individuals and their ideas. As the saying goes, "All music was once new." The same is true with all ideas. As a teacher, you foster creativity when you encourage, expect, and respect creative responses.

Creativity—What Is It?

One of the challenges with creativity is knowing what it is—what does creativity look like when you see it? Treffinger (2009) asked what creativity means to educators: "Does it refer to artistic ability, to a set of cognitive skills, or to inventiveness or imagination?" (p. 245). Of course, creativity can be evidenced in all of those dimensions. A teacher who places a premium on creativity will be looking for creative responses in answers, questions, and a variety of products.

Myths about creativity abound. Many people misunderstand what creativity looks like and think that creativity is mainly found among artists. Of course, artists are creative, but creativity also describes thinking that can be done in science, language arts, history, and mathematics. Many educators think they are encouraging creativity if the student writes a poem, paints a picture, or performs a skit. Those products can be creative, but they are not necessarily so. Creativity is evidenced in ideas as well as in products. Young people must be encouraged to think about ideas in fresh ways and to process their thinking from a new perspective or vantage point.

Survival Secrets About the Essence of Creativity With Young Children

Allison Bemiss

"Creativity is the key to innovation. It is up to you to use it as a tool." —Easton LaChappelle, *Founder of Unlimited Tomorrow*

Creativity is imperative to critical thinking in early childhood and throughout life. So often in schools and homes we limit creativity to a colorful art project or fantastical short story—and those are beautiful examples of creativity. However, when we limit creativity to only these types of projects, we put a ceiling on the children's potential. Creativity can be discovering plants and animals outside, creativity can be wondering why soda fizzes but juice doesn't, or creativity can be pulling items out of the recycling bin to create your own invention. Creativity should not be seen as only evident in the arts; creativity should also be defined as a tool to guide innovation and critical thinking.

There are many ways to inspire creativity in our youngest learners. The first thing to consider when attempting to develop a schema for creative thinking is the environment. I like to think of the term *environment* as a two-part concept: physical environment and emotional environment.

Physical Environment for Creativity

This term refers to the physical setup of the space where learning occurs. When thinking of a classroom or home environment, one of the most important things to remember is this should be the child's space. If all of the materials (e.g., books, artwork, scissors) are placed at the adult's eye level or on a high shelf, the child will have a difficult time being independent in that environment. As simple as it sounds, one of the best things you can do is put your eyes at the child's level and take a look at the space. Are the materials easily accessible for your little learners? If not, bring everything down to their level. The next question you want to ask yourself while viewing the space is, "What materials are available in this space to inspire creating, exploring, and thinking?" A child's environment should have a variety of items, including magnifying glasses, books on topics of interest, art supplies, and dramatic play materials. A Makerspace box or basket of loose parts (collected from recycling or on nature walks) is also a wonderful tool for children to use to discover and create. Using a combination of dramatic play and Makerspace is one of my favorite ways to inspire creativity in young children. Children learn to problem solve and develop so many wonderful literacy skills through dramatic

165

play. Combining this important thinking strategy with a Makerspace box or loose part lab pushes the child's problem-solving skills to a new level. An example of this would be if a child were dressed as a doctor and were fixing their bear's leg. Rather than the parent helping to bandage the leg, encourage the child to use the loose parts lab or Makerspace box to invent something to help the bear. The children love it; this is play-based learning at its best.

Emotional Environment for Creativity

The emotional environment in which a child explores and discovers is extremely important. When children are asked to think at high levels, they will need to feel comfortable taking risks. Children should feel comfortable expressing their ideas and participating in candor (open and honest discussions) so that they learn how to cope and move forward from the mistakes that are a natural part of true learning. We hear a lot about growth mindset these days, and rightfully so. But for our youngest learners, we must remember that we are teaching them not only how to learn from mistakes, but also how to handle the BIG emotions that come from making mistakes. It is for this reason that I would encourage teachers and families of young children to teach about growth mindset and use mindfulness strategies such as breathing exercises. There are many wonderful mindfulness breathing strategies and exercises for young children on the web. Take 5 Breathing (turtle breathing) is one of my favorites. When a child creates and the project fails or breaks, having a self-regulatory strategy like this really helps them move forward to begin the process of learning from the mistake.

The last, but perhaps most important, consideration to keep in mind when teaching young children to be creative thinkers is to help them understand how to share their thinking. Very young children, even infants, are capable of making inferences and thinking at a higher level. When an infant sees a bottle, then they will infer that "I will get to eat soon." We must remember that although the children are capable of these higher order thinking strategies, they do not always have the language to express those ideas. I ask students to use the phrase, "I wonder . . ." as a sentence stem as they are exploring and creating together. If I want them to make inferences, I'll encourage them to use the phrase, "Maybe if. . . ." Sharing and modeling sentence starters allows students to feel success in communicating their ideas while collaborating with a small group.

As Easton LaChappelle states, creativity really is the key to innovation. It is the foundation for which critical thinking and problem solving are built.

—Allison Bemiss
Educator and Author

Strategies to Foster Creativity

Remain Neutral in Responses

When leading a discussion in which you want creative responses, you need to remain fairly neutral. If you were to respond, "That is a great idea," others may be cautious about entering the conversation. Likewise, they may be reluctant to risk offering a creative idea if someone else's idea had been greeted with an unfavorable response. Keep the discussion going with comments such as "That's one response" or "What is another way to accomplish the task?"

Include Creativity in the Rubric

Be sure to include creativity in the rubric for a product. The DAP Tool (Roberts & Inman, 2015a) uses creativity as one of four components to guide students in completing products and you, the teacher, in assessing the products (see Figure 21). The other three components of the DAP Tool are content, presentation, and reflection. Teamed with creativity, those four components are the same, with only the presentation component changing as the product changes. Consequently, the DAP Tool is a protocol to guide students as they develop products and teachers as they assess them. Too often, student products will be more similar than different unless creativity is one expectation that you specify for the students to address. Students will know you expect them to be creative about their work if you include it as a component in the rubric.

Teach Creativity Thinking Skills

Ensure that the children know creative thinking skills (i.e., fluency, flexibility, originality, and elaboration) and can apply them. They need to know what each creative thinking skill is and how to incorporate these skills as they write, think about content, and complete project-based learning. Thinking skills (critical, creative, and their combinations in problem-solving skills) need to be taught and encouraged from the time students enter school until they emerge ready to use these thinking skills in postsecondary opportunities.

167

Figure 21
Poster Tier 2–DAP tool

POSTER Tier 2—DAP TOOL

CONTENT	• Content is accurate.	0 1 2 3 4 5 6
	• Content has depth and complexity of thought.	0 1 2 3 4 5 6
	• Content is organized.	0 1 2 3 4 5 6
PRESENTATION		
TEXT	• Title enhances the poster's purpose and is well placed. Text highlights most important concepts in topic.	0 1 2 3 4 5 6
GRAPHICS	• Graphics (illustrations, photos) add information and are appropriate for the topic.	0 1 2 3 4 5 6
LAYOUT	• Layout design clearly emphasizes graphics in an organized and attractive manner. Text is placed to clearly describe/explain all graphic images. Spacing is carefully planned with consideration of space not used.	0 1 2 3 4 5 6
CREATIVITY	• Individual insight is expressed in relation to the content.	0 1 2 3 4 5 6
	• Individual spark is expressed in relation to the presentation.	0 1 2 3 4 5 6
REFLECTION	• Reflection on the learning of the content through product development is apparent.	0 1 2 3 4 5 6
	• Reflection on what the student learned about self as a learner is apparent.	0 1 2 3 4 5 6

Comments

_____

_____

Meaning of Performance Scale:
6—PROFESSIONAL LEVEL: level expected from a professional in the content area
5—ADVANCED LEVEL: level exceeds expectations of the standard
4—PROFICIENT LEVEL: level expected for meeting the standard
3—PROGRESSING LEVEL: level demonstrates movement toward the standard
2—NOVICE LEVEL: level demonstrates initial awareness and knowledge of standard
1—NONPERFORMING LEVEL: level indicates no effort made to meet standard
0—NONPARTICIPATING LEVEL: level indicates nothing turned in

Note. From *Assessing Differentiated Student Products: A Protocol for Development and Evaluation* (2nd ed., p. 182), by J. L. Roberts and T. F. Inman, 2015, Taylor & Francis. Copyright 2015 by Taylor & Francis. Reprinted with permission.

Bring Individuals Who Value Creativity Into the Classroom

Bring in individuals from business and industry, as well as the arts, to talk about creativity and how important it is in their lives—professional and otherwise. Make as many connections as you can for the students—connections between their interests and goals and creativity.

Provide Time to Nurture Creativity

Give students time to be creative. In a short time, it is easy to answer who, what, when, and where questions, but it takes time to wonder and reflect in order to produce more creative ideas on a topic. It takes time to engage in problem-based learning.

Reward Creativity

Reward creativity on an ongoing basis, and let students know that being creative is important. Too often creative ideas and questions are discouraged with comments such as "We don't have time for that question now" or "Ask questions that stick to the facts." Truthfully, you can google for right answers, and innovation requires putting ideas together in new and innovative ways.

Be Open to Surprises

Be open to surprise findings. The 2010 Nobel Prize in physics was awarded to Andre Geim and Konstantin Novoselov for discovering graphene, the thinnest and strongest substance yet known. The discovery of graphene was the result of an unexpected discovery. Examples like this one can help students value creative thinking skills like brainstorming and understanding the importance of trial and error.

Let Students Learn About Creative Thinkers

Expose your students to creative thinkers through biographies, films, and stories about discovery. Remember that professionals from many different fields, including business and industry, employ creative thinking to solve everyday problems in innovative ways. Perhaps these creative individuals can be highlighted in biographies, linking student interest with the biographies to be read.

Expect Creativity in All Disciplines

Remember that creativity is not limited to the visual and performing arts. Creative ideas are to be encouraged and expected in all content areas. Interdisciplinary learning promotes thinking in ways that depend on multiple disciplines; thus, making connections between and among disciplines encourages students to make linkages when they are learning within and beyond the classroom.

Watch for Signs of Creativity

Not only is it important for you to encourage creative thinking, but you also must be watching for signs of creativity. One early sign of creative thinking is using something in a way other than its intended use. As one example, the child finds a LEGO piece to substitute for a person as they tell a story with prompts. Or another student may choose to substitute a new material to improve a product. Perhaps rescuing something from the trash can leads to a new use for that "found object." When you see signs of creativity, make sure you note that use in a positive way.

Synectics

Another way to encourage creative thinking is to use synectics. William Gordon (1961) defined synectics as "the joining together of different and apparently irrelevant elements" (p. 1). He wrote that "synectics theory applies to the integration of diverse individuals into a problem-stating problem-solving group" (p. 1), and it includes combining ideas in a variety of ways. Gordon put together people from various disciplines in order to solve problems.

Synectics is based on metaphorical thinking. How is something like something else? Asking metaphorical questions stimulates young people to think at high levels and in different ways than they usually would be thinking. You might ask, "Your birthday is like what kind of flower, and why?" Or you may ask, "What kind of weather is like exploration?" Of course, you always ask "why" to see what connection the student is making between the two items. These questions would not have a content base, but they would limber up the students' thinking abilities before using metaphorical thinking in a discussion. Wouldn't you stretch before doing physical exercise? The same is true for mental exercise.

One step in synectics is to look at compressed conflicts, which requires students to look at words that don't seem to go together and to think of what they know that fits both descriptors. For example, "What do you know that is both delicate and strong or loved and dreaded?" A spider web, a parent's love, or an egg might be responses to the query of what is both delicate and strong, but they provide only the starting point of possibilities. Such questions provoke many responses that come from one's own experiences. Until you ask such questions, students may never stretch to think of something from two different perspectives.

The Creative Thinking Jot Down

Behaviors typical of creative thinkers are shown in the Creative Thinking Jot Down in Figure 22. You also can go back to Chapter 5 to see Table 1, which compares behaviors of high achievers, gifted learners, and creative thinkers.

Classroom teachers sometimes don't appreciate creative thinkers. Young students often ask a lot of questions that may not have ready answers. But stop and think for a minute. Good questions are really more important than right answers. Questions move thinking forward, whereas a right answer is simply a right answer. Good minds will move our society forward with new approaches and innovations. One of the best ways to encourage creative thinking is to show that you value good questions. In fact, you may encourage parents to ask their children at the end of a school day if they asked any good questions today and then follow up with asking what that question was. That type of thinking is very important.

The Innovation Wheel

In a magnet program that started as part of Project Gifted Education in Mathematics and Science (GEMS), a partnership between The Center for Gifted Studies at Western Kentucky University and the Warren County Schools, innovation is the universal theme that guides the curriculum. Of course, innovation is a theme that could be applied across the curriculum. The heuristic in Figure 23 includes both critical and creative skills. Words were carefully chosen to encourage students to wonder, imagine, anticipate, revise, produce, and conceptualize. The figure illustrates various ways one thinks that lead to innovation; the beginning point is wondering.

The Innovation Wheel has been conceptualized to guide teachers' questions and spark student thinking in ways that lead to creative approaches to content as well as to issues and problems related to the content. Each of the verbs requires thinking—inquire, create, analyze, enhance, communicate, and connect. There is really no starting or stopping point on the wheel. It is intended that each step in the process will be repeated as the innovation process continues.

Conclusion

Creativity is vitally important for the future—the future of young people as well as the future of the community, the county, and the globe. Consequently, it is crit-

Figure 22

Creative Thinking Jot Down

Date _____ / _____ / _____
        Mo.   Day   Yr.

Brief description of
observed activity: _____

_____

Teacher _____

Grade _____ School _____

1. As students show evidence of the following creative thinking characteristics in comparison with age peers, jot their names down in the appropriate box/es.

2. When recommending students for gifted services, use this identification jot down as a reminder of student performances as creative thinkers.

Offers many ideas (fluency).	Displays ability to switch categories or change ideas (flexibility).	Develops ideas with details (elaboration).	Offers ideas no one else may have thought of (originality).
Asks questions about everything and anything (alert and curious).	Appears bored with routine tasks and may refuse to complete them.	Uses imaginative and a strong sense of fantasy.	Appears to be daydreaming at times.

Figure 22, continued

May be uninhibited with ideas or opinions; is sometimes radical or tenacious in expressing ideas.	Is a high risk taker with an adventurous and speculative spirit.	Has high energy level that may cause the student to get in trouble.
Offers ideas others may view as wild and crazy.	May not read rules or may question the rules.	Enjoys spontaneous activities; sometimes without considering the consequences.
		Sees humor in situations others do not see (keen sense of humor).
		Appears reflective or idealistic.

Note. From *Jot Downs* [unpublished manuscript], by M. A. Evans and L. Whaley, n.d., The Center for Gifted Studies, Western Kentucky University, Bowling Green, KY. Reprinted with permission of the authors.

Figure 23
The Innovation Model

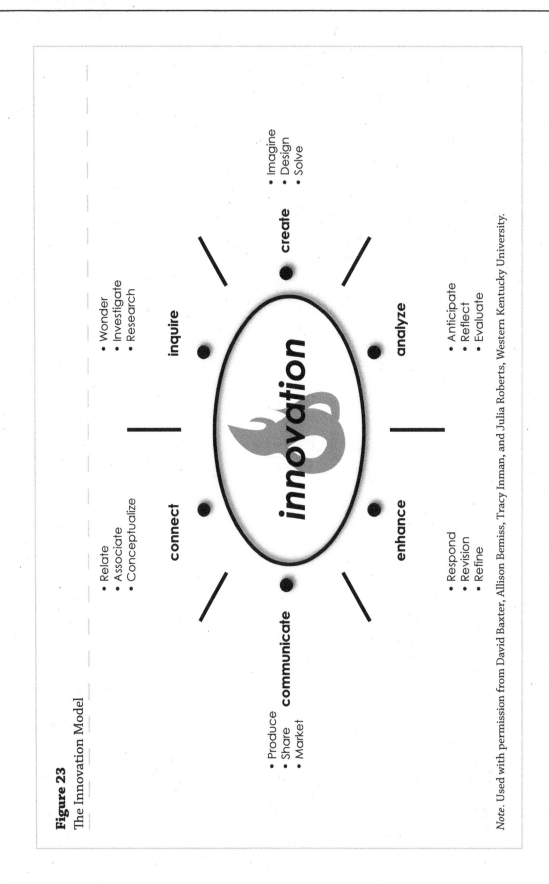

- Imagine
- Design
- Solve

create

- Wonder
- Investigate
- Research

inquire

- Anticipate
- Reflect
- Evaluate

analyze

- Relate
- Associate
- Conceptualize

connect

- Respond
- Revision
- Refine

enhance

- Produce
- Share
- Market

communicate

Note. Used with permission from David Baxter, Allison Bemiss, Tracy Inman, and Julia Roberts, Western Kentucky University.

ical that creative thinking is not only encouraged but also expected in assignments of various products. Too often educators expect creativity to be the domain of the visual and performing arts. Instead, creativity should be noticed and rewarded in all content areas.

Survival Tips

- As you nurture and encourage creative thinking, you are preparing designers, inventors, and entrepreneurs of the future.
- Parents need to know that creativity is going to be a key factor in the future success of their child. In a world in which you can search Google for answers, it will be the creative problem solvers who will likely be most successful in their careers.

Survival Toolkit

- The Torrance Center (https://coe.uga.edu/directory/torrance-center) is dedicated to creativity and carrying out the mission established by the work of E. Paul Torrance. The center offers professional development and special events dedicated to creativity.
- Other resources include:
  - Bemiss, A. (2019). *Inspiring innovation and creativity in young learners: Transforming STEAM education for pre-k–grade 3.* Prufrock Press.
  - Freeman, M. (2020). *Born curious: 20 girls who grew up to be awesome scientists.* Simon & Schuster.
  - Smutny, J. F., & van Fremd, S. E. (2009). *Igniting creativity in gifted learners, K–6: Strategies for every teacher.* Corwin Press.

- Valuable children's books include:
  - Beaty, A. (2007). *Iggy Peck, architect.* Abrams.
  - Yamada, K. (2016). *What do you do with an idea?* Compendium.
  - Spires, A. (2014). *The most magnificent thing.* Kids Can Press.

Chapter 17

Nurturing Leaders

A Necessity, Not an Option

"The very essence of leadership is that you have to have vision. You can't blow an uncertain trumpet."—Theodore M. Hesburgh

Gifted children will not be the only leaders of the future, but they all will have numerous opportunities to lead in their areas of expertise. The key is to provide experiences that will prepare them to be ethical and effective leaders. They need to be resilient leaders, ones who can problem solve. Leaders may come with natural leadership ability, but all will need opportunities for leadership skills to be nurtured on an ongoing basis.

Leadership is optimally developed when there is an agreed-upon model of leadership that focuses on the skills of effective leaders. Without such a focus for leadership development in a classroom and school, providing experiences that could develop effective leaders is a hit-or-miss proposition. The uncertainty of reaching that destination is reminiscent of *Alice's Adventures in Wonderland* (Carroll, 1865/2000) when the Cheshire Cat tells Alice that if you don't know where you are going, any road will get you there. Having an agreed-upon destination enhances the possibility of getting there.

DOI: 10.4324/9781003238553-18

The Leadership to Make a Difference Model

The Leadership to Make a Difference Model (Figure 24) provides an array of skills that are important for effective leadership development. There are numerous ways to teach and reinforce each of these skills in the classroom as well as in school and extracurricular activities. However, without a focus on specific skills, activities commonly done in the name of leadership development may miss the mark. Not only should the activities have a skill or skills as their goal, but also discussion should both precede and follow any learning experiences with leadership skills embedded. Others may call the discussions debriefings. Questions can address how nonverbal communication was perceived, how planning could have been more effective, and so on. Reflecting on the experience or debriefing is essential in making the opportunity to develop leadership skills more effective the next time (not just walking in place). The purpose would be to develop leaders who will make a positive difference in their communities and beyond.

Expert Mariam G. MacGregor describes leadership development and suggests opportunities to ensure that young people learn about becoming effective leaders.

Survival Secrets for Developing Students' Leadership Skills

Mariam G. MacGregor

More than we might like to admit, it's been common for student leadership development to be optional in the K–12 experience instead of treated as a set of essential skills needed for lifelong success. Student council, clubs, or spirit committees overshadow abundant opportunities to strengthen leadership skills from kindergarten to graduation. Younger generations increasingly want to have voice in their schools, communities, and future. These are valuable reasons for incorporating leadership development, ranging from leadership classes to mentoring and service-learning activities, integrating leadership across the curriculum, and engaging youth in decisions that positively affect school and community culture. Many can be accomplished within the context of existing instructional minutes, regardless of subject area. When a school or district sets expectations that every student will graduate with leadership skills that can serve them well in whatever career path they choose, it's easy to get parents on board.

There are plenty of leadership theories, research, and expertise available to create an effective leadership program. But most young people don't need textbook

Figure 24
The Leadership to Make a Difference Model

Leadership to Make a Difference Model

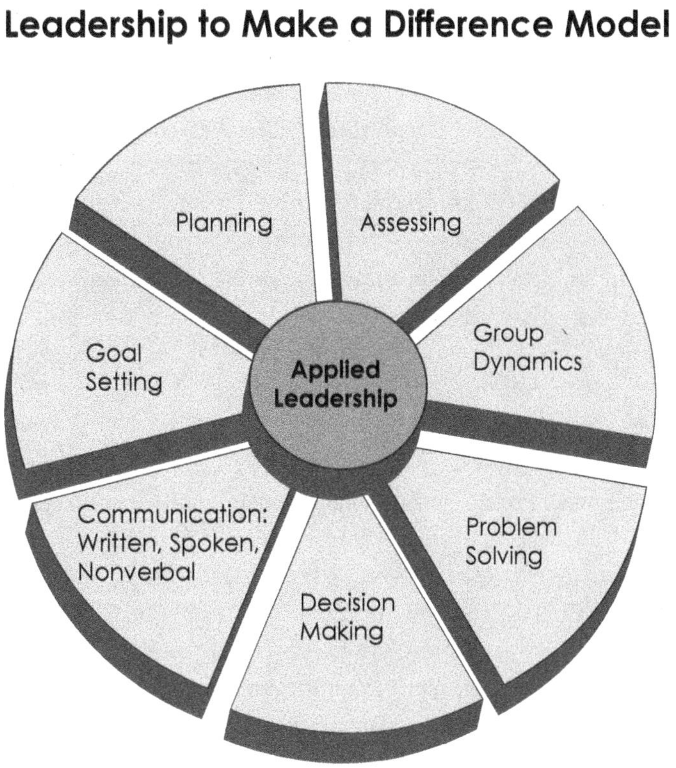

Note. Developed by J. L. Roberts, 2010, The Center for Gifted Studies, Western Kentucky University. Reprinted with permission of the author.

definitions or leadership theories to explain what it means to be a leader. One way to help kids build leadership competency is to create a program that yields a "yes" to this fundamental question:

> Would you be your own next-door neighbor? Would you give a house key to the "you" next door, trusting yourself to be responsible for your "neighbor's" house, children, pets, and monetary valuables?

Whether failing or earning straight A's at school, troubled or not—when youth of all ages are asked this question, they grasp the profound understanding that it's not what people see on the outside that influences their actions, attitudes, and character; it's who they are on the inside. Whether someone admits a willingness to live next door to themselves or not, everyone benefits from having opportunities to build leadership skills that will make them a "good neighbor." Because I work with students and employees from 18 to 80 years old, I have a lot of experience being able to assess who will succeed in a role. It's the ones who can describe what makes them a good neighbor—and consistently demonstrate those behaviors—who become strong team members and formal or informal organizational leaders.

To get there, leadership development deserves thoughtful attention.

Even in those perceived as being natural leaders, leadership skills left untended will not blossom. In fact, leadership talent applied without guidance or limits can produce lenient leaders, unconcerned with ethics, fairness, or inclusiveness and more likely to act in reckless, unwise, or arbitrary ways. Leadership cultivated intentionally from a young age, with deliberate training in essential skills such as communication, teamwork, conflict management, cultural competence critical thinking, and self-awareness, creates extraordinary individuals others want to follow.

Leadership is as much an attitude as it is a set of skills. By accepting this notion, leaders will be seen all around us—in fact, *they are us!*—in everyday settings, not powerful positions, free of publicity and special attention, and no less important.

Good leaders can easily be overlooked because bad leaders call attention to themselves with brash errors and poor judgment. To find good leaders, we are reminded to look beyond the loudest and most boisterous people to find those quietly leading with integrity and humility. These are the everyday leaders, who possess clear expectations for their own behavior and how others should be treated, and who inspire others to set high standards as well.

Educators willing to try new things and integrate leadership lessons into their classroom culture and content are instrumental in inspiring legions of leaders. Educators willing to relinquish power by creating situations where students can take action, express their opinions, and influence sustainable change are confident leaders. Educators capable of drawing out the shy, underestimated kids as equally as they do the extroverted ones are themselves stewards of leadership.

Exceptional leaders are the educators who model for all students what it means to lead and succeed at one's highest level; who challenge and prod students regardless of individual abilities, limitations, or self-doubt; and who set all students, in all circumstances, on a path to become true leaders in return.

—Mariam G. MacGregor
Author and Leadership Consultant, Leadership Is a Life Skill: Preparing Every Student to Lead and Succeed *and the* Building Everyday Leadership *curriculum series*

Identifying Leadership Talent or Potential Talent

How do you identify leadership talent? There are several possibilities, and they are most effective when used in combination. The Leadership Jot Down in Figure 25 focuses your attention on behaviors that are characteristic of leadership talent. Remember that no child shows evidence of all of the behaviors in a particular Jot Down, but rather the overall demonstration of behaviors typical of a child with leadership ability. Look for a pattern with a particular child's name being noted for demonstrating particular behaviors associated with leadership.

A leadership portfolio is another way to gather evidence of leadership potential and interest. Children and young people, perhaps with the assistance of a teacher or counselor, put together pieces that provide evidence of leadership interest and experiences. These pieces could include reflections on leadership projects from school, youth organizations, or community activities. Letters from adults who have worked with the young person in activities outside the school would provide important information about students' interest in leadership and their experiences initiating and implementing leadership projects.

A sociogram (a graphic representation of a person's social links) can provide insight into whom the children in the class consider to be the leaders. A sociogram can be completed informally by asking students to anonymously answer questions like who they would they want to include in their group if they were completing a science project or designing a mural.

The Everyday Leadership Skills and Attitudes Inventory (MacGregor, 2010) is an assessment of one's leadership skills and attitudes. It provides the opportunity for self-assessment, as well as a means to measure growth in important leadership skills and change of attitudes.

Events to Showcase to Learn about Leadership

Numerous experiences can be planned to showcase leadership learning, including the following suggestions.

- *An Evening of Notables*. Have a culminating activity in which students dress as a leader (current or historical) and carry on conversations in keeping with what they know about the individual figures.
- *Lunch With Leaders*. Invite community or school leaders in for lunch with your class. Have questions about leadership prepared beforehand to use in

Figure 25
Leadership Jot Down

Brief description of observed activity: ____
____
____

Date ______ / ______ / ______
Mo. Day Yr.

Teacher ______________________

Grade ________ School ______________________

1. As students show evidence of the following characteristics in comparison with age peers, jot their names down in the appropriate box/es.
2. When recommending students for gifted services, use this identification jot down as a reminder of student performances in leadership.

Gets others to work toward desirable or undesirable goals.	Is looked to by others when something must be decided.	Initiates activities that involve peers.
Figures out what is wrong with an activity and shows others how to make it better.	Transmits his or her enthusiasm for a task to others.	Judges abilities of others and finds a place for them.
May appear "bossy" at times.	Interacts easily with both children and adults.	

Figure 25, continued

Is sought out by other students for play/activities.	Displays a sense of justice and fair play.	Organizes ideas and people to reach goal.	Displays self-confidence.
Is often the captain of teams or a leader in the classroom.	Displays charismatic qualities.	Communicates effectively to make things happen.	May be frustrated by lack of organization or progress toward goal.

Note. From *Jot Downs* [unpublished manuscript], by M. A. Evans and L. Whaley, n.d., The Center for Gifted Studies, Western Kentucky University, Bowling Green, KY. Reprinted with permission of the authors.

conversations with them. Students might enjoy having lunch with older student leaders (e.g., the student body president of your district's high school) and finding out how they developed their leadership skills.

- *Panel of Community Leaders.* Have leaders who represent various professions in the community serve on a panel. Ask them questions about leadership, including questions about their leadership roles when they were in elementary, middle, and high school.
- *Leader Study.* Conduct a study of a leader, perhaps one who ties to something being studied in history, science, mathematics, literature, the arts, or any area of interest. Focus on skills they had or lacked that led to their accomplishments or lack thereof.

Conclusion

The basic learning experiences that develop leadership ability will have a focus on skills like communication and collaboration. Those experiences can be ongoing and occur in every classroom. The important thing to remember is to talk about how the various skills form the basis of what it means to be a leader.

Survival Tips

- Leadership does not just develop, but rather it is nurtured. Educators can provide experiences that will help students learn to be outstanding leaders.
- Young people need opportunities to hone their leadership skills as they set goals and work with others in order to reach their goals. Gifted children will grow up to be leaders in their professions, organizations, and communities. Make sure they are prepared to be effective leaders.

Survival Toolkit

Resources on this topic include:

- Boswell., C., Christopher, M., & Colburn, J. J. (2018). *Leadership for kids: Curriculum for building intentional leadership in gifted learners (grades 3–6)*. Prufrock Press.
- Karnes, F. A., & Bean, S. M. (2010). *Leadership for students: A guide for young leaders* (2nd ed.). Prufrock Press.
- MacGregor, M. (2014). *Building everyday leadership in all kids: An elementary curriculum to promote attitudes and actions for respect and success*. Free Spirit.
- MacGregor, M. (2015). *Building everyday leadership in all teens: Promoting attitudes and actions for respect and success*. Free Spirit.

Chapter 18

Creating a Gold Standard School and District

"Gold Standard Schools are places in which gifted children and young people thrive, but so do all other children." (Roberts & Inman, 2010, p. 21)

As you work to improve services offered at your school, you need a target. The NAGC 2019 Pre-K–Grade 12 Gifted Programming Standards will provide guidance for you and your colleagues to measure progress in terms of student outcomes. In fact, these standards can guide you as you work to enhance the following components in your classroom and school:

1. Learning and Development
2. Assessment
3. Curriculum and Instruction
4. Learning Environments
5. Programming
6. Professional Learning

The standards document is available at https://www.nagc.org/resources-publ ications/resources/national-standards-gifted-and-talented-education/pre-k-grade-12.

DOI: 10.4324/9781003238553-19

Checklist for the Gold Standard School

Another source to guide you is the checklist for a Gold Standard School (Roberts & Inman, 2010; see Figure 26). This checklist will assist you in planning with fellow educators in your school and district to address the learning needs of gifted students.

You will be most effective in your role if you work well with others. Collaboration is key to improving student learning. Two experts discuss the topic of collaboration in the following sections: Mary Evans describes important considerations for working with your principal, and Virginia H. Burney highlights points to remember as you work with other teachers.

Survival Secrets for Working With Your Principal

Mary Evans

The key to working with your principal effectively is communication. Set up a time to meet with your principal and ask what their vision for gifted education is at the school. Share your vision for what you want gifted education to look like in your school. What should the students, parents, classroom teachers, and administrators be doing in a school that meets the needs of gifted students? Make sure your principal is aware of and understands the implications of state regulations and local school district policies that impact gifted students. Share the Pre-K–Grade 12 Gifted Programming Standards with your principal. Volunteer to conduct a needs assessment to determine your school's level of implementation of best practices in gifted education.

Once the needs assessment has been conducted, discuss the results with the principal and ask to form a committee to review the data and set long- and short-term goals for the school. When principals understand their schools' needs, they will find ways to meet those needs, whether it is storage space, teaching space, help with scheduling, or additional resources. Professional learning is frequently identified as a need. Talk to the principal about the ongoing professional development initiatives for the school and ways that gifted education can be integrated into those initiatives.

The gifted resource teacher is the only person in the building whose total focus is on gifted and talented education. Be positive, proactive, and always looking for ways to better serve gifted students. Volunteer to be on curriculum committees,

Figure 26
Gold Standard School Checklist

Characteristic 1: Focus on Continuous Progress
- 1.1 The school mission statement specifies that every child will realize his potential or each child will make continuous progress.
- 1.2 Preassessment is routine and establishes the interests, preferred ways of learning, and levels of readiness of all students.
- 1.3 Grouping for instructional purposes is a standard practice in order to facilitate all children (remember that includes gifted children) learning at appropriately challenging levels. Most groupings are flexible to allow students to be regrouped as the level of readiness changes with different content or topics as well as when interest shifts into high gear.
- 1.4 Assessment is ongoing to see that all children are learning. This type of assessment is called formative, and it is important because it monitors progress to make certain that a child is neither practicing skills incorrectly nor misunderstanding content.
- 1.5 Lessons are differentiated to match the level of challenge to the needs of individual students or clusters of students. Differentiated learning experiences are not "just different" no r are they simply more of the same.

Characteristic 2: Talent Development
- 2.1 Opportunities in a variety of content and talent areas are sought out, announced, and encouraged.
- 2.2 Achievements in a variety of content and talent areas are recognized and celebrated.

Characteristic 3: Policies That Remove the Learning Ceiling
- 3.1 A policy for acceleration is in place.
- 3.2 A policy for performance assessment is established.
- 3.3 A policy for educational enhancement is adopted.
- 3.4 Policies and practices do not inhibit continuous progress.

Characteristic 4: Ongoing Professional Development
- 4.1 Professional development about gifted education and talent development is embedded throughout a school year.

Note. From "A Checklist to Guide Advocacy for a Gold Standard School," by J. L. Roberts and T. F. Inman, December 2010, *Parenting for High Potential*, p. 23. Copyright 2010 National Association for Gifted Children. Reprinted with permission.

nominate students and colleagues for awards, and offer to work a booth at the Fall Festival or open house events so that you are very visible in the building and seen as a dedicated member of the school team. Show your passion for meeting the needs of all students, including gifted students.

If you chair the building's gifted and talented committee, make sure the principal knows when the meetings are and receives an invitation to attend. Make sure they receive a copy of the agenda in advance of the meeting. Ask the principal to give a welcome speech when you hold parent meetings, brief the principal on parent concerns, and discuss solutions. Keep the principal well informed about the achievements of the gifted students, and ask the principal to help make students aware of opportunities that are available, such as Saturday enrichment classes, contests, programs at local museums, and so on. Offer to write a paragraph for the school newsletter or make a flyer about enrichment opportunities available in the community.

Collect quantitative and qualitative data to show the principal the value of gifted education for students. What percentage of identified students score at the highest level on the state assessment? If academically gifted students are not scoring at the highest levels, work with the principal and classroom teachers to determine why. Set and monitor learning goals for gifted students just as is done for other students with specialized learning needs. All students should make continuous progress in learning, including gifted students.

Work with your principal and colleagues to develop a range of services to address the needs of gifted students. Share what your students and parents are saying about the services provided. Take pictures and share them through a website. Include student quotes as captions to the pictures.

Communicate, communicate, communicate in every way you can so the principal has a full picture of the gifted students in the school. Find ways to show that raising the level of learning for gifted students raises the level of learning for all students.

—Mary Evans, Ed.D.
Former Principal, Cumberland Trace Elementary School,
Warren County Schools, Bowling Green, KY

Survival Secrets for Gifted Resource Teachers on Working Effectively With Other Teachers

Virginia H. Burney

The gifted resource teacher has the potential to transform education for gifted students and influence the faculty in terms of understanding the characteristics and needs of gifted students. You will share responsibility for the education of certain students, but you are also in a position to know what is going on in the classrooms of other teachers. The challenge is to establish positive relationships, trust, and clear expectations of the other faculty members. How can you do this?

Gain Clarity

Request a meeting with the district gifted coordinator and the principal to gain clarity on your role and its implementation. Before you meet, outline for yourself what you think that role is, your exact responsibilities, and how the logistics of sharing student instruction might be designed. This will help you clarify your own thinking and questions. During the meeting, the coordinator can clarify the district design for services, K–12, as well as offer suggestions for implementation. The principal will know the challenges and opportunities of the particular student population, faculty, and how the scheduling is to be organized. Together, develop written guidelines for what your role is so that other faculty can also have clarity. It will be time well spent and will establish the support of your principal and coordinator.

Offer to Assist and Establish Credibility

If you are already knowledgeable, offer to lead a book study or staff mini-lesson on some aspect of gifted education. Possible topics include the characteristics of gifted children, the social and emotional needs of this population, and differentiating to provide challenge. If you are not yet confident in your own knowledge, or if you want further development, ask the principal for support for your own professional development in gifted education. Ask to share in the schoolwide duties assigned to regular classroom teachers. Having bus duty, recess duty, cafeteria duty, and other responsibilities can demonstrate your competence in student management, makes you a member of the team, and provides you the opportunity to see the gifted students within the larger social milieu.

Establish Trust

Think of working with your colleagues in the same way we think of working with gifted children. Strive to understand both their cognitive and affective needs in order to be effective. Frame your work together as jointly influencing maximum growth in student achievement; this will establish common goals and benefits. Remember that it can be intimidating to other teachers for you to know so well what goes on in their classrooms. Be sensitive to that position, be positive about their strengths, share the joys and challenges of knowing the shared students, and be on the same team.

By establishing clear expectations for your role and the support of your administration, you should be in a position to establish your class or classroom support to maximum benefit. Seek to be a resource for the faculty as well as the students to gain team membership and leadership.

—Virginia H. Burney, Ph.D.
Assistant Professor of Educational Psychology, Ball State University, and Consultant

Influencing Change

The NAGC 2019 Pre-K–Grade 12 Gifted Programming Standards and the Gold Standard Schools checklist discussed earlier offer guidelines for what good gifted programming should encompass, but how do you go about making changes in your program or school? Expert Anita Davis provides guidance for upgrading your school district's services for gifted young people through her firsthand experiences in making changes to the gifted education policy in her district.

Survival Secrets for Making a District Outstanding in Gifted Education

Anita Davis

Our journey to change gifted education in our district started with the willingness to acknowledge the brutal facts presented by our parents, staff, and students. Dr. Phil's life law of "You can't change what you don't acknowledge" is so true, and until the leaders in our schools and district acknowledged that we were not providing the type of services our kids needed, no meaningful changes happened. Someone has to be willing to shine a light on what's happening and ask some hard questions.

We were very fortunate to have a superintendent who did this in our district. If those at the top don't own the problem and make it a priority, it is nearly impossible to affect radical and evolutionary change (which is so desperately needed in many areas of K–12 education, especially gifted education).

But acknowledging the problem isn't enough—change comes only when folks roll up their sleeves and do something! We brought a task force together to analyze our current reality, study the research and best practices, and make recommendations about what needed to be done differently in our classrooms, schools, and district. The task force was comprised of representatives from our various stakeholders so that all had a voice in the process. The task force's first task was to articulate a vision statement, goals, and parameters for gifted education in our district. The committee then divided its findings and recommendations into five key areas: organization, identification, services, communication, and professional learning. This report was shared with the board of education, which adopted the report as a multiyear action plan for immediate implementation. We now had the blueprint needed to build the type of gifted education services we envisioned.

At the same time the task force was working, administrative staff meetings were used to build shared knowledge about gifted education. All administrators were asked to do three things in relation to our study about gifted education: (1) be willing to be disturbed, (2) be willing to confront their biases, and (3) have a sense of urgency. We read numerous articles, examined the myths and truths about gifted students, looked at school through the eyes of our most capable students, and confronted some difficult realities about our practices and beliefs. Taking time to develop this type of understanding with our building and district leaders was pivotal and foundational to the change that ensued. They understood the vision and blueprint once it was presented to them by the task force and were better able to implement the recommendations in their respective buildings.

Throughout the process, the most critical factor that created understanding and ownership was our focus on always looking at things through the eyes of the gifted child. Putting folks in scenarios and making them see what the child experiences in the classroom and in life was extremely powerful. We knew that research and best practice appeal to the head, the rational, logical part of us all; we were committed to making sure we appealed to the heart as well, that part of us that drove us to be teachers.

—Anita Davis
Former Assistant Superintendent, Curriculum and
Instruction, Oldham County Schools, Buckner, KY

Conclusion

Moving toward implementing programming standards characterized by best practices for all children, including those who are gifted and talented, will be easier when you have a clear target in mind and you have key educators and parents on board. Use the information in this chapter as your blueprint for what you want to put in place and how you should work to accomplish your goals. Resist any need to reach your goals on your own. Instead educate and collaborate with decision makers in your school and district to move along together in establishing a Gold Standard School and implementing the NAGC 2019 Pre-K–Grade-12 Gifted Programming Standards.

Survival Tips

- Become familiar with the Pre-K–Grade 12 Gifted Programming Standards and the components of a Gold Standard School to help determine changes that need to be made to your gifted programming.
- Parents need to know what policies and practices could be in place in a school that would allow all students to thrive, including those who are gifted and talented. Such knowledge improves advocacy efforts by parents.
- Make sure that information about standards and best practices is available via the school and district websites and in other places educators and parents can access.

Survival Toolkit

- This webpage (https://www.nagc.org/resources-publications/resources/national-standards-gifted-and-talented-education/pre-k-grade-12) includes a link to the downloadable booklet that outlines the NAGC 2019 Pre-K–Grade 12 Gifted Programming Standards.
- For more on the Gold Standard School, see: Roberts, J. L., & Inman, T. F. (2010, December). A checklist to guide advocacy for a gold standard school. *Parenting for High Potential*, 21–23.

Chapter 19

Working With All Special Area Teachers as the Gifted Child's Best Resources

"Never apologize for talent! Talent is a gift! And that is my special talent, encouraging talent!"—Madame Morrible, *Wicked: The Grimmerie: A Behind-the-Scenes Look at the Hit Broadway Musical*

Key Question

- In what ways can special area teachers be talent developers for children and young people in your school?

The special area teachers in your school will likely include the librarian, music teacher, art teacher, and physical education teacher. In middle school and high school you also will look to teachers of graphic design, theater, business, agriculture, and family and consumer sciences as resources, in addition to content teachers in core subjects. These teachers can be helpful resources to children who are gifted and talented, developing both interests and talents in their areas of expertise. Ongoing conversations between you and the special area teachers can benefit the students who show special interests and talents in the teachers' areas of expertise. You and the special area teachers can partner to see that talents blossom during each school

 DOI: 10.4324/9781003238553-20

year. They can give you suggestions and strategies for incorporating a talent area in your lesson plans for specific children with special interests or talents like art, music, dance, or the visual arts. They can recognize potential talent, and they can implement strategies and extend opportunities for students to develop their talents at the next level.

Working With the School Librarian

School librarians usually have more resources at their disposal than any other educators in the school. Becoming a lifelong learner requires accessing resources that allow students to both answer and ask good questions. The librarian certainly will help students access resources for research, but they can facilitate learning in other ways as well.

For a librarian, working with gifted students can come in many different forms. Book studies with small groups provide an excellent opportunity for librarians to interact with gifted students. Often students are asked to focus on plot points or comprehension of reading materials in class. A book group will give the students a chance to focus on higher level thinking skills and delve into the complexities of a story or novel. Some great resources for finding appropriate reading material are:

- "Biographies for Talented Readers, A Bibliography" (http://aea11gt.pbworks. com/f/Biographies_forGT+Rdrs.pdf) by Ann Robinson from the University of Arkansas at Little Rock is a bibliography of biographies suitable for gifted children. The list includes the reading levels for each book.
- Hoagies' Gifted Education Page (http://www.hoagiesgifted.com/reading_ lists.htm) provides several lists of recommended books for advanced readers on a variety of topics.
- Halsted, J. W. (2009). *Some of my best friends are books: Guiding gifted readers from preschool to high school* (3rd ed.). Great Potential Press.
- Hauser, P., & Nelson, G. A. (1988). *Books for the gifted child* (Vol. 2). Bowker.

One challenge that many parents and teachers of gifted students face is finding material that is high-level reading and also high-interest and age-appropriate. Librarians need to stay in tune with what students are interested in and update their collection with the needs and wishes of these children in mind. It is also important to mention that gifted students often prefer nonfiction books. Biographies are an excellent option to capture gifted learners' interest.

Finding authors who write books that capture the interests of gifted students can be a challenge. Some authors we've found to be favorites of gifted kids include

Lloyd Alexander, Jodi Lynn Anderson, Laurie Halse Anderson, Louise Arnold, E. D. Baker, Blue Balliett, Dave Barry, Ted Bell, Jeanne Birdsall, Pseudonymous Bosch, Berkeley Breathed, Georgia Byng, Beverly Cleary, Andrew Clements, Susan Cooper, Roald Dahl, Kate DiCamillo, Marguerite Henry, Anthony Horowitz, Polly Horvath, Erin Hunter, Brian Jacques, Robin Jarvis, Philip Kerr, E. L. Konigsburg, Madeleine L'Engle, Lois Lowry, Robert McCloskey, Marissa Moss, Christopher Paolini, Gary Paulsen, Katherine Paterson, Rodman Philbrick, Ellen Potter, Guillaume Prevost, Rick Riordan, J. K. Rowling, Jon Scieszka, Lemony Snicket, Trenton Lee Stewart, Vivian Vande Velde, E. B. White, and Jane Yolen.

Bibliotherapy is an important way to help gifted students understand a variety of different issues that they may encounter. There are so many wonderful picture books that can help explore the social-emotional issues that gifted students experience. Don't let the term *picture books* limit their use to elementary children. In fact, some of these books are useful for getting important points about gifted children's needs understood by educators and parents, as well as by middle and high school students. Some favorites include:

- *Archibald Frisby* by Michael Chesworth (1996): This is an excellent book about a little boy whose mother worries that he is missing out on the rest of the world because he is too focused on science and reading. She ships him off to camp, where Archibald helps everyone at camp discover that science can be fun. It is a wonderful illustration of how gifted kids don't have to change to be happy.
- *The Big Orange Splot* by Daniel Pinkwater (1993): All of the houses in the neighborhood look exactly the same until one day a bird drops a can of orange paint on Mr. Plumbean's house. The neighborhood panics that his house looks different. Mr. Plumbean embraces the difference and uses his artistic abilities to create a multicolored masterpiece. Eventually the rest of the neighborhood realizes that creativity is better than conformity.
- *Eggbert, the Slightly Cracked Egg* by Tom Ross (1997): Even though he is a talented artist, Eggbert is banished from his home in the refrigerator when the other eggs discover he has a slight crack. Eggbert initially tries to disguise the fact that he is different, but eventually he discovers that there are many things in this world that are wonderful because they are different.
- *Ish* by Peter H. Reynolds (2004): Ramon loves creating art until his older brother teases him about his artwork. Ramon loses his passion for drawing until his younger sister shows him that art doesn't have to be perfect. This book is helpful for students who worry about perfection.
- *The Little Cupcakes* by Anthony King (2005): Caitlin is so excited to take cupcakes to school to share with her classmates. Some of the cupcakes have vanilla frosting, and some have chocolate frosting. When the box is opened, the teacher decides to cut off all of the tops so that they will all be the same. When Caitlin returns home, devastated, her father comforts her by explain-

ing that it is wonderful and important to celebrate all of the differences in the world. This book is a tale about the importance of diversity and tolerance.

- *Michael* by Tony Bradman (1997): Although Michael enjoys math, reading, art, and science, he does not enjoy how his teachers are teaching those subjects. Michael is considered by his teachers to be the "worst boy in school," and they do nothing to get him interested in school. Michael doesn't mind being unique and busies himself in each subject with his own projects. In the end, all of Michael's projects combine to surprise everyone with his accomplishment.
- *Odd Velvet* by Mary Whitcomb (1998): Velvet is a unique little girl who brings a milkweed pod to show-and-tell while other girls are bringing their dolls. When the other students first meet her, they think she is odd, but Velvet has great confidence in herself. Her confidence and her unique talents eventually win over her classmates.
- *Something Else* by Kathryn Cave (1998): A little creature is told by the other animals in town that he is not like them and that he "doesn't belong." He tries to fit in but to no avail. When another unique creature shows up at the door, Something Else initially rejects it, saying that it doesn't belong there. In the end, they become fast friends. This is a wonderful story about accepting each other's differences and a subtle nod to the Golden Rule.
- *Stand Tall, Molly Lou Melon* by Patty Lovell (2001): Molly Lou is a tiny, bucktoothed, clumsy first grader. Her grandmother gives her wonderful advice about embracing each of her unique characteristics. When she moves to a new school, she encounters a bully but rises above each of his insults with panache.
- *Violet: The Pilot* by Steve Breen (2008): Violet is different from her classmates because she prefers her set of tools to tea sets. She lives with her parents next to the junkyard and is a mechanical genius. As she grows up, her inventions become much more complex and often are flying machines. Her constant companion and only friend is her dog, Orville. Violet ignores the taunts of her classmates and instead focuses on creating a flying machine for the upcoming Air Show. As she travels to the Air Show in her new machine, she has to stop and rescue a Scout Troop. In the end, the town celebrates Violet's heroism, and Violet makes it on the cover of her favorite scientific magazine. This is a beautifully illustrated tale of a girl who is seen as different because she is passionate about science and engineering.

Working With the Art Teacher

Classroom teachers also need to recognize artistic talent and provide opportunities to highlight skills and interests in art as young people learn in other subject areas. Experts Judy K. Bellemere and Mary Judith Stallard provide suggestions for art teachers and classroom teachers to use to develop students' talent in art.

Survival Secrets for Developing Artistic Talent

Judy K. Bellemere and Mary Judith Stallard

It is easy to identify the children in your art class who are gifted in art. Those gifted children will be doing art at every possible moment, usually volunteering for any extra work having to do with art, and consistently creating art that catches the eye of the observer. They are able to creatively and/or meticulously combine the elements of design through drawing, painting, and three-dimensional projects in a way that delights the viewer.

The harder part is encouraging development of the gift and broadening the scope. Today's art teachers often have large numbers of students. Because of the nature of the subject and its limited time allocations, the attention of the art teacher is in constant demand, and the individual projects and use of media are in varying stages, from those barely started to those nearing completion. Many art students are in the class not because of talent. These students must still be encouraged and assisted, and like many other situations, end up needing most of the attention. And herein lies the difficulty—how to give quality encouragement and experience to the gifted and those showing profound interest in the subject when your teaching must be shared with the other students. Three words to keep in mind when developing a student's artistic talent are not unlike those we pursue in any of the disciplines: EXPOSE, INVOLVE, AFFIRM. The suggestions below address these three categories that could be workable for students of any age, with teacher and parent support and approval, and help the teacher meet the needs of all students while providing support to the gifted.

Let's first consider the soul of these talented students. Most of us react positively to recognition and praise, to be singled out for accomplishment. Therefore, offer private gallery spaces in the art room, on the wall, shelves, or counter, in addition to your usual displays, for those who are deserving and interested. Matting or backing material to enhance presentation could be made available. Pieces could be changed out at will. All students could have a chance to be the subject of attention at some scheduled time if that would prove prudent. Let the gifted students be in charge of their own display and assisting others. This can help their promotion and free you to help elsewhere where needed. Most art teachers commonly use this technique in a public area of the school. Further enhance the honor and attention factor by selecting some gifted students to design and execute a permanent mural for the school or elsewhere in the community. Work with the journalism staff to let a talented student submit a cartoon, political or otherwise, to their publication and for teacher bulletins, etc.

Have the students keep a journal, handmade or purchased, for art's sake or in conjunction with written dialogue. This should be the student's personal playground, full of thumbnail sketches and notations on a variety of subjects. Notes can pair with the drawings as to coloration, locality, and so forth. It's good to have ways they can express themselves in addition to standard projects. Students might be encouraged to enlarge some of these images to create a sizable composition. It could be true to the sketch or abstracted. If there is no class time available for such opportunity, consider a voluntary home based project for which extra credit could be given.

Arrange field trips to area art museums. This is especially important for the many gifted children who are not introduced to the arts as part of their home life.

Give art a purpose. If it is not possible to take the children on site to see how and why art fits into a profession, try to bring some willing representatives into your classroom to demonstrate and discuss. This provides awareness and can protect the art teacher from time away from other classes or afterschool involvements. These target areas could include architects, workers at an advertising agency, photographers, commercial gallery owners, functional and art ceramicists, sculptors, jewelers, computer graphic artists, cartoonists, and illustrators. Watching artists make art is an enlightening experience.

Keep a folder of art materials available to those students who are often seeking additional projects. Attach a list of suggested but not compulsory projects. Learning can take place, and the children can get beyond rainbows. Seeing such a folder of expanded opportunity can be helpful to parents seeking additional projects to encourage art at home as well as to demonstrating your attempts to meet the needs of their gifted child. Associated display area should be adjacent, tacked up and arranged by participating student.

If time allows, sponsor an afterschool art club for gifted students. Meeting one afternoon a month could be not so taxing, and perhaps an interested parent or two could help to sponsor. Teacher, parents, and students could all help select the project or field trip of greatest interest and fun. If circumstances allow, supply students and their parents with class schedules at an area art institute or art museum. Try to interest parent-teacher groups to help sponsor this kind of opportunity for students unable to afford the experiences.

Have library resources, changed periodically, available to those students who love looking at art and reading and learning about the artists and art periods in history. Art history can be a special involvement. Often parents and children alike don't realize the professional positions available in our prominent art galleries and museums of art. We support those who like to do art and those who study and appreciate.

To summarize, let us remember that to keep the gifted, young artist interested is paramount. Within the short time available to you, expose this student to the best you have to offer, always affirming that their creations are special and worthy of notice. This is the kind of attention and guidance that will provide stimulus and opportunities that take them beyond the boundaries of mediocrity.

—Judy K. Bellemere
Former Shawnee Mission School District Art Teacher

—Mary Judith Stallard
Shawnee Mission School District Art Teacher,
Middle School Art Teacher, Pembroke Hill School

Working With the Theater/ Drama Teacher

Other students have talents in drama. Tapping into their interests can improve their willingness to learn in various content areas. Expert Harper Lee highlights strategies for letting students learn content as they develop their interests and talents in drama. Some students thrive when they have opportunities to use their interests and talents in drama to show what it is that they have learned through projects like skits, videos, and podcasts.

Survival Secrets for Developing Talent in Drama

Harper Lee

Just before starting the fifth grade, I got "bit by the theatre bug" when I performed in my very first play. In the following years, I signed up for dance classes, sang in the choir, and auditioned for every play I heard about. In high school, I happily spent long evenings doing my homework backstage, and in college, I majored in theatre and seriously considered pursuing graduate studies in acting. Ultimately, I followed a different path, but my early passion for performing helped shape my chosen career. And I also continue to write, create, dance, and perform.

I was lucky. I had experienced teachers and mentors who knew how to foster a young actor like me and understood the value of giftedness in drama.

But what does it mean to be gifted in drama? What does it look like? What can it mean for a child's future? I myself am not a scholar—I can only speak from my own experience. However, here I have gathered just a handful of thoughts on gift-edness in drama based on my childhood:

1. **I was a kinesthetic learner.** Children who crave performing tend to have a great deal of energy (I did— apologies to *all* of my teachers), and I would wager that for many of them, their preferred mode of learning is doing. To this day, I do not feel like I have truly learned my lines or know a play inside and out until I have learned the character's movements and gestures and spent time in the physical performance space. As a child, it was very hard for me to sit in a desk all day long and be quiet. It was hard for me to internalize information just by listening or just by reading. I wanted to touch things, hold things, interact with others, get out of my seat, and actually move through the learning. I was drawn to theatre because it is about doing, and I learn by doing. A child who is a gifted performer may present as a problem in a traditional classroom setting, and it is possible they will be more fully engaged by a kinesthetic approach to learning.

2. **I was fascinated by people.** I was a talker as a child. I was very curious about other people, and I always had a lot of questions for them: Where were they from? What did they like when they were in school? What was their favorite food? Did they have pets? Why did they not like the color blue? I had a remarkable memory for people's answers. Even as a little girl, I practiced accents, and I could make my people laugh when I did impressions or told jokes. These might seem like strange hobbies for a child. But in ret-rospect, I was practicing the things that actors do: crafting the inner life of another, curating the expression of that inner life, and holding the attention of an audience.

3. **I was a hard worker.** In high school, my schedule was almost entirely AP classes, and I spent my evenings in dance class or in rehearsal. I was sad if I wasn't in a play. I would sit next to a dim blue light backstage and read my history book or work through math problems. I didn't sleep much, but I loved every minute of what I was doing. I always had a little more energy to give if it meant I could do theatre.

4. **I kept at it.** When I started taking ballet classes, many of the young people in my class had been dancing for a lot longer than I had. I was behind and embarrassed. But I loved dancing, and I wanted to dance in productions, so I just kept showing up until I got better and better and better. Later, when I was applying to graduate school, I had a terrible audition. I cried and cried after finding out that I didn't get a callback from the schools I wanted to hear from. But then, I pulled myself together, grabbed my headshots, and just started visiting schools on my own. I got offers from great places because I refused to give up.

As an adult, these innate qualities that drama cultivated in me continue to serve me well. I continue to be a hard worker who doesn't like to call it quits. My curiosity about people has translated to invaluable soft skills like listening and empathy.

If you have a student in your class who is climbing the walls or behaving like a classic class clown, try involving them in a play or exposing them to theatrical improvisation. It could be that they are gifted in drama.

—Harper Lee
Writer

Identifying Talent in the Arts

The special area teachers in your school can be terrific resources in the identification process for the visual and performing arts. Tap into their expertise for both the screening and the identification of talent in art, music, drama, and dance.

The Jot Downs for the Visual Arts and for Music (Figures 27 and 28) provide guidance for teachers as they observe behaviors of students, looking for indicators of talent in the visual arts and music. Teachers with specialization in these areas are valuable resources to take the lead in the identification process of children who are gifted and talented in the visual and performing arts.

Conclusion

Using the expertise of all teachers in your building contributes to making your school one that prides itself on each child developing their potential. A team effort is always stronger than a single person trying to accomplish the same purpose. That's what a talent development school offers its students—an array of opportunities to develop their talents to advanced levels.

Figure 27
Visual Arts Jot Down

Date _____ / _____ / _____
Mo.   Day   Yr.

Brief description of
observed activity: _____

_____

Teacher _____
Grade _____ School _____

1. As students show evidence of the following characteristics in comparison with age peers, jot their names down in the appropriate box/es.
2. When recommending students for gifted services, use this identification jot down as a reminder of student performances in the visual arts.

May be asked by others to do artwork.	Likes to comment on colors, shapes, and structure of things.	May be critical of own artwork and work of others.	Enjoys and takes pride in doing visual art well.
Draws or doodles often in school or at home.	Does outstanding original artwork.	Likes the opportunity to choose to express self through the use of many different materials.	Enjoys talking about art and collecting works of art.

Figure 27, continued

Masters basic art skills quickly and easily.	Has a keen sense of humor; makes unusual connections with drawing.	Concentrates on art projects for long periods; may shut out other things going on.	Creates exceptional charts, graphs, models, or other visuals when given the opportunity.
Provides detailed artwork (elaboration).	Has a sensitive use of line/color/texture.	Enjoys open-ended art activities; shows frustration with art projects that are very specific.	Notices and shows appreciation for beauty and aesthetic qualities.

Note. From *Jot Downs* [unpublished manuscript], by M. A. Evans and L. Whaley, n.d., The Center for Gifted Studies, Western Kentucky University, Bowling Green, KY. Reprinted with permission of the authors.

Figure 28
Music Jot Down

Brief description of
observed activity: _____

Date _____/_____/_____
          Mo.   Day   Yr.

Teacher _____
Grade _____ School _____

1. As students show evidence of the following musical characteristics in comparison with age peers, jot their names down in the appropriate box/es.
2. When recommending students for gifted services, use this identification jot down as a reminder of student performances in music.

Perceives fine differences in sound.	Remembers melodies and can reproduce them accurately.	Is sensitive to rhythm; may tap fingers or feet while working.	Has sustained interest in musical activities.
Expresses feelings or emotions through music.	Makes up original tunes.	May hum or sing to break the silence.	Displays interest in musical symbols and learns them easily.

Figure 28, continued

Identifies rhythmic patterns as same or different.	Likes to perform musically.	Sings on pitch.	Performs musically with a high degree of technical difficulty.
Displays interest in musical instruments and various ways to produce sound.	Enjoys musical performances.	Plays or would like to play a musical instrument.	Prefers to work with music playing.

Note. From *Jot Downs* [unpublished manuscript], by M. A. Evans and L. Whaley, n.d., The Center for Gifted Studies, Western Kentucky University, Bowling Green, KY. Reprinted with permission of the authors.

Survival Tips

- Plan with all school personnel, including the special area teachers, to build a network of professionals who are on board to develop the talents of all children who express interest and demonstrate potential in any content or talent area.
- Parents need to know that all school personnel are resources for talent development for their children.
- Be the collector of all information coming into the school about contests and competitions in order to share opportunities with children. Many of these opportunities will be in the visual and performing arts.

Survival Toolkit

- "Biographies for Talented Readers, A Bibliography" (http://aea11gt.pbworks.com/f/Biographies_forGT+Rdrs.pdf) by Ann Robinson from the University of Arkansas at Little Rock is a bibliography of biographies suitable for gifted children. The list includes the reading levels for each book.
- Hoagies' Gifted Education Page (http://www.hoagiesgifted.com/reading_lists.htm) provides several lists of recommended books for advanced readers on a variety of topics.
- SEM-R bookmarks (https://gifted.uconn.edu/semr-resources) are useful for teachers at the elementary and middle school levels, as they provide prompts that can be used many times to encourage higher level thinking.
- Other resources include:
  - Cukierkorn, J. R. (2008). *Arts education for gifted learners*. Prufrock Press.
  - Halsted, J. W. (2009). *Some of my best friends are books: Guiding gifted readers from preschool to high school* (3rd ed.). Great Potential Press.

Chapter 20

Opportunities Galore

"When I was a child, my family was poor. No lawyers or judges lived in my neighborhood. I knew nothing about the Supreme Court . . . . You cannot dream about something you do not know about. You have to learn to dream big. Education exposes you to what the world has to offer, to the opportunities open to you." —Supreme Court Justice Sonia Sotomayor

Key Questions

- What contests, competitions, summer and Saturday programs, travel, and other opportunities are available in your school and community?

- What are sources for financial support for young people to take advantage of the opportunities that are available?

Be a talent development coordinator. Let the principal, the counselor, and all staff in the office know that you would like to have copies of all announcements

 DOI: 10.4324/9781003238553-21

about contests and competitions. As you gather announcements, you can share information with individual students or with classes if you think several students' interests and talents would match the opportunities available. They are also available for parents.

Your students may have passion areas you will not know about unless you ask for that information, so be sure to solicit information from students about their interests and talents outside of school, as well as more in-depth information about those interests and talents you know about from school. Then, keep track of those passion areas. Doing so will give you optimal possibilities for matching opportunities to your students. This information about student interests also lets you get to know your students better. What an asset that is!

Contests and Competitions

Contests and competitions provide opportunities for children to share their talents and incentives for working hard to improve skills in their talent areas. Recitals and other performances encourage young people to get ready to perform for others. Such events are important steps in talent development, as a young person notches up their skills and interests as they prepare for the contest or competition. Some contests and competitions provide prizes, and others result in recognition. Either way, the experience can be very motivating to children and young people. In fact, participating in the process is a great experience in and of itself. Usually such contests provide opportunities for students to get to know others of their age, ones who share their interests. What a win it is for all concerned when children have opportunities to perform in their interest and talent areas and to meet like-minded peers who may be thought of as idea-mates.

The product, whether it is a slogan or an aria, is the critical component of a contest or competition. Clear expectations of the product itself are essential if the product is to be high quality. How can you make that happen? You could outline expectations for every product for every student interested in the competition. Or you could provide a guide that not only helps the student in developing the product, but also encourages them to consider creativity and the content expressed.

DAP Tools can be used to prepare and instruct students on what components are important in specific products. (See Figure 21 in a previous chapter.) The presentation component of the DAP Tool identifies the essential ingredients of a podcast, an essay, an experiment, a speech, or any other product that the contest requires. Even if you do not have experience with the wide range of products that may be required in a contest, the DAP Tool for that specific product can guide the student in creating an outstanding product. DAP Tools for multiple products can be found in *Assessing Differentiated Student Products* by Roberts and Inman (2015a).

Another possibility is to link the student with someone who has experience and, hopefully, talent in the product or performance area. Feedback from another person who has expertise helps the student prepare for the contest or competition. Remember that experts are usually very happy to share with young people, happy to find others who are interested in something that they are. In fact, they often want to encourage interest in their profession or hobby, so they welcome opportunities to do so. You may want to check with the Chamber of Commerce, a local university or community college, an artists' guild, as well as with other groups in your community to identify volunteers to guide your students.

Invite students who have been in a contest to come back and share what they learned from that experience. Did they have a good time? What did they learn from the experience? Do they still have the product so they could show the others or could they describe it? Could they do a similar performance? What would they do differently the next time? Will they enter the contest or competition another time?

Contests and competitions are available in all content areas. Some of them focus on creative thinking and problem solving, like Odyssey of the Mind, Destination Imagination, and the Future Problem Solving Program. Others focus on engineering tasks like FIRST LEGO League's robotics competition. *Competitions for Talented Kids* (2005) by Karnes and Riley listed contacts for an array of contests and competitions. Search out contests for a child or group of young people who have a special interest, or encourage the student to conduct an Internet search for possibilities. Keep a record of all contests and competitions for current and future use. Make a calendar of contests and their deadlines to have for reference, and post it in a prominent place.

Talent Searches

Another source of opportunities for young people can be found through programs sponsored by regional talent search centers. These centers cover all states, with each center handling students within a particular region. They conduct talent searches for students generally in seventh grade, providing the opportunity for young people to take the ACT or the SAT, assessments intended for graduating seniors. The centers also offer programming on weekends and during the summers, as well as other advanced learning opportunities. Check out these websites for information on the different talent searches available across the country:

- The Center for Talented Youth at Johns Hopkins University (https://cty.jhu.edu)
- The Talent Identification Program at Duke University (https://www.tip.duke.edu)

- The Center for Talent Development at Northwestern University (https://www.ctd.northwestern.edu)
- The Center for Bright Kids in Denver, CO (https://www.centerforbrightkids.org)

Many of these centers now offer programs for younger students, often through online learning programs. These distance-learning courses can be used to supplement students' talents or help them try out areas that interest them in a short summer or afterschool course. Information on applying and qualifying for these programs can be found at each of the websites listed.

Travel and Field Trips

Travel is another engaging opportunity that promotes learning. Sometimes students can travel to a nearby city or another part of the country to enhance their learning, and other times their travel experiences may take them to another part of the world, especially in study abroad or cultural exchange programs. In a time when globalization describes the world scene, opportunities to interact with individuals from other cultures are important.

Virtual field trips are an excellent opportunity for teachers to guide small groups or individual students on an adventure. Because there are costs associated with field trips, virtual field trips often provide the experience desired. When taking a field trip on the computer, you can travel around the world in seconds and explore inside places you couldn't easily go. Virtual field trips are a great tool to educate and motivate students. The following sections provide resources for travel, virtual field trips, and other interactive experiences in key content areas.

Math

- Geometry Center (http://www.scienceu.com/geometry): This website allows students to explore patterns, shapes, and symmetry in an interactive format.
- Max's Math Adventures (http://teacher.scholastic.com/max/index.htm): Max and his best friend Ruth love math. At this site, Max will lead your students on an exploration of math concepts including patterns, graphs, addition, and subtraction.
- Tessellations (https://www.uen.org/themepark/patterns/tessellation.shtml): On this virtual field trip, students will learn about and create tessellations. The site also directs you to other high-level websites that can lead to some wonderful discussions.

- Internet Field Trips (http://teacher.scholastic.com/fieldtrp/math.htm): There are many different math concepts discussed on these websites. Students can explore concepts including estimation, geometry, number sense, patterns, and the history of mathematics.
- Villainy, Inc. (http://villainyinc.thinkport.org/default.asp): This creative site allows students to take a trip "thwarting world supremacy through mathematics." The site explores statistics and probability, algebra, geometry, decimals, percentages, negative numbers, and more.

Science

- The Heart: The Engine of Life (https://www.fi.edu/learn/heart): This virtual field trip allows students to explore the heart's development and structure. Students can follow the blood, travel through the body system, and learn how to take care of and monitor their bodies to maintain a healthy heart.
- Microbe Zoo (http://commtechlab.msu.edu/sites/dlc-me/zoo): When students visit Microbe Zoo, they can learn all about "the worlds of hidden microbes." The Information Booth guides students through Dirt Land, Animal Pavilion, Water World, Space Adventure, and the Snack Bar.
- Volcanoes (http://satftp.soest.hawaii.edu/space/hawaii/vfts/kilauea/kilauea.vfts.html): Students will enjoy this trip to learn more about volcanoes. Students can view remote sensing images of a volcano, take ground and radar tours around Kilauea Crater, and watch a video of lava entering the ocean.
- Slime in Space (https://www.weareteachers.com/slime-space-virtual-field-trip): Nickelodean and two astronauts teamed up to show what happens to slime in microgravity. Students then do the same experiments back on Earth,
- Aquariums: Watch the jellyfish on the Monterey Bay Aquariums Live Jelly Cam (https://www.montereybayaquarium.org/animals/live-cams/jelly-cam). The Maritime Aquarium has a variety of virtual programs for families to experience (https://www.maritimeaquarium.org/virtual-programs). Take a tour of Seattle's National Aquarium (https://samuraivirtualtours.com/example/nadc/index.html). Watch the webcam from Georgia Aquarium's Ocean Voyager (https://www.georgiaaquarium.org/webcam/ocean-voyager).
- Nature Lab (https://www.nature.org/en-us/about-us/who-we-are/how-we-work/youth-engagement/nature-lab): The Nature Conservatory has eleven virtual field trips in its youth curriculum.

Language Arts

- Author, Author (http://www.tramline.com/lit/author): This virtual field trip is a wonderful resource for children to learn how authors do what they do. Authors on the trip include Eric Carle, Stan and Jan Berenstain, and Judy Blume.
- Literary Virtual Field Trips (https://www.educationworld.com/a_lesson/virtual-field-trips-literature-books.shtml): This site has virtual fields trips connected with authors and series including: Anne of Green Gables, Little House on the Prairie, and Edgar Allan Poe.
- Two Writing Teachers (https://twowritingteachers.org/2020/04/17/all-aboard-field-trips-and-writing-experiences): Enjoy fun writing activities after going on virtual field trips to exciting places like Disney, Paris, and Washington, DC.

Social Studies

- Ancient Egyptian Pyramids (https://www.pbs.org/wgbh/nova/pyramid): This virtual field trip allows students to journey through the Great Pyramid's chambers and passageways. Students follow a group of archaeologists and learn about pharaohs.
- Europe (https://www.virtourist.com/europe/index.html): Students can explore their way around the European continent on this site. Photographs of each locale are beautiful, and the tours are very descriptive.
- U.S. Capitol Tour (https://www.capitol.gov): This trip allows students to click on various places in and around the U.S. Capitol.
- White House Tour (https://www.360virtualtour.co/portfolio/the-white-house-google-virtual-tour): Students can click on different areas of the White House to view its rooms and grounds.
- Museum Virtual Tour (https://www.bostonchildrensmuseum.org/museum-virtual-tour): This is a wonderful site to take a virtual tour of Boston's Children's Museum.
- Google Arts & Culture (https://artsandculture.google.com): Visit more than 2,000 museums in more than 80 countries with this wonderful site.

Art

- Destination Modern Art (https://www.moma.org/interactives/ destination/#): This trip follows a little alien through New York's Museum of Modern Art. When students click on a piece of art, they are able to learn about the artist, interesting facts about the art, and tips to create their own pieces of art.

- Leonardo da Vinci (http://www.tramline.com/tours/cross/leo/_tourlaunch 1.htm): Students will be able to take a journey through Leonardo da Vinci's life and art.
- The Met (https://artsandculture.google.com/partner/the-metropolitan-museum-of-art): Experience the Metropolitan Museum of Art online with any of the 26 online galleries. Enjoy a gallery walk of everything from ball gowns to works of art.
- The Louvre (https://www.louvre.fr/en/visites-en-ligne#tabs): Visit all of the amazing exhibits of The Louvre Museum in Paris, France.

Advice on out-of-school opportunities is offered by expert Paula Olszewski-Kubilius. How do educators and parents determine what opportunities are available and which ones would provide the type of opportunity their students are ready to experience?

Survival Secrets for Accessing and Selecting Out-Of-School Talent Development Opportunities

Paula Olszewski-Kubilius

When thinking about outside-of-school programs such as weekend, summer, or online programs for gifted students, an important first question is "Why do them?" I always like to say, "Some talents are developed primarily outside of school, such as dance and sport—and some are developed primarily in school, such as mathematical or scientific talent. But no talent, even academic ones, is developed completely in school." And research backs this up, showing that a larger dose of STEM experiences prior to college studies, including those acquired outside of school, is associated with a higher rate of creative productivity in these fields in adulthood.

The benefits of outside-of-school programs are numerous, including: learning about a field or domain not studied in school (e.g., anatomy); using an outside-of-school course to accelerate progress in a chosen domain (e.g., taking algebra in sixth grade); instruction from expert teachers; interactions with other similarly interested, able, and supportive peers; guidance and advising from adult professionals; early exposure to higher education; opportunities to do authentic, real-life work in a domain; socialization into the values and ideals of a domain; and guidance and advising regarding educational and career paths.

How Can Educators Help?

Some schools can provide summer and/or weekend programming geared specifically for advanced learners. Most often, though, students are on their own to find these opportunities. However, educators can assist students and families in accessing supplemental gifted programming in many ways, including directing families to organizations and universities that offer these opportunities; convincing parents of their value, particularly if they are residential, outside the immediate community, or interfere with other family plans; helping students make selections of specific programs and courses; and assisting families in applying for or obtaining financial aid if needed. This kind of support from educators is especially important for lower income students, who are may be more reliant on schools to help identify and implement talent development pathways.

Choosing an Outside-Of-School Program or Course

Summer, online, and weekend programs vary, and the goal is to find one that is a good match to a student's interests, personality, and academic needs. For younger students, dabbling in areas of interest via short courses may be the best fit, particularly if there is a need for more intellectual stimulation than is offered in most play-oriented preschools. Weekend and summer courses can accommodate an early and advanced reader or a child with exceptional interests in the natural world or mathematics. These advanced enrichment opportunities enable children to explore their interests, see what "sticks," acquire content knowledge and develop higher level thinking skills, and foster creativity. They also give children opportunities to socialize with peers.

As children develop, outside-of-school programs should be selected that address their demonstrated strengths, talent areas, and interests. Summer, online, and weekend programs for gifted students tend to increase the instructional pace and complexity of the content in response to students' intellectual capacities and are not meant to shore up relatively "weaker areas." Middle school-age students who attend schools with limited advanced offerings might want to select a program that allows earlier access to courses such as biology or algebra. Students whose main purpose in seeking an outside-of-school program is to connect with peers might choose a residential program or one that includes significant face-to-face contact hours with other students.

Parents or students considering a residential program should evaluate a student's readiness to be away from home and independent study and time management skills as well as self-care skills. Students who are hesitant to leave home should opt for a commuter program or online course, or a shorter residential program (1 or 2 weeks). Parents who want to build their child's capacity to live and study away from home might start with a shorter program and build to a program that is 3 or more weeks in duration in subsequent summers. Some summer program models consist of studying one subject intensely, while others enable student to take several different courses simultaneously. There are advantages to either approach, and the choice is a matter of interest level and preference. Residential programs have the advantage of providing a very diverse student population, as they draw students from across the U.S. and internationally. In addition to the quality of the academic program, families should assess aspects of the residential program such as levels and kinds of supervision, after-class activities, and qualifications of the residential staff.

High school-age students will benefit from programs or courses that allow them to work with professionals such as scientists, artists, engineers, IT professionals, or journalists to get a preview of real-life work and learn about professional standards and authentic problems within a domain of interest. These kinds of courses tend to include more field-based or project-/product-oriented work and can assist students in thinking about potential educational and career paths.

Online courses are a good option for students who do not want to leave home or cannot commit to or accommodate the time frame of a summer or weekend program due to other responsibilities or interests, yet desire or need more academic stimulation. There is an increasing pool of vendors for online programs, and families will want to be sure to choose a provider that is attuned to gifted students' need for faster pacing and higher level content. A key feature to assess is the degree to which the course operates as a self-paced, independent study with significant one-on-one interaction with an instructor, which is most appropriate for a student seeking to fit in an extra course or take one earlier than offered in their school— versus a cohort model with online virtual class meetings, which is a good fit for students seeking significant interaction with peers. Online courses are especially appropriate for students with well developed, independent study skills.

Finally, school policies vary widely in whether they will count a summer, weekend or online class towards fulfilling course requirements. It is always best to check this before signing up for a course that is meant to replace a typical school requirement (e.g., algebra or biology). Some schools will accept credits from an outside-of-school program, while others may not give credit but will place the student in the next higher course.

Parents and students should also consider the likelihood of an increased level of challenge within supplemental programs designed for gifted students, when compared to their regular school courses. This challenge can come not only from the content but also from intellectual peers and a residential environment. Parents and students can prepare for increased challenge by learning about the supports that the program provides, such as teaching assistants and residential counselors, by discussing good coping strategies before attending the program and by having reasonable expectations for performance.

—Paula Olszewski-Kubilius
Director, Center for Talent Development, Northwestern University

Centers for Gifted Education

Another source for information on programming options to extend the learning would be centers of gifted education. Most centers are located on university campuses. Contact the closest center and find out what opportunities are provided that would match the interests of your students. If you are not located close to one of these centers, call a university near you to see what they offer for children. Then encourage them to offer programming if they do not currently do so. A few of the centers that offer programming for young people in addition to the talent search centers are:

- The Belin-Blank Center for Gifted Education at the University of Iowa (https://www.education.uiowa.edu/belinblank): The Belin-Blank Center is a full-service gifted education center offering assessment, counseling, outreach, and consultation. It directs professional learning opportunities and sponsors a variety of educational opportunities for students, including summer programming, school-year programs (Challenge Saturdays), and the Belin-Blank Exceptional Student Talent Search.
- The Jodie Mahony Center for Gifted Education at the University of Arkansas at Little Rock (https://ualr.edu/gifted): The Center for Gifted Education provides opportunities for parents, students, and educators. The opportunities for educators include professional learning and Pre-AP and AP instruction. It also has precollege programs and the 3-week Summer Laureate program for students in grades K–7.
- The Center for Gifted Education at William & Mary (https://education.wm.edu/centers/cfge): The Center for Gifted Education is a research and development center. The center provides a variety of services and professional learning for adults interested in learning more about working with gifted individuals. These services include an AP Institute, National Curriculum Network Conference (NCNC), and customized professional learning.
- The Center for Gifted and Talented Education at the University of Northern Colorado (https://www.unco.edu/cebs/gifted-talented-center): The Center for the Education and Study of Gifted, Talented, Creative Learners provides opportunities for students, parents, and educators. Student programming includes the Summer Enrichment Program, the Summer Enrichment Day

Program, the Leadership Enrichment Program, the Young Child Program, and Creativity Quest. The center offers workshops and symposia for parents and educators of gifted children.

- The Center for Gifted Studies at Western Kentucky University (https://wku.edu/gifted): The Center for Gifted Studies offers year-round opportunities for young people who are gifted as well as for educators and parents. Professional learning opportunities include an Advanced Placement Institute, workshops on social-emotional development of gifted children, leadership development, and twice-exceptional children. The center offers summer programming for elementary, middle, and high school students and Super Saturdays for first through eighth graders. The center has advocacy as one major primary focus.

- The Frances A. Karnes Center for Gifted Studies at the University of Southern Mississippi (https://www.usm.edu/education-human-sciences/gifted-studies): The Karnes Center for Gifted Studies provides a variety of opportunities for youth, parents, and educators. The programming for youth includes Saturday, summer, and leadership studies programs. The Center also offers the Summer Program for Academically Talented Youth (SPATY). Parent resources include the Parenting Gifted Children Conference. The programming for educators includes the annual Day of Sharing for Teachers of the Gifted.

- The Gifted Education Research and Resource Institute at Purdue University (https://www.education.purdue.edu/geri): The Gifted Education Research and Resource Institute (GER$_2$I) offers a variety of programs for gifted youth including summer and Saturday programs as well as Diversity Initiatives for Gifted Students (DIGS). The program also offers consulting and online professional development and resources for educators of gifted students.

Conclusion

Opportunities abound, and you may be the one, perhaps the only one, to connect young people with opportunities that match their strengths and interests. It is so important to know your students; in fact, that is a "must" if you are able to match students with various contests, competitions, extracurricular opportunities, virtual or actual travel and experiences, as well as summer and Saturday programs. Such opportunities can help students find interests that last a lifetime, and they may introduce students to a content area that ends up morphing into a career.

Survival Tips

- You may be the only one to let a young person know about a contest or competition, a Saturday or summer program, or any other opportunity that you think matches their interests, skills, and talents. Don't miss the chance to do so.
- Competitions and contests, as well as Saturday and summer programs, often are the deciding factors as to what the young person decides to major in during their college years. These opportunities are not frivolous but essential in helping students make friends who share their interests and goals, as well as for engaging students in learning in a high-interest content or talent area.

Survival Toolkit

- "Contests and Awards" (https://www.hoagiesgifted.org/contests.htm) from the Hoagies' Gifted Education Page offers links to contest and scholarship opportunities for gifted students.
- "Summer and Saturday Enrichment Programs" (https://www.hoagiesgifted.org/summer.htm): from the Hoagies' Gifted Education Page provides links to hundreds of opportunities for gifted kids, organized by state.
- NAGC (https://www.nagc.org/resources-publications/resources-parents/planning-summer) features links to articles on the benefits of summer camps and programs for gifted students, along with access to the NAGC Resource Directory, which lists many such programs.
- Other resources include:
  - Berger, S. L. (2018). *The best summer programs for teens: America's top classes, camps, and courses for college-bound students* (4th ed.). Prufrock Press.
  - Karnes, F. A., & Riley, T. L. (2005). *Competitions for talented kids: Win scholarships, big prize money, and recognition.* Prufrock Press.
  - Roberts, J. L., & Inman, T. F. (2015). *Assessing differentiated student products: A protocol for development and evaluation* (2nd ed.). Prufrock Press.

Chapter 21

Unlocking Considerations That Often Mask Giftedness

"Foster a supportive ecosystem that nurtures and celebrates excellence and innovative thinking. Parents/guardians, education professionals, peers, and students themselves must work together to create a culture that expects excellence, encourages creativity, and rewards the successes of all students regardless of their race/ethnicity, gender, socioeconomic status, or geographical locale." (National Science Board, 2010, p. 3)

Key Questions

- What are barriers that sometimes keep gifted children from being recognized as gifted—those who underachieve, who are in kindergarten or first grade, who are twice-exceptional, who have high energy (or ADHD), or who have a language other than English as their first language?

- What can teachers do to remove barriers that stand in the way of young children, children who are twice-exceptional, those who speak English as an additional language, and those who underachieve?

DOI: 10.4324/9781003238553-22

Gifted children may have their talents masked by underachievement, a disability, a lack of opportunity, others' expectations of their abilities for their age, or speaking English as a second language. Many factors can disguise or cover up the gifts or strengths that some children possess, unless the children have opportunities to demonstrate what they can do.

Underachievement

When children do not have opportunities to learn new things on an ongoing basis (remember the Bill of Rights in Chapter 8), they have not learned to be resilient when faced with academic challenge and persistent when they need to work through a problem. They have not developed a work ethic on academic tasks, as it is not possible to really work hard when what is being required is not difficult but rather perfunctory. Think for a moment about something you are asked to do that has become very routine, such as running the vacuum. There is no way for you to do a better job, no matter how many times you vacuum, assuming that you know how to vacuum in the first place.

Underachievement is pervasive in classrooms in which young people get high grades and praise for "good work" without working hard. It is easy for children who have not been challenged to underachieve when faced with a challenge. Underachievement is very common among advanced learners.

The best way to deal with underachievement is to prevent it from happening. Teachers who preassess and match the learning experiences to the preassessment results are unlikely to face underachievement problems. It is so much better to prevent underachievement than to try to reverse it, as bad habits develop when children are not challenged. For example, idle time can result in behaviors that are unwanted in a classroom—rushing through tasks to get them done or seemingly not paying attention in class, but doing the work.

Expert Del Siegle provides a description of underachievement, with recommendations for addressing this pervasive problem.

Survival Secrets for Reversing Underachievement Among Gifted Students

Del Siegle

Julia believes English is not important and seldom completes her English writing assignments. Carlos dislikes his history teacher and refuses to put any effort into history projects. Damian believes mathematics is too difficult and does not attempt any work associated with it. Each of these students is underachieving for a different reason. All students have the ability to learn and attain self-fulfillment; however, many students are at risk of failing to achieve their academic potential. The reasons often vary from student to student.

Gifted students are one group of learners who are not normally considered at risk for academic failure; however, the seeming lack of motivation of many academically gifted students is an area of frustration and concern for many parents and teachers. Underachievement is the most frequently cited concern of educators of the gifted (Renzulli et al., 1991). Low academic motivation affects students' current performance and their persistence at completing tasks; it ultimately limits their future choices. The underachievement of gifted students is not only a resource loss for the nation, but also a personal loss of self-fulfillment for the underachieving individual.

Underachievement tends to appear in middle school and often continues into high school. Almost half of the gifted students who underachieve in seventh grade continue to underachieve throughout junior high and high school (Peterson & Colangelo, 1996), and although many attend college, only about half finish college in 4 years (Peterson, 2000). In the largest longitudinal study of underachievers conducted to date, McCall et al. (1992) found that 13 years after high school, the educational and occupational status of high school underachievers paralleled their grades in high school, rather than their abilities. They also found that underachievers were less likely to complete college and remain in their jobs.

Generally, underachievers are more likely to be male than female. The ratio of male underachievers to female underachievers appears to be at least 2:1 (Baker et al., 1998; Matthews & McBee, 2007; McCall, 1994; McCoach, 2002; McCoach & Siegle, 2001; Peterson & Colangelo, 1996; Richert, 1991; Siegle et al., 2006).

Peer issues may influence the achievement and underachievement of adolescents. High-achieving peers can contribute to some students' reversal of their underachievement (Reis et al., 1995). Likewise, negative peer attitudes often relate to underachievement (Clasen & Clasen, 1995; Weiner, 1992). Underachieving students frequently report peer influence as the strongest force impeding their achievement, and many report peer pressure or the attitude of the other kids, including friends, as the primary force against getting good grades (Clasen &

Figure 29
Siegle and McCoach Achievement-Orientation Model

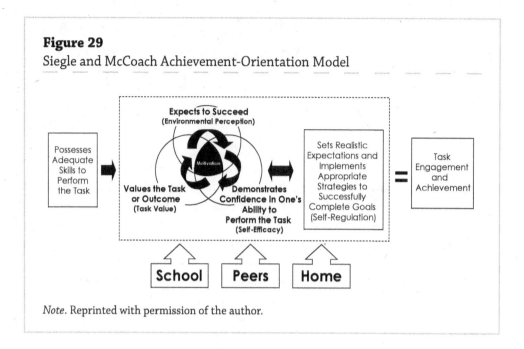

Note. Reprinted with permission of the author.

Clasen, 1995). Students with friends who care about learning demonstrate better educational outcomes than those in less educationally oriented peer groups (Chen, 1997). When examining students' fall and spring grades, students' grades more closely resemble their friends' at the end of the school year than they do at the beginning of the school year; students' grades tend to decrease between fall and spring if their friends have lower grades in the fall. Although peer achievement levels do relate to students' academic achievement, it is unclear whether the choice to associate with other nonachievers is a cause or a result of gifted students' underachievement. Although some gifted students underachieve because they have not had opportunities to develop their potential, others choose not to develop their potential. Siegle and McCoach (2002) suggested that students who underachieve may espouse one of three problematic beliefs: (1) They do not believe they have the skills to do well (self-efficacy) and are afraid to try and fail; (2) they do not see the work they are being asked to do as meaningful (task value); or (3) they believe the "deck is stacked against them" (environmental perceptions) and any effort they put forth will be thwarted. When any one of these negative beliefs exists, students tend not to perform well (see Figure 29).

Students must believe they have the skills to perform a task before they will attempt it. For example, students must believe they are capable in mathematics before they will attempt a difficult math problem. If they believe mathematics is too difficult, they are unlikely to put forth appropriate effort. Motivated students believe they have the skills to do well in school. It is also imperative that students recognize their own role in developing these skills (Siegle, 2008). Students who believe their abilities are not innate but have been developed are more likely to attempt challenging tasks (Dweck, 2000). Gifted students are at risk for believing their abilities are simply innate, particularly if others in their lives have not discussed their giftedness with them. It is important for gifted children to recognize that the talents they possess are acquired, that they have something to do with mastering them, and that they are capable of further developing these talents and even learning new ones.

For many students, school is not meaningful. This is particularly true for many gifted students who are not being intellectually challenged in their classrooms. When students value the goals of school, they are more likely to engage in academics, expend more effort on their schoolwork, and do better academically (Pintrich & DeGroot, 1990; Wigfield, 1994). There is a positive relationship between students' interest in a subject area and their assessment of their skill in that area. Students who report being interested in an area tend to do well; those with lower interest also have lower self-reported achievement (Siegle et al., 2010). Educators can make learning meaningful by helping students develop a personal value for learning by reflecting on how their lives will be different by learning, or not learning, given school content (Kaplan, 2006). Educators must also do a better job of sharing why content is pertinent (Brophy, 2008).

Students' perceptions of their environment play an important role in their achievement motivation. Students must expect to succeed and know that those around them will support their efforts. They must trust that their efforts will not be thwarted by external factors and that putting forth effort is not a waste of time and energy. Students who view their environment as friendly and reinforcing may be more likely to demonstrate motivated behavior. Phrases such as "My teacher does not like me" or "I cannot learn the way he teaches" may be signs that students do not view their environment as friendly or that they have developed a belief that their efforts do not affect outcomes. Some environmental factors are within an individual's control; others are not.

People put their effort into areas where they believe they can be successful and in environments where they believe they are supported (Ogbu, 1978).

Although each of the three attitudes discussed is important, it is their interaction that results in engagement and performance. Motivated students feel good about their abilities, find the tasks in which they are engaged meaningful, and feel supported and appreciated in their environment. The intensity of the attitudes in the three areas need not be equally strong; however, attitudes must be positive in each area. Ultimately, the three attitudes direct a resultant behavior (self-regulation) that results in achievement. If any one of the three components is low, regardless of the strength of the others, motivation is hindered. When students value the task or outcome and have positive perceptions of themselves and their opportunities for success, they are more likely to implement self-regulation strategies that result in students setting realistic expectations and applying appropriate strategies for academic success.

—Del Siegle, Ph.D.
University of Connecticut

Young Gifted Children

Young gifted children constitute a special group that contains much promise that can be blunted if their schools do not offer ongoing opportunities to learn new things (because these children already have learned much of what is expected at that level). Thus, young gifted children often have their abilities masked and, consequently, they may learn to underachieve.

Expert Patrice McCrary discusses the challenges that can be offered in an early childhood classroom, and she describes what young children can achieve when the learning ceiling is removed.

Survival Secrets on Influencing Early Childhood Learning

Patrice McCrary

As a curriculum coordinator for an elementary school, I had the enjoyable task of assessing primary students whom teachers nominated for the primary talent pool. Often those students amazed me with their knowledge in certain content areas well beyond expectations for a child that age. I always eagerly asked, "Who taught you that?" The comment was always something along the lines of a parent or even a grandparent. Never did I hear the response, "My teacher." I became concerned that we were building classrooms of middle-of-the-road expectations. What could I, as a regular education teacher, do to make certain a child's response was, "My teacher taught me that!" when asked about a brilliant piece of knowledge? I requested to return to the classroom as a kindergarten teacher with a mission. Yes, the students who struggled would receive the support they needed, but those students ready to fly would soon soar.

My earlier years of teaching were filled with making certain I followed the teacher editions to cover the content. I should have been busy having the children uncover the content and following their needs. I became an avid kid watcher/assessor/facilitator. Assessments became driving forces in the classroom. If a child already knew the content, then they were ready to move beyond that level. How exciting it became to assess a child in reading in the kindergarten classroom and discover students ready to read second-, third-, even eighth-grade-level materials! Math preassessment made it easy to group children. I now love working with 5-year-olds as they determine whether or not a particular number is a prime number. The children in room 80 have never been told they will learn more about a concept later. In our classroom, later is now.

When parents tell me their child has gone beyond their own level of knowledge, my heart sings. In science, the children learn about neutral buoyancy through inquiry learning experiences. In math, they discover that a square is a rectangle, but a rectangle is not a square. In reading, they quickly share that they are reading with inflection as a visitor stops nearby to listen. A group of children gather around a globe to determine which countries are on what continents . . . just because they want to know. Every kindergarten student and every classroom can have these experiences. It simply takes a teacher willing to remove the ceiling of learning. My students soar, and I love being the flight attendant.

—Patrice McCrary
Retired Kindergarten Teacher, Cumberland Trace Elementary School, Bowling Green, KY; 2003 Kentucky Teacher of the Year; 2009 National Teacher Hall of Fame Inductee; Member of the Kentucky Board of Education

Expert Jeane Adams-Smith recounts the experience of her highly gifted daughter when she was in elementary school. Her behaviors were a problem until an educator suggested a solution.

Survival Secrets of the Parent of a Young Student

Jeane Adams-Smith

Abby was in second grade when we encountered some difficulty with her teachers. She was young for her grade and physically small, but Abby had a big personality. She scored 140 on an IQ test in kindergarten. She was reading by age 3 and excelling early in many areas of cognitive development. In first grade she wanted to take her periodic table to show and share.

But most of all, Abby wanted to read and run. It was hard for her to sit still. As her parent, I knew she was different than other kids her age. She did not like to color or draw and wanted to talk about subjects that were way out of the range of most kids her age. Her fine motor skills were late developing as were some social skills.

We had her tested but nothing was ever conclusive. I have always thought that Abby was just a really smart kid who vibrated at a different level than most. It was never a problem until we hit second grade. I had already put Abby on an IEP to help her get any help she needed with her delayed motor skills and social skills. The Individualized Education Program (IEP) was put in place to minimize obstacles to learning and enhance Abby's education environment. We specifically put it into place to create strategies to improve her fine motor skills like handwriting and to have school support with her social skills.

At first it seemed to help. But two of her teachers seemed to "not know what to do with Abby." They complained to me that she was disruptive and did not want to sit still. I am sure to this day that she was bored. I was tired of complaints with no solutions. I used the IEP as an excuse and called a meeting with the school's counselor, her teachers, and the school district's accommodations supervisor.

I was nervous about calling such attention to Abby. Would this backfire? But I was tired of her being punished in class. I was afraid she would start to hate school. One of the teacher complaints was that she would want to read all of the time during class activities. I mentioned in the meeting that this was really not a bad thing! The supervisor was the one that saved the day.

"She needs a job," she said. "Abby needs to have something at school that is her own." The supervisor suggested that Abby become an aide in the library for part of the day. She could be around books and feel ownership over something at school. She was also asked to read to the kindergarten class during their reading time.

This turned out to be exactly what Abby needed. She became more focused in class. She could be sent out to deliver books and would not wander off. She enjoyed her time so much at the library that when the librarian left to take another job, she cried about leaving Abby.

Sometimes it is not about punishment or discipline; it is about finding the right path for the unique and gifted student. Abby continued working in the school library through middle school. She also created a fundraiser for her public library branch, and donated books to her middle school library. Abby needed to feel empowered, that her needs and thoughts were important.

She found that in her school library.

—Jeane Adams-Smith
Abby's Mother

Gifted Students With Disabilities

A category of gifted children that is often new to educators is the gifted student who also has a disability, commonly referred to as a twice-exceptional student. For many of these students, their disabilities mask their gifts, leaving them unidentified for advanced programs. In some cases, a student's gifts can mask their disabilities, making teachers think the student is working at a level average to their peer group.

Because there are various definitions of twice-exceptionality, the National Twice-Exceptional Community of Practice (2e CoP) was organized in 2014 to represent voices in the field and agree upon a definition. This group represented the organizations in gifted and special education as well as professionals who are actively involved with providing services to this group of dually identified children. The goal was to collaborate on a definition. That definition is one that represents the work of the 2e CoP (Baldwin et al., 2015):

> Twice exceptional individuals evidence exceptional ability and disability, which results in a unique set of circumstances. Their exceptional ability may dominate, hiding their disability; their disability may dominate, hiding their exceptional ability; each may mask the other so that neither is recognized or addressed.
>
> 2e students who may perform below, at, or above grade level require the following
>
> - Specialized methods of identification that consider the possible interaction of the exceptionalities,
> - Enriched/advanced educational opportunities that develop the child's interests, gifts, and talents while also meeting the child's learning needs,
> - Simultaneous supports that ensure the child's academic success and social-emotional well-being, such as accommodations, therapeutic interventions, and specialized instruction, and
> - Working successfully with this unique population requires specialized academic training and ongoing professional development.

A special issue of *Gifted Child Today* (December, 2015) was devoted to the definition, the history of the field, and shared perspectives of members of various role groups regarding ways that they can use this definition.

Experts Elizabeth Nielsen and Dennis Higgins make recommendations to help parents and educators understand the needs of this group of young people.

Survival Secrets for Understanding the Needs of Twice-Exceptional Children

Elizabeth Nielsen and Dennis Higgins

As the population of gifted students who also have disabilities or challenge areas increases, so does the challenge a classroom teacher faces in order to meet the needs of these unique, often emotional students. It is especially difficult when the needs of the twice-exceptional student behave like a moving target. Just when the teacher feels the right path has been located and success is on the horizon, the challenge seems to morph into an additional, more difficult condition. This is the reality for children whom the field of gifted education describes as twice-exceptional learners. The difficulties these children raise are neither intentional nor purposeful on the students' part. It is the honest but confusing reality these individuals present to teachers and parents.

The characteristics of a twice-exceptional child read like a Mobius strip acts: superior vocabulary, but poor social skills; advanced ideas and opinions, but high sensitivity to criticism; penetrating insight into complex issues, but difficulty with written expression. These learners are frequently underidentified, misunderstood, disconnected, mysterious, bright, alone, scared, and extremely independent. When so many discrepant, opposing characteristics appear within one individual, solutions and strategies to address this enigma are not always at the educator's or family's disposal.

There have been sharp debates and numerous articles about the most "appropriate" approach to instructing the twice-exceptional child. Should the teacher address the gifted needs first and then turn to the challenge areas? Or should the approach take the opposite focus? Should the teacher only address the giftedness and allow the gifts to overtake the challenge? Should the teacher address the challenges and hope the giftedness will take care of itself? Should the teacher focus on the emotional side of the student first and foremost? Unfortunately, these are the easier questions. The more difficult issue concerns the long-term effects of instruction on the lives of twice-exceptional children. How will the experience in the classroom of today influence the reality of the students' tomorrows? How can we prepare these children to work in situations where the environment is not accepting of their challenge? How can we help these children negotiate a life filled with exogenous factors? How can we help these students take charge of their own amazing promise?

John Dewey has emphasized the need for experiential, inquiry-based instruction, stating that experience is *of* as well as *in* nature. It is how the individual experiences the event that is important. Educating and raising a twice-exceptional learner is destined to be a powerfully rewarding experience for everyone involved. The process does not always guarantee a product, and the conclusions are not necessarily universal. But it is a road that must be traveled.

—M. Elizabeth Nielsen, Ph.D.
Associate Professor of Special Education at the University of New Mexico, Retired; Honorary Member of the Colorado Academy of Educators for the Gifted, Talented, and Creative

—L. Dennis Higgins, Ed.D.
Adjunct Professor of Gifted Education at the University of New Mexico, Retired; Honorary Member of the Colorado Academy of Educators for the Gifted, Talented, and Creative

One of the best strategies for bringing out the best in gifted children who also have a disability is to focus on their strengths while accommodating their disabilities. It is unproductive to focus on deficiencies alone. Temple Grandin (Peif, 2011), a professor and researcher with autism, has said that schools focus too much on socialization skills and need to spend more time on hands-on learning. She said, "I was making things all the time as a child. Things I got fixated on, I got motivated on. Teachers need to harness that fixation" (para. 15).

ADHD or High Energy

Another issue that can cloud appropriate educational opportunities for children concerns the appropriate identification of a child as having Attention Deficit/ Hyperactivity Disorder (ADHD). Sometimes a child with high energy is misdiagnosed as having ADHD when the child is actually gifted and demonstrating behaviors that are characteristic of gifted children and of children with ADHD. Sharon Lind (1996) put together a chart (see Table 5) that described behaviors that are characteristic of a child who is gifted and of one who has ADHD. This chart allows parents and teachers to distinguish between behaviors typical of each label.

English Language Learners

English language learners (ELLs) constitute a category of children that includes those who are gifted and talented; however, it may be difficult to identify them as advanced learners as they are currently learning a new language. Often their ability in math reveals itself before abilities in other areas, as the language barrier hampers the child's chance to show their verbal abilities. Using nonverbal assessment is preferable for recognizing exceptional ability for English language learners.

Conclusion

All children deserve opportunities to achieve their potentials, including those who are gifted and talented. The phrase "all children" also includes children of all ages, those from all economic levels and geographic regions, as well as those who may appear to be gifted due to their behaviors, language, or disability. Although issues can cloud the picture for some gifted young people to achieve what their

Table 5

Checklist to Consider Before Referring a Gifted Child for ADHD Evaluation

Gifted?	Need More Information	ADD/ADHD?
Contact with intellectual peers diminishes inappropriate behavior		Contact with intellectual peers has no positive effect on behavior
Appropriate academic placement diminishes inappropriate behavior		Appropriate academic placement has no positive effect on behavior
Curricular modifications diminish inappropriate behavior		Curricular modifications have no effect on behavior
The child has logical (to the child) explanations for inappropriate behavior		Child cannot explain inappropriate behavior
When active, child enjoys the movement and does not feel out of control		Child feels out of control
Learning appropriate social skills has decreased "impulsive" or inappropriate behavior		Learning appropriate social skills has not decreased "impulsive" or inappropriate behavior
Child has logical (to the child) explanations why tasks, activities are not completed		Child is unable to explain why tasks, activities are not completed
Child displays fewer inappropriate behaviors when interested in subject matter or project		Child's behaviors are not influenced by his or her interest in the activity
Child attributes excessive talking or interruptions on need to share information, need to show that he/she knows the answer, or need to solve a problem immediately		Child cannot attribute excessive talking or interruptions to a need to learn or share information
Child who seems inattentive can repeat instructions		Child who seems inattentive is unable to repeat instructions
Child thrives on working on multiple tasks—gets more done, enjoys learning more		Child moves from task to task for no apparent reason
Inappropriate behaviors are not persistent—seem to be a function of subject matter		Inappropriate behaviors persist regardless of subject matter

Table 5, continued

Gifted?	Need More Information	ADD/ADHD?
Inappropriate behaviors are not persistent—seem to be a function of teacher or instructional style		Inappropriate behaviors persist regardless of teacher or instructional style
Child acts out to get teacher attention		Child acts out regardless of attention

Note. Developed by Sharon Lind. Copyright 1996 by Sharon Lind. Reprinted with permission of the author.

potentials would predict, you and your colleagues can educate parents and teachers in order for them to be aware of barriers and strategies to overcome the barriers. Our society cannot afford to lose talent; instead you must be in the business of talent development.

Survival Tips

- Gifted children may have their talents masked by a disability, a lack of opportunity, a preconceived idea of what ADHD and/or high energy looks like and what a young child should be able to do, or having English as a second language.
- Keep learning about issues that mask giftedness.
- Parents need to know that giftedness will not always reveal itself.
- Consult with professionals who are knowledgeable about gifted children about any special issues regarding your children who have been identified as gifted and talented or that you suspect should be.

Survival Toolkit

- Bridges Academy (https://www.bridges.edu/resources.html) has numerous resources on twice-exceptional children.
- 2e News (https://www.2enews.com) offers a wide variety of resources to parents and teachers of gifted students with learning disabilities.
- Other resources include:

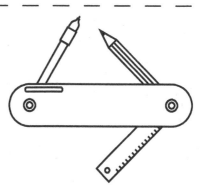

Baum, S. M., Schader, R. M., & Owen, S. V. (2017). *To be gifted and learning disabled: Strength-based strategies for helping twice-exceptional students with LD, ADHD, ASD, and more* (3rd ed.). Prufrock Press.

Equity in Gifted/Talented Education. (n.d.). *The varied faces of gifted/talented students.* http://www.gtequity.org/equity-and-gt/varied-faces.php

Iseman, J. S., Silverman, S. M., & Jeweler, S. (2010). *101 school success tools for students with ADHD.* Prufrock Press.

Matthews, M. S. (2008). *Working with gifted English language learners.* Prufrock Press.

Roffman Shevitz, B., Stemple, M., Barnes-Robinson, L., & Jeweler, S. (2011). *101 school success tools for smart kids with learning difficulties.* Prufrock Press.

Weinfeld, R., Barnes-Robinson, L., Jeweler, S., & Roffman Shevitz, B. (2006). *Smart kids with learning difficulties: Overcoming obstacles and realizing potential.* Prufrock Press.

Webb, J. T., Amend, E., Webb., N. E., Kuzujanakis, M., Olenchak, F. R., & Goerss, J. (2016). *Misdiagnosis and dual diagnoses of gifted children and adults: ADHD, bipolar, OCD, Asperger's, depression, and other disorders* (2nd ed.). Great Potential Press.

Survival Toolkit, continued

Chapter 22

Book Studies for *Teacher's Survival Guide: Gifted Education*

This book could be used as a text for a class or as a book study for a PLC or any cluster of educators interested in being up to date on gifted education and talent development. This book could also be interesting for a group of parents to read and discuss together. Three versions of a book study are included to provide choice and to differentiate the opportunity to learn about this very important topic.

Book Study 1

The first way to engage in a book study is to use the questions at the beginning of each chapter to focus your discussion. The second and third book study options are included for you to check out and engage in discussing.

Wishing you a "good read" and insightful discussions!

 DOI: 10.4324/9781003238553-23

Book Study 2

1. This book is written for those new to gifted education (perhaps new to teaching but not necessarily). What experiences have you had that provide information about children and young people who are gifted and talented?
2. What definition of giftedness is in place in your state?
3. Of the various myths about gifted children (ones in the book or others you know) that are prevalent among people you have encountered, which ones do you consider to be the most harmful to gifted students? In what ways are those myths barriers to gifted children having the best experience they can have in school?
4. Looking at characteristics of children who are gifted, high achievers, and creative thinkers, what gets in the way of parents and educators understanding the differences?
5. Differentiation is more than different. What are key points from the reading about differentiation that are very important to remember in order to differentiate?
6. Acceleration is far more than grade-skipping. What other ways can teachers accelerate students at the level at which you teach?
7. What do you consider "success" for a student? Is it an A? If not, how do you assess success for students?
8. Who in a school is responsible for the development of students' talents? Special teachers? Classroom teachers? School leaders? You? In what ways is each responsible for developing talent?
9. Advocating is speaking out on behalf of an idea, or it could be speaking out for a person. In what ways can you or do you advocate for children with gifts and talents?

Book Study 3

1. List three myths that, if believed, interfere with making continuous progress. What is the conflict with the myth and students making continuous progress?
2. Add another myth about gifted children that isn't included in the list of 10 myths. Are there other myths that are alive and well in your school or community? How could you and your colleagues work to turn the myths to truths about gifted children or programming options that are based in research?

3. What policies are in place in your school and district to support gifted children and their learning needs (remember, needs of gifted children are created by their strengths)?

4. What policies need to be added to current policies to ensure that children with advanced abilities thrive in school?

5. "No talent is developed in the absence of appropriate opportunities for education, training, or coaching" (Olszewski-Kubilius et al., 2018, p. 12). Discuss this quote and what could it mean for discovering and developing talent in your school. What could be put in place to make your school a center for talent development?

6. "Unless you find a child's specific talent—and provide him or her with the exact means needed to express it—it may go undiscovered" (Scheve, 2010, para. 3). In what ways does this quote about talent provide you with important information that will inform your best practice as a teacher?

7. "Because talents manifest in numerous domains, children remain a very heterogeneous group of people; as children, few to no claims would be equally true for the entire group of gifted students" (Cross, 2018, p. 56). Think of gifted children you have known. What characteristics have they demonstrated that might make others look over them as potentially being nominated for consideration for assessment for some category of giftedness?

8. Best practice in identification is to have the opportunity open for being assessed (not a one-time opportunity). Check on the practice in your school to see if identification remains open.

9. What are the assessments (performance and paper-and-pencil) that your school uses to identify students as gifted and talented in the categories that your district and state recognize?

10. What are current practices in your school that support acceleration (various types) and differentiation to ensure opportunities for students to make continuous progress?

11. What do school leaders, classroom teachers, special education resource teachers, and the gifted resource teacher need to know about twice-exceptional children so they can recognize them and provide services to encourage their giftedness and support their learning needs?

12. "People will forget what you said, people will forget what you did, but people will never forget how you made them feel."—Maya Angelou. What are the implications for gifted children in regard to their academic challenge and opportunities to learn with idea-mates . . . to find idea-mates?

13. Locate the APA (2017) principles that relate to creativity, preassessment, differentiation, assessment, and learning. Assess how your school is doing with meeting the intent of the principles of learning.

CONCLUDING THOUGHTS

There are such great opportunities ahead for you to challenge your gifted students, but you will need to embark on this journey one step at a time. Start at the very beginning:

- Learn about gifted education in your school, school district, and state.
- Find colleagues who share your interests in talent development.
- Participate in decision-making groups whenever possible. Volunteer for a curriculum committee or a committee to interview a prospective faculty member. It is so important to be "in the room" when decisions are made.
- Take the opportunity to participate in professional development related to gifted education and get fellow educators to do the same.
- Join your state advocacy organization—and the local one too, if one is established.

Use *Teacher's Survival Guide: Gifted Education* as a ready reference as you work to make your school one that is known as a great place for all children to learn. Just remember that the phrase "all children" includes children who differ in many ways—those who learn at different paces, who have a wide array of interests, who have both abilities and disabilities, and who come from all backgrounds. In a school known for fulfilling its mission to develop talent, all children will thrive, and you will, too.

The final chapter provides a book study guide for this book. Gather others around you and discuss the ideas and how they apply to classrooms in your school.

Perhaps your entire school could engage in a book study through PLCs. Learn together and, when you do so, children and young people are the winners, all of them—including those who are advanced and ready for more complex content than their age-mates.

REFERENCES

Adams, C. M., & Pierce, R. L. (2006). *Differentiating instruction: A practical guide to tiered lessons in the elementary grades*. Prufrock Press.

American Psychological Association, Center for Psychology in Schools and Education. (2017). *Top 20 principles from psychology for preK-12 creative, talented, and gifted students' teaching and learning*. https://www.apa.org/ed/schools/teaching-learning/top-twenty/creative-talented/index

Anderson, L., & Krathwohl, D. R. (Eds.). (2001). *A taxonomy for learning, teaching, and assessing: A revision of Bloom's taxonomy of educational objectives* (Complete ed.). Longman.

Assouline, S. G., Colangelo, N., Lupkowski-Shoplik, A., Forstadt, L., & Lipscomb, J. (2009). *Iowa acceleration scale* (3rd ed.). Great Potential Press.

Assouline, S. G., Colangelo, N., VanTassel-Baska, J., & Lupkowski-Shoplik, A. (Eds.). (2015). *A nation empowered: Evidence trumps the excuses holding back America's brightest students* (Vol. 2). The University of Iowa, The Connie Belin & Jacqueline N. Blank International Center for Gifted Education and Talent Development.

Baker, J. A., Bridger, R., & Evans, K. (1998). Models of underachievement among gifted preadolescents: The role of personal, family, and school factors. *Gifted Child Quarterly, 42*(1), 5–14. https://doi.org/10.1177/001698629804200102

Baldwin, L., Baum, S., Perles, D. & Hughes, C. (2015). Twice-exceptional learners: The journey toward a shared vision. *Gifted Child Today, 38*(4), 206–214. https://doi.org/10.1177/1076217515597277

Bloom, B. S. (Ed.). (1985). *Developing talent in young people*. Ballantine Books.

Brophy, J. (2008). Developing students' appreciation for what is taught in school. *Educational Psychologist, 43*(3), 132–141. https://doi.org/10.1080/0046152 0701756511

Carroll, L. (2000). *Alice's adventures in wonderland.* Signet Classic/New American Library. (Original work published in 1865)

Chen, X. (1997, June). *Students' peer groups in high school: The pattern and relationship to educational outcomes* (NCES 97-055). U.S. Department of Education.

Clasen, D. R., & Clasen, R. E. (1995). Underachievement of highly able students and the peer society. *Gifted and Talented International, 10*(2), 67–75. https://doi.org /10.1080/15332276.1995.11672824

Colangelo, N., Assouline, S. G., & Gross, M. U. M. (Eds.). (2004). *A nation deceived: How schools hold back America's brightest students* (Vols. 1 & 2). The University of Iowa, The Connie Belin & Jacqueline N. Blank International Center for Gifted Education and Talent Development.

Cross, T. L. (2018). *On the social and emotional lives of gifted children* (5th ed.). Prufrock Press.

de Wet, C. F., Gubbins, E. J., & Vahindi, S. (Eds.). (2005). *The NRC/GT instrument bank* [CD]. University of Connecticut, The National Research Center on the Gifted and Talented.

Dweck, C. S. (2000). *Self-theories: Their role in motivation, personality, and development.* Psychology Press.

Dweck, C. S. (2016). *Mindset: The new psychology of success.* Ballantine Books. (Original work published 2006)

Evans, M. A., & Whaley, L. (n.d.). *Jot downs* [Unpublished manuscript]. The Center for Gifted Studies, Western Kentucky University, Bowling Green, KY.

Friedman, T. L. (2009, June 27). *Invent, invent, invent.* The New York Times. https:// www.nytimes.com/2009/06/28/opinion/28friedman.html

Friedman, T. L. (2010, February 23). *U.S.G. and P.T.A.* The New York Times. https:// www.nytimes.com/2010/11/24/opinion/24friedman.html

Frost, L. (2017, September 14). *The achievement trap: How American is failing millions of high-achieving students from lower-income families.* http://www.schoolinfosystem. org/2007/09/14/the_achievement

Gardner, H. W. (1993, July). Educating for understanding. *The American School Board Journal, 180*(7), 20–24.

Gewertz, C. (2010, August 18). *ACT scores deliver good and bad news.* Education Week. https://blogs.edweek.org/edweek/curriculum /2010/08/ act_scores.html

Gladwell, M. (2008). *Outliers: The story of success.* Little, Brown.

Gordon, W. J. J. (1961). *Synectics.* Harper & Row.

Hébert, T. P. (2020). *Understanding the social and emotional lives of gifted students* (2nd ed.). Prufrock Press.

Henderson, A., Jacob, B., Kernan-Schloss, A., & Raimondo, B. (2004). *The case for parent leadership.* KSA Plus Communications/Prichard Committee for Academic Excellence.

Higher Education Opportunity Act, Pub. L. 110-315 (2008). https://www.congress.gov/110/plaws/publ315/PLAW-110publ315.pdf

Jacob K. Javits Gifted and Talented Students Education Program, 20 U.S.C. § 7294 (2015). https://congress.gov/114/plaws/publ95/PLAW-114publ95.pdf

Johnsen, S. K. (Ed.). (2018). *Identifying gifted students: A practical guide* (3rd ed.). Prufrock Press.

Kanevsky, L. S. (2003). Tiering with Venn diagrams. *Gifted Education Communicator, 34*(2), 42–44.

Kaplan, S. (2006, July). *Gifted students in a contemporary society: Implications for curriculum* [Keynote presentation]. 29th Annual University of Connecticut Confratute, Storrs, CT, United States.

Karnes, F. A., & Riley, T. L. (2005). *Competitions for talented kids: Win scholarships, big prize money, and recognition.* Prufrock Press.

Kingore, B. (2004). *Differentiation: Simplified, realistic, and effective.* Professional Associates Publishing.

Kingsolver, B. (2002, Winter). Congratulatory letter. *The Challenge, 8,* 9.

Kulik, J. A. (1992). *An analysis of research on ability grouping: Historical and contemporary perspectives.* University of Connecticut, The National Research Center on the Gifted and Talented.

Lind, S. (1996). *Before referring a gifted child for ADD/ADHD evaluation.* https://www.sengifted.org/post/before-referring-a-gifted-child-for-add-adhd-evaluation

Loveless, T., Farkas, S., & Duffett, A. (2008). *High-achieving students in the era of NCLB.* Thomas B. Fordham Institute.

Lupkowski-Shoplik, A., Behrens, W. A., & Assouline, S. G. (2018). *Developing academic acceleration policies: Whole grade, early entrance & single subject.* The University of Iowa, The Connie Belin & Jacqueline N. Blank International Center for Gifted Education and Talent Development, National Association for Gifted Children, the Council of State Directors of Programs for the Gifted.

MacGregor, M. (2010). *Everyday leadership skills and attitude inventory.* Free Spirit.

Marland, S. P., Jr. (1972). *Education of the gifted and talented: Report to the Congress of the United States by the U.S. Commissioner of Education and background papers submitted to the U.S. Office of Education,* 2 vols. U.S. Government Printing Office. (Government Documents, Y4.L 11/2: G36)

Matthews, M. S., & McBee, M. T. (2007). School factors and the underachievement of gifted students in a talent search summer program. *Gifted Child Quarterly, 51*(2), 167–181. https://doi.org/10.1177/0016986207299473

McCall, R. B. (1994). Academic underachievers. *Current Directions in Psychological Science, 3*(1), 15–19. https://doi.org/10.1111/1467-8721.ep10769838

McCall, R. B., Evahn, C., & Kratzer, L. (1992). *High school underachievers: What do they achieve as adults?* SAGE.

McCoach, D. B. (2002). A validity study of the School Attitude Assessment Survey (SAAS). *Measurement and Evaluation in Counseling and Development, 35*(2), 66–77. https://doi.org/10.1080/07481756.2002.12069050

McCoach, D. B., & Siegle, D. (2001). A comparison of high achievers' and low achievers' attitudes, perceptions, and motivations. *Academic Exchange Quarterly, 5*(2), 71–76.

McTighe, J., & O'Connor, K. (2005). Seven practices for effective learning. *Educational Leadership, 63*(3), 10–17.

National Association for Gifted Children. (2010). *Redefining giftedness for a new century: Shifting the paradigm* [Position statement]. https://www.nagc.org/sites/default/files/Position%20Statement/Redefining%20Giftedness%20for%20a%20New%20Century.pdf

National Association for Gifted Children. (2011). *Starting and sustaining a parent group to support gifted children.* https://www.nagc.org/sites/default/files/Parent%20CK/Starting%20and%20Sustaining%20a%20Parent%20Group.pdf

National Association for Gifted Children. (2019a). *A definition of giftedness that guides best practice* [Position statement]. https://www.nagc.org/sites/default/files/Position%20Statement/Definition%20of%20Giftedness%20%2820 19%29.pdf

National Association for Gifted Children. (2019b). *2019 Pre-K–Grade 12 Gifted Programming Standards.* http://www.nagc.org/sites/default/files/standards/Intro%202019%20Programming%20Standards.pdf

National Science Board. (2010). *Preparing the next generation of STEM innovators: Identifying and developing our nation's human capital.* National Science Foundation.

No Child Left Behind Act, 20 U.S.C. §6301 (2001). https://www.congress.gov/107/plaws/publ110/PLAW-107publ110.pdf

Ogbu, J. U. (1978). *Minority education and caste.* Academic Press.

Olszewski-Kubilius, P., Subotnik, R. F., & Worrell, F. C. (Eds.). (2018). *Talent development as a framework for gifted education: Implications for best practices and applications in schools.* Prufrock Press.

Partnership for 21st Century Learning. (2019). *Framework for 21st century learning.* https://static.battelleforkids.org/documents/p21/P21_Framework_Brief.pdf

Passow, A. H. (1982). Differentiated curriculum for the gifted/talented: A perspective. In S. N. Kaplan, A. H. Passow, P. H. Phenix, S. M. Reis, J. S. Renzulli, J. S. Sato, I. Smith, E. P. Torrance, & V. S. Ward (Eds.), *Curriculum for the gifted: Selected proceedings of the first national conference on curriculum for the gifted and talented* (pp. 4–30). Ventura County Superintendent of Schools Office.

Peif, S. (2011, February 7). *Temple Grandin: Hands-on learning is key to education.* Greeley Tribune. https://www.greeleytribune.com/article/200110207/NEWS/702079978

Peterson, J. S. (2000). A follow-up study of one group of achievers and underachievers four years after high school graduation. *Roeper Review, 22*(4), 217–225. https://doi.org/10.1080/02783190009554041

Peterson, J. S., & Colangelo, N. (1996). Gifted achievers and underachievers: A comparison of patterns found in school files. *Journal of Counseling and Development, 74*(4), 399–406. https://doi.org/10.1002/j.1556-6676.1996.tb01886.x

Pintrich, P. R., & DeGroot, E. V. (1990). Motivational and self-regulated learning components of classroom academic performance. *Journal of Educational Psychology, 82*(1), 33–40. https://doi.org/10.1037/0022-0663.82.1.33

Plucker, J. A., Burroughs, N., & Song, R. (2010). *Mind the (other) gap! The growing excellence gap in K–12 education.* Center for Evaluation and Education Policy.

Reis, S. M., Hébert, T. P., Diaz, E. P., Maxfield, L. R., & Ratley, M. E. (1995). *Case studies of talented students who achieve and underachieve in an urban high school* (RM95120). University of Connecticut, The National Research Center for the Gifted and Talented.

Reis, S. M., & McCoach, D. B. (2000). The underachievement of gifted students: What do we know and where do we go? *Gifted Child Quarterly, 44*(3), 152–170. https://doi.org/10.1177/001698620004400302

Reis, S. M., & Renzulli, J. S. (2009). Myth 1: The gifted and talented constitute one single homogeneous group and giftedness is a way of being that stays in the person over time and experience. *Gifted Child Quarterly, 53*(4), 233–235. https://doi.org/10.1177/0016986209346824

Reis, S. M., Westberg, K. L., Kulikowich, J., Caillard, F., Hébert, T. P., Plucker, J., Purcell, J. H., Rogers, J. B., & Smist, J. M. (1993). *Why not let high ability students start school in January? The curriculum compacting study* (RM93106). University of Connecticut, The National Research Center for the Gifted and Talented.

Renzulli, J. S. (2007). A practical approach for developing the gifts and talents of all students. In B. Z. Presseisen (Ed.), *Teaching for intelligence* (2nd ed., pp. 245–287). Corwin Press.

Renzulli, J. S., Heilbronner, N. N., & Siegle, D. (2010). *Think data: Getting kids involved in hands-on investigations with data-gathering instruments.* Prufrock Press.

Renzulli, J. S., Reid, B. D., & Gubbins, E. J. (1991). *Setting an agenda: Research priorities for the gifted and talented through the year 2000.* University of Connecticut, The National Research Center for the Gifted and Talented.

Renzulli, J. S., & Reis, S. M. (2014). *The Schoolwide Enrichment Model: A how-to guide for talent development* (3rd ed.). Prufrock Press.

Richert, E. S. (1991). Patterns of underachievement among gifted students. In M. Bireley & J. Genshaft (Eds.), *Understanding the gifted adolescent: Educational, developmental, and multicultural issues* (pp. 139–162). Teachers College Press.

Roberts, J. L. (n.d.). *PLAN model* [Unpublished manuscript]. The Center for Gifted Studies, Western Kentucky University, Bowling Green, KY.

Roberts, J. L. (2005). *Enrichment opportunities for gifted learners.* Prufrock Press.

Roberts, J. L. (2008). Multiple ways to define academic success: What resonates with you? *The Challenge, 21*, 13.

Roberts, J. L. (2020, June). *Reducing gaps so gifted children thrive.* Gifted Awareness Week New Zealand. New Zealand Centre for Gifted Education.

Roberts, J. L., & Inman, T. F. (2010, December). A checklist to guide advocacy for a gold standard school. *Parenting for High Potential*, 21–23.

Roberts, J. L., & Inman, T. F. (2015a). *Assessing differentiated student products: A protocol for development and evaluation* (2nd ed.). Prufrock Press.

Roberts, J. L., & Inman, T. F. (2015b). *Strategies for differentiating instruction: Best practices for the classroom* (3rd ed.). Prufrock Press.

Rogers, K. B. (2007). Lessons learned about educating the gifted and talented: A synthesis of the research on educational practice. *Gifted Child Quarterly, 51*(4), 382–396. https://doi.org/10.1177/0016986207306324

Scheve, T. (2010, September 9). *How can you tell if your child is a prodigy?* https://health.howstuffworks.com/pregnancy-and-parenting/ parenting/child-prodigy.htm

Siegle, D. (2007, September). Gifted children's Bill of Rights. *Parenting for High Potential*, 3, 30.

Siegle, D. (2008). The time is now to stand up for gifted education: 2007 NAGC Presidential Address. *Gifted Child Quarterly, 52*(2), 111–113. https://doi.org/ 10.1177/0016986208315848

Siegle, D. (2018, July 23). *Why increasing equity in gifted education is important and what you can do about it* [Keynote presentation]. Edufest, Boise, ID, United States.

Siegle, D., & McCoach, D. B. (2002). Promoting a positive achievement attitude with gifted and talented students. In M. Neihart, S. M. Reis, N. M. Robinson, & S. Moon (Eds.), *The social and emotional development of gifted children: What do we know?* (pp. 237–249). Prufrock Press.

Siegle, D., Reis, S. M., & McCoach, D. B. (2006, June). *A study to increase academic achievement among gifted underachievers* [Poster presentation]. Institute of Education Sciences Research Conference, Washington, DC, United States.

Siegle, D., Rubenstein, L. D., Pollard, E., & Romey, E. (2010). Exploring the relationship of college freshman honors students' effort and ability attribution, interest, and implicit theory of intelligence with perceived ability. *Gifted Child Quarterly, 54*(2), 92–101. https://doi.org/10.1177/0016986209355975

Singer, D. G., & Ravenson, T. A. (1996). *A Piaget primer: How a child thinks*. International Universities Press.

Smarick, A. (2013). *Closing America's high-achievement gap: A wise giver's guide to helping our most talented students reach their full potential*. The Philanthropy Roundtable.

Southern, W. T., & Jones, E. D. (2004). Types of acceleration: Dimensions and issues. In N. Colangelo, S. G. Assouline, & M. U. M. Gross (Eds.), *A nation deceived: How schools hold back America's brightest students* (Vol. 2, pp. 5–12). The University of Iowa, The Connie Belin & Jacqueline N. Blank International Center for Gifted Education and Talent Development.

Stanley, J. C. (2000). Helping students learn only what they don't already know. *Psychology, Public Policy, and Law, 6*(1), 216–222. https://doi.org/10.1037/ 1076-8971.6.1.216

Tannenbaum, A. J. (1962). *Adolescent attitudes toward academic brilliance*. Teachers College Press.

Tomlinson, C. A. (2005). Traveling the road to differentiation in staff development. *Journal of Staff Development, 26*(4), 8–12.

Treffinger, D. J. (2009). Myth 5: Creativity is too difficult to measure. *Gifted Child Quarterly, 53*(4), 245–247. https://doi.org/10.1177/0016986209346829

U.S. Department of Education. (1993). *National excellence: A case for developing America's talent*. U.S. Government Printing Office.

Weiner, I. B. (1992). *Psychological disturbance in adolescence* (2nd ed.). Wiley.

Wigfield, A. (1994). The role of children's achievement values in the self-regulation of their learning outcomes. In D. H. Schunk & B. J. Zimmerman (Eds.), *Self-regulation of learning and performance: Issues and educational applications* (pp. 101–124). Erlbaum.

Winebrenner, S. (with Brulles, D.). (2018). *Teaching gifted kids in today's classroom: Strategies and techniques every teacher can use* (4th ed.). Free Spirit.

Wyner, J. W., Bridgeland, J. M., & DiIulio, J. J. (2007). *Achievementrap: How America is failing millions of high-achieving students from lower-income families*. Jack Kent Cooke Foundation.

APPENDIX
Top 20 Principles From Psychology

1. Students' beliefs or perceptions about intelligence and ability affect their cognitive functioning and learning.
2. What students already know affects their learning.
3. Students' cognitive development and learning are not limited by general stages of development.
4. Learning is based on context, so generalizing learning to new contexts is not spontaneous but instead needs to be facilitated.
5. Acquiring long-term knowledge and skill is largely dependent on practice.
6. Clear, explanatory, and timely feedback to students is important for learning.
7. Students' self-regulation assists learning, and self-regulatory skills can be taught.
8. Student creativity can be fostered.
9. Students tend to enjoy learning and to do better when they are more intrinsically rather than extrinsically motivated to achieve.
10. Students persist in the face of challenging tasks and process information more deeply when they adopt mastery goals rather than performance goals.
11. Teachers' expectations about their students affect students' opportunities to learn, their motivation, and their learning outcomes.
12. Setting goals that are short-term (proximal), specific, and moderately challenging enhances motivation more than establishing goals that are long-term (distal), general, and overly challenging.
13. Learning is situated within multiple social contexts.

14. Interpersonal relationships and interpersonal communication are critical to both the teaching-learning process and the social development of students.
15. Emotional well-being influences educational performance, learning, and development.
16. Expectations for classroom conduct and social interaction are learned and can be taught using proven principles of behavior and effective classroom instruction.
17. Effective classroom management is based on (a) setting and communicating high expectations, (b) consistently nurturing positive relationships, and (c) providing a high level of student support.
18. Formative and summative assessments are both important and useful but require different approaches and interpretations.
19. Students' skills, knowledge, and abilities are best measured with assessment processes grounded in psychological science with well-defined standards for quality and fairness.
20. Making sense of assessment data depends on clear, appropriate, and fair interpretation.

Note. From *Top 20 Principles From Psychology for PreK–12 Creative, Talented, and Gifted Students' Teaching and Learning*, by American Psychological Association, Center for Psychology in Schools and Education, 2017, https://www.apa.org/ed/schools/teaching-learning/top-twenty/creative-talented/index. Copyright 2017 by American Psychological Association. Reprinted with permission.

ABOUT THE AUTHORS

Julia Link Roberts, Ed.D., is the Mahurin Professor of Gifted Studies at Western Kentucky University. She is the Executive Director of The Center for Gifted Studies and The Carol Martin Gatton Academy of Mathematics and Science in Kentucky. Dr. Roberts is president of the World Council for Gifted and Talented Children and a board member of The Association for the Gifted (a division of the Council for Exceptional Children) and the Kentucky Association for Gifted Education. Dr. Roberts received the first David W. Belin NAGC Award for Advocacy and the NAGC Ann F. Isaacs Founding Member's Award. She is coauthor with Dr. Tracy F. Inman of *Strategies for Differentiating Instruction: Best Practices for the Classroom* (2009 Legacy Award winner for the outstanding book for educators in gifted education by the Texas Association for the Gifted and Talented) and *Assessing Differentiated Student Products: A Protocol for Development and Evaluation.* She also is editor with Dr. Jennifer H. Robins and Dr. Inman of *Introduction to Gifted Education*, which received the Legacy Book Award in the Scholar category Dr. Roberts directs summer and Saturday programs for children and young people who are gifted and talented. Dr. Roberts and her husband Richard live in Bowling Green, KY. They have two daughters, Stacy Moots and Julia Boggess, and four granddaughters, Elizabeth, Caroline, Jane Ann, and Claire.

Julia Roberts Boggess, M.A., M.S., is an elementary librarian at Pearre Creek Elementary School in Williamson County, TN. She has taught in the primary grades and has been a gifted resource teacher. In 2008, Mrs. Boggess was awarded an $8,000 Jenny's Heroes grant from the Jenny Jones Foundation. In 2018, she was recognized for the outstanding book fair in the country by Scholastic. She has taught drama and literature to elementary and middle school students in Saturday and summer programs offered by The Center for Gifted Studies at Western Kentucky University. Mrs. Boggess earned a bachelor's degree in elementary education, a master's degree in elementary education with an endorsement in gifted education, and a master's degree in library media education at Western Kentucky University. She lives in Tennessee with her husband, Mark, and her delightful daughter, Claire.